T0068909

Helping the Patient with Advanced Disease

A workbook

Edited by

Claud Regnard

Radcliffe Medical Press

Radcliffe Medical Press Ltd
18 Marcham Road
Abingdon
Oxon OX14 1AA
United Kingdom

www.radcliffe-oxford.com
The Radcliffe Medical Press electronic catalogue and online ordering facility.
Direct sales to anywhere in the world.

―――――――――――――――――

British Library Cataloguing in Publication Data

A catalogue record for this book is available from the British Library.

ISBN 1 85775 964 8

Typeset by Joshua Associates Ltd, Oxford
Printed and bound by TJ International Ltd, Padstow, Cornwall

CLIP worksheets

Introduction

Background

Helping others to learn about caring for people with advanced disease has always been a fundamental part of effective palliative care. The aim is to resource existing professionals, carers and teams with the knowledge and skills needed in their daily work. Many opportunities exist for learning: academic courses such as diplomas, degrees, local courses, journals and books. There is also a variety of methods of delivery such as workshops, lectures, on-line degrees, and on-line information sites. Despite this, it can be difficult for carers to find time to update themselves, and tutors can find it difficult to find suitable materials to incorporate in their existing teaching.

The CLIP worksheets grew from the idea of a 'coffee update'. The principle was to develop a flexible learning material that could be used over a coffee break, but could also be used in a variety of settings.

Evaluation of CLIP worksheets

CLIP worksheets have been evaluated formally by the Open University and have been used by the editor and colleagues at St Oswald's Hospice and the Freeman Hospital, Newcastle upon Tyne for over five years in a variety of settings.

The Open University carried out a two-year evaluation using the CLIP worksheets, comparing delivery in a face-to-face tutorial setting with that over a videoconferencing link.* They found that:

- the level of satisfaction was high
- 88% showed an increase in learning scores
- learning scores increased by 17–18%
- the worksheets were as effective in face-to-face tutorials as over a videoconferencing link
- effectiveness increased if the worksheets were sent out prior to the session
- the worksheets were considered to be 'well-designed activity-based lessons'.

*van Boxel P, Anderson K and Regnard C (2003) The effectiveness of palliative care education delivered by videoconferencing compared with face-to-face delivery. *Palliative Medicine.* 17: 344–58.

Our experience has been that the worksheets can be used in a variety of settings: self-learning, one-to-one with a tutor, small groups, large groups and even in lecture-theatre settings of 100, although interaction is less with larger groups. We find that:

- Learners comment that the worksheets
  - can be used interactively during sessions
  - double as handouts
  - can be used later as updates or reminders.
- Tutors comment that the worksheets
  - give structure to a discussion
  - can be easily incorporated into a presentation
  - provide a 'change of pace'
  - encourage further discussion.

Suggestions on ways of using the worksheets follow.

Using the worksheets in different settings

Format of worksheets

All the worksheets are in four sections:

1. Title, information on that worksheet, instructions and case study.
2. Information page. This gives answers to all the activities and questions on the work page.
3. Work page. Activities and questions.
4. A suggested further activity (optional) and further reading.

Learning levels

Each worksheet has been assigned a learning level (Introductory, Intermediate, Advanced) to give an indication of how much prior experience or knowledge is required for that worksheet.

Order of worksheets

Each worksheet is self-contained, but later worksheets in a series may assume knowledge in previous worksheets. Use of intermediate worksheets assumes knowledge in the introductory worksheets, while use of the advanced worksheets assumes knowledge in the introductory and intermediate worksheets.

Self-learning setting

Since the worksheets are self-contained they can be used by individuals in different ways:

- introduction to a new subject
- update or reminder of a subject.

In this setting, a worksheet takes approximately 15 minutes.

Small group setting

Worksheets can be used by tutors in different ways:

- as preparation prior to a presentation
- as the main component of a workshop
- as an illustration of an issue to stimulate discussion
- as a different format for variety in a longer presentation or workshop
- as handouts for 'further reading'.

In the first four formats, discussion means that each worksheet will take 20–30 minutes.

Lecture theatre setting

The CLIP worksheets have been used with groups of 20, and on occasions with up to 100, with the following observations:

- There is inevitably less interaction.
- Most discussion comes from a few individuals, but most use the worksheets.
- Even limited discussion can be enjoyed by other learners.
- All those present need copies of the worksheet which double as handouts.
- The worksheets should be used between other presentation methods for variety.

Advice for using the worksheets

Advice for learners

Aim of these worksheets: To consider aspects of palliative care.

How to use each worksheet:

- Choose a worksheet at the level you want (Introductory, Intermediate or Advanced).
- You can work through the worksheet by yourself or with a tutor (this may be in a small tutorial, in a lecture setting or over a videoconferencing link).
- Read the case study, then work on the questions.
- The work page is on the right side, the information page is on the left.
- Work any way you want: you can try answering from your own knowledge (in which case cover the information page), you can use the information page (this is not cheating – you learn as you find the information) or you can use other sources of information.
- It should take you about 15 minutes working through the worksheet by yourself – if anything is unclear, discuss it with a colleague.
- Finally, use the 'Further Activity' on the last page of each worksheet to put your learning into practice.

Advice for tutors

Decide on:
- The subjects to be covered – these are best chosen by the learners.
- The level that is appropriate for the learner's experience and knowledge:
  - *Introductory* if this is new to the learner
  - *Intermediate* if the learner has some experience of the subject
  - *Advanced* for the learner already experienced in the subject.
- The setting can be:
  - self-learning as an introduction to a subject
  - self-learning as an update
  - small group work
  - lecture theatre setting
  - over a videoconferencing link.

Process:
- Read out the case study.
- Start working through the questions.
- Expand on the information as time allows.
- Encourage discussion and debate.
- Encourage groups of 2–3 to complete tasks.
- Consider setting the learners the activity or suggest an alternative one yourself.

In a tutorial setting:
- Allow up to 30 minutes for each worksheet.
- Encourage individual feedback.
- Be flexible about time.

In a lecture setting:
- Ensure everyone has a copy of the worksheet.
- Keep more closely to the worksheet and to time.
- Accept that only some learners will feedback.

Choosing a worksheet

Intro = Introductory; *Intmd* = Intermediate;
Adv = Advanced

Introduction to palliative care

1	What is palliative care?	*Intro*
2	Meeting the very ill adult for the first time	*Intro*
3	Making sensible decisions	*Intro*

Helping the patient with pain

1	What is pain?	*Intro*
2	Issues in assessing pain	*Intro*
3	Diagnosing the cause of pain	*Intmd*
4	Choosing an analgesic	*Intmd*
5	Using morphine	*Intmd*
6	Alternatives to morphine	*Adv*
7	Changing opioids	*Adv*
8	Persisting pain	*Adv*
9	Managing severe pain	*Adv*

Helping the patient with symptoms other than pain

1	Constipation	*Intro*
2	Fatigue, lethargy, drowsiness and weakness	*Intmd*
3	Breathlessness	*Intro*
4	Oral problems	*Intro*
5	Nausea and vomiting	*Intmd*
6	Bowel obstruction	*Intmd*
7	Oedema	*Intmd*
8	Lymphoedema	*Adv*
9	Confusion	*Intmd*
10	Recognising emergencies	*Intmd*
11	Issues around resuscitation	*Intmd*

Moving the ill patient

1	General principles	*Intro*
2	Equipment, adaptations and improving the environment	*Intmd*

Psychological needs

1	Fostering hope	*Intro*
2	Helping the person to share their problems	*Intro*
3	Breaking difficult news	*Intmd*
4	Helping the anxious person	*Intmd*
5	Helping the angry person	*Intmd*
6	Answering difficult questions	*Intmd*
7	Helping the withdrawn patient	*Adv*
8	Collusion and denial	*Adv*

Helping the patient with reduced hydration and nutrition

1	Maintaining the environment for eating and drinking	*Intro*
2	Balancing the diet	*Intmd*
3	Enriching and fortifying the diet	*Intmd*
4	Decisions in hydration and nutrition	*Intmd*
5	Thinking about swallowing problems	*Intmd*
6	Using non-oral routes	*Adv*
7	Managing a gastrostomy	*Adv*
8	The cachexia syndrome	*Adv*

Procedures in palliative care

1	Setting up a Graseby syringe driver	*Intmd*
2	Problems with a subcutaneous infusion	*Intmd*
3	Spinal analgesia: problems with two drugs	*Adv*
4	Spinal analgesia: problems with the line	*Adv*

Helping the person with communication difficulties

1	Conditions causing communication difficulties	*Intro*
2	Identifying distress	*Intro*
3	Down's syndrome	*Intmd*
4	Epilepsy	*Intmd*
5	Dementia	*Intmd*

The last hours and days

1	Adjustments	*Intmd*
2	Managing distress	*Intmd*
3	The death	*Intro*
4	A friend dies . . .	*Intro*

Bereavement

1	The loss begins . . .	*Intro*
2	The effect of death on staff	*Intro*
3	Assessing risk	*Intmd*

List of contributors

Sarah Alport
Senior Nurse
St Oswald's Hospice, Newcastle upon Tyne

Christine Armstrong
Senior 1 Occupational Therapist
NHS Beacon Palliative Care in Learning Disability Team,
Northgate Hospital, Northumberland

Christine K Armstrong
Clinical Coordinator
NHS Beacon Palliative Care in Learning Disability Team,
Northgate Hospital, Northumberland

Lisa Bushby
Occupational Therapist
St Oswald's Hospice, Newcastle upon Tyne

Jackie Chaplin
Marie Curie Centre, Newcastle upon Tyne

Sue Clark
Head Speech and Language Therapist
Royal Victoria Infirmary, Newcastle upon Tyne

Sylvia Dryden
Staff Development Officer
Marie Curie Centre, Newcastle upon Tyne

Tracey Forrester
Head of Children's Services
St Oswald's Hospice, Newcastle upon Tyne

Lynn Gibson
Senior Physiotherapist
NHS Beacon Palliative Care in Learning Disability Team,
Northgate Hospital, Northumberland

Andrew Hughes
Consultant in Palliative Medicine
St Oswald's Hospice, Newcastle upon Tyne,
and Gateshead NHS Trust

Janet Jackson
Chaplain
St Oswald's Hospice, Newcastle upon Tyne

Christine Jensen
Occupational Therapist
Palliative Care in Learning Disability Team,
Northgate Hospital, Northumberland

Margaret Kindlen
Head of Education
St Oswald's Hospice, Newcastle upon Tyne

Laura Lowes
Senior Physiotherapist
Palliative Care in Learning Disability Team,
Northgate Hospital, Northumberland

Paul McNamara
Consultant in Palliative Medicine
St Oswald's Hospice, Newcastle upon Tyne,
and Northumberland NHS Trust

Dorothy Matthews
Senior Nurse
NHS Beacon Palliative Care in Learning Disability Team,
Northgate Hospital, Northumberland

Kathryn Mannix
Consultant in Palliative Medicine
Marie Curie Centre, Newcastle upon Tyne,
and Newcastle City Hospitals NHS Trust

Tessa Nichol
Social Worker
St Oswald's Hospice and Newcastle Social Services,
Newcastle upon Tyne

Gail Nicholson
Senior Nurse, Outpatient Services
St Oswald's Hospice, Newcastle upon Tyne

Claud Regnard
Consultant in Palliative Medicine
St Oswald's Hospice, Newcastle upon Tyne,
Newcastle City Hospitals NHS Trust
and Northgate and Prudhoe NHS Trust
Honorary Lecturer in Pharmacological Sciences
University of Newcastle upon Tyne

John W Thompson
Emeritus Professor of Pharmacological Sciences
University of Newcastle upon Tyne

Rev Bryan Vernon
Lecturer in the Ethics of Health Care
Department of Primary Health Care,
University of Newcastle upon Tyne

Tom Walwyn
SHO in Paediatrics
Sunderland Royal Infirmary

Margaret Younger
Children's Unit Project Manager
St Oswald's Hospice, Newcastle upon Tyne

Acknowledgements

Development of the following worksheets was supported by Help the Hospices for the IMPACT project: *Using morphine, Constipation, Breathlessness, Nausea and vomiting, Bowel obstruction, Helping the anxious person, Helping the angry person, Helping the withdrawn patient, Setting up a Graseby syringe driver, Problems with a subcutaneous infusion, Spinal analgesia: problems with the line, Adjustments, Managing distress, The death, A friend dies . . . .*

Development of the following worksheets was supported by the NHS Executive BEACON initiative, Northgate Palliative Care Team NHS Beacon site: *General principles, Equipment, Adaptations and improving the environment, Decisions in hydration and nutrition, Thinking about swallowing problems, Using non-oral routes, Managing a gastrostomy, The cachexia syndrome, Conditions causing communication difficulties, Identifying distress, Down's syndrome, Epilepsy, Dementia, The loss begins . . . , The effect of death on staff, Assessing risk.*

Development of the following worksheets was supported by Help the Hospices for the IMPACT project and by the NHS Executive BEACON initiative, Northgate Palliative Care Team NHS Beacon site: *Diagnosing the cause of pain, Balancing the diet, Enriching and fortifying the diet.*

About the editor

Claud Regnard is Consultant in Palliative Medicine, at St Oswald's Hospice, Newcastle City Hospitals NHS Trust and Northgate and Prudhoe NHS Trust, and Honorary Lecturer in Pharmacological Sciences, University of Newcastle upon Tyne.

He can be contacted via email at claudregnard@stoswaldsuk.org

INTRODUCTION TO PALLIATIVE CARE

1 What is palliative care?

Claud Regnard
Tom Walwyn
Tracey Forrester
Margaret Kindlen

INTRODUCTORY LEVEL

Aim of this worksheet

To review the basic principles of palliative care in adults and children.

How to use this worksheet

- You can work through this worksheet by yourself, or with a tutor.

- The work page is on the right side, the information page is on the left.

- Work any way you want: you can try answering from your own knowledge (in which case, fold over the information page), you can use the information page (this is not cheating – you learn as you find the information) or you can use other sources of information.

- It should take you about 15 minutes. If anything is unclear, discuss it with a colleague.

- If you think any information is wrong or out of date, let us know.

- Use the activity on the back page and take this learning into your workplace.

INFORMATION PAGE

Defining palliative care in adults and children

Palliative care:
- is the right of every adult and child and the duty of every professional
- is about the holistic care of adults and children with life-limiting and life-threatening illness
- closely involves the partner, family or relatives
- includes care of the dying and bereavement support (although 60% of adults and nearly 100% of children in many hospices will return home after their first admission)
- can occur in any setting, but both adults and children spend most of their illness at home
- aims to support existing services, collaborating with them to tailor the care to the patient
- requires good symptom control (physical and psychological)
- is not limited to cancer (up to 18% of adults and 90% of children in hospices do not have cancer)
- has no age limits (although adult and children's services usually work separately)
- is the alternative to euthanasia.

It has also been called 'A safe place to suffer' (Averil Stedeford (1987) *Palliative Medicine.* **1**: 73–4):
- Effective physical symptom control is essential.
- Some psychological suffering will be left.
- It is therapeutic for this suffering to be expressed.
- Expression will only occur if it is safe.
- Removal of the suffering is not always possible.
- Expression can be enabled almost anywhere (i.e. it is not dependent on a hospice building).

Symptoms left unrelieved

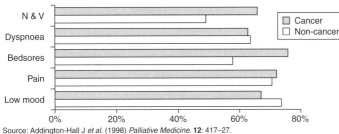

Two-thirds of adults remain very distressed by their symptoms. This figure of unrelieved distress is about the same for non-cancer adults.
There are no comparative figures for children with life-threatening or life-limiting illness.
There is still much work to be done in palliative care.

Source: Addington-Hall J *et al.* (1998) *Palliative Medicine.* **12**: 417–27.

Palliative care in children

1100 children die each year from conditions for which there is no reasonable hope of cure: 40% from cancers, 20% from heart disease and 40% from other life-limiting conditions. There are many similarities with adult palliative care (*see* above), but there are also important differences: 1) a wider range of conditions, 2) the longer time span of conditions (often years), 3) issues around their physical and intellectual development, 4) much less involvement with cancer (since these children are treated by oncological teams), 5) the fact that conditions may affect several members of the same family, 6) the intensity of support needed for the whole family, 7) the presentation of symptoms, 8) the effects of drugs on young children and 9) legal issues of treating and caring for children.

When should palliative care start?

Adults: In cancer patients palliative care may start at diagnosis, although it is more usual for it to start when cure is no longer possible. In neurological disease such as motor neurone disease, palliative care can start at diagnosis for patients since their prognosis can be much worse than many cancers. For other neurological diseases (e.g. multiple sclerosis) they may be first seen by the rehabilitation services, and only referred at a late stage to palliative care. In AIDS patients, treatment today is aimed at controlling the disease and this has greatly limited the need for referral to palliative care services, but patients do continue to succumb to AIDS, and palliative care now sees more patients with AIDS-related dementia.

Children: Four groups are recognised:
- Group 1: conditions for which cure is possible, but may fail (e.g. cancer, irreversible failure of heart, liver or kidney)
- Group 2: conditions where long-term treatment aims to prolong life, but death is still possible (e.g. cystic fibrosis)
- Group 3: progressive conditions lasting many years (e.g. Batten's disease, mucopolysaccharidoses)
- Group 4: conditions causing severe disability which increase susceptibility to health complications which may cause sudden deterioration (e.g. disabilities following severe brain or spinal cord injury, including some with cerebral palsy).

Groups 1 and 2 may need palliative care at times of uncertainty or in the terminal stages. Groups 3 and 4 may need support from palliative care services on a regular basis.

NB. As medical care improves, some of these children are now growing into their teens and early adulthood.

WORK PAGE

 Think The following have all been used to describe palliative care. (Ring) those descriptions that you feel are the closest to reality

The right of every patient	Terminal care	Cancer care
Macmillan care	Symptom control	Euthanasia
The duty of every professional	Hospice care	Home care
Care of advanced, progressive disease	Care of the dying	A safe place to suffer

 Think In one study, what percentage of cancer adults do you think remained very distressed by the following symptoms?

Pain	less than 20%	50%	Two-thirds	80%
Nausea and vomiting	less than 20%	50%	Two-thirds	80%
Breathlessness	less than 20%	50%	Two-thirds	80%

 Think Do you think these figures would be different for non-cancer patients?

Lower About the same Higher

List the similarities and differences in the palliative care of adults and children.

Similarities	How are children different?
. . . .	. . . .
. . . .	. . . .
. . . .	. . . .
. . . .	. . . .
. . . .	. . . .
. . . .	. . . .
. . . .	. . . .

 Think When should palliative care start?

For a cancer adult	at diagnosis	when cure is no longer possible	in the last weeks
For motor neurone disease	at diagnosis	when cure is no longer possible	in the last weeks
For a child with severe cerebral palsy	at diagnosis	when cure is no longer possible	in the last weeks

FURTHER ACTIVITY

Over the next week observe:

- how many patients have palliative care needs now

- how many patients may have palliative care needs in the future.

FURTHER READING

Journal articles

Belasco JB, Danz P, Drill A, Schmid W and Burkey E (2000) Supportive care: palliative care in children, adolescents, and young adults – model of care, interventions, and cost of care: a retrospective review. *Journal of Palliative Care.* 16(4): 39–46.

Fainsinger RL (2000) A century of progress in palliative care. *Lancet.* 356: 24.

Gilmer MJ (2002) Pediatric palliative care: a family-centered model for critical care. *Critical Care Nursing Clinics of North America.* 14(2): 207–14.

Goldman A (2001) Recent advances in palliative care. Importance of palliative care for children is being increasingly recognised. *BMJ.* 322: 234.

Horsburgh M, Trenholme A and Huckle T (2002) Paediatric respite care: a literature review from New Zealand. *Palliative Medicine.* 16(2): 99–105.

Kane JR, Barber RG, Jordan M *et al.* (2000) Supportive/palliative care of children suffering from life-threatening and terminal illness. *American Journal of Hospice and Palliative Care.* 17(3): 165–72.

Makin W, Finlay IG, Amesbury B *et al.* (2000) What do palliative medicine consultants do? *Palliative Medicine.* 14(5): 405–9.

Oliver D and Webb S (2000) The involvement of specialist palliative care in the care of people with motor neurone disease. *Palliative Medicine.* 14(5): 427–8.

Roy DJ (2000) The times and places of palliative care. *Journal of Palliative Care.* 16(Suppl): S3–4.

Shuster JL Jr (2000) Palliative care for advanced dementia. *Clinics in Geriatric Medicine.* 16(2): 373–86.

Szlosarek PW (2001) Recent advances in palliative care. United Kingdom continues to lead in palliative care. *BMJ.* 322: 234.

Thorns AR, Gibbs LM and Gibbs JS (2001) Management of severe heart failure by specialist palliative care. *Heart.* 85(1): 93.

Twycross RG (1999) Palliative care in the past decade and today. *European Journal of Pain.* 3(Suppl. A): 23–29.

Webster J and Kristjanson LJ (2002) 'But isn't it depressing?' The vitality of palliative care. *Journal of Palliative Care.* 18(1): 15–24.

Resource books and websites

2000 Directory of Hospice and Palliative Care Services in the United Kingdom and Republic of Ireland. London: Hospice Information Service at St Christopher's.

Doyle D, Hanks GWC and Calman K (eds) (2003) *Oxford Textbook of Palliative Medicine* (3e). Oxford University Press, Oxford.

Providing a Palliative Care Service: towards an evidence base. (1999) Oxford University Press, Oxford.

Twycross R (2003) *Introducing Palliative Care* (4e). Radcliffe Medical Press, Oxford.

www.act.org.uk – Association for Children with Life-threatening or Terminal Conditions and their Families.

www.stchristophers.org/hic – Information on available palliative care services in the UK.

INTRODUCTION TO PALLIATIVE CARE

2 Meeting the very ill adult for the first time

Claud Regnard
Sarah Alport
Margaret Kindlen

INTRODUCTORY LEVEL

Aim of this worksheet

To understand that very ill adults are simply people who happen to be very ill!

How to use this worksheet

- You can work through this worksheet by yourself, or with a tutor.

- Read the case study below, then work on the questions overleaf.

- The work page is on the right side, the information page is on the left.

- Work any way you want: you can try answering from your own knowledge (in which case, fold over the information page), you can use the information page (this is not cheating – you learn as you find the information) or you can use other sources of information.

- It should take you about 15 minutes. If anything is unclear, discuss it with a colleague.

- If you think any information is wrong or out of date, let us know.

- Use the activity on the back page and take this learning into your workplace.

Case study

Mary is a 29-year-old lady, married with two young children. Eight months ago she was found to have an advanced pelvic tumour which was inoperable. She received radiotherapy but the tumour persisted and she now has problems with pain and nausea. You are new to this area of work and are seeing Mary for the first time.

INFORMATION PAGE

Meeting a very ill person for the first time

It may feel more difficult if:
- you feel so nervous you forget to introduce yourself
- you ask only about clinical issues
- you don't listen to what Mary is saying
- Mary is quiet or nervous
- you are still struggling with the effects of a bereavement
- you are afraid you will do Mary some psychological harm by saying the wrong thing.

It may feel easier if:
- you remember to be polite
- you ask about her feelings
- you remember that you won't do any psychological harm if you listen to what Mary is saying
- Mary is chatty and friendly
- you have had previous contact with ill people
- you care about Mary's problems.

What do you say?

How about treating her like a fellow human being!

If you met her in any other circumstance, you would welcome her in with a smile, shake hands, introduce yourself and say why you are there.

Meeting a very ill person for the first time is uncomfortable for most of us.

Answering difficult questions

Difficult questions are difficult because they're difficult and uncomfortable to answer:
- they're NOT difficult because you haven't got the right skills
- skills help you cope with such questions, but they remain difficult questions!

They're difficult because of two conflicting feelings:
- we all have a desire to 'fix it' or 'make it better' (and not distress the person) but
- this is not something we can fix (which is going to upset the person).

1 F: Telling it 'like it is' assumes that a) you have asked her if she wants to know and b) that you know exactly what is going on. If you're new to this type of work both are unlikely. (*See also* CLIP worksheet *Breaking difficult news*.)

2 F: You can avoid the question by asking about her pain, but she will immediately notice this avoidance and may not ask you again. (That may be more comfortable for you, but has it helped her?)

3 T: Honesty is always appreciated by patients and is *never* a loss of face or professionalism.

4 T: If you ask why she's asking this question, this acknowledges that you have heard and acknowledged the importance of her question. She may be willing to talk more about it. She knows you won't give her the answers but you will have helped by making it safe for her to express her fears. Just remember you don't have to fix them!

5 T: This is the right thing to do if you can't answer, but be sure to say it politely, e.g. 'Please ask one of the doctors or nurses. If you want, I can let them know you asked.' Also make sure that the person(s) you direct them to can help with their question.

What happens if she gets upset?

This is often the biggest anxiety for professionals (it's part of the 'fix-it/make-it-better' syndrome). Use care and common sense:
- Acknowledge that she's upset, e.g. 'I can see you're upset.' (Professionals often forget this step.)
- Make contact through touch, e.g. a hand lightly on an arm. (But withdraw if she withdraws.)
- Stay silent for a while (the hardest thing to do for 'fix-it' people!).
- Ask her if she wants to continue or needs a break. (Leave her in control.)

If you feel Mary needs more help, remember to include the GP and Macmillan nurse, the team social worker or another professional with counselling training.

WORK PAGE

Think What factors do you think will affect how you get on with Mary?

Factors that will make it harder   Factors that will make it easier

. . . .

. . . .

. . . .

. . . .

. . . .

Think As Mary comes in to see you, what can you say?

. . . .

. . . .

. . . .

. . . .

. . . .

MCQ Mary asks you how ill you think she is.

How do you respond?

1 Tell it like it is	True	False
2 Ask about her pain	True	False
3 Explain that you're new and don't know the answer	True	False
4 Ask her why she's asking that question	True	False
5 Ask her to ask someone else	True	False

Think Mary looks anxious and upset. What can you do? Who else could you ask to be involved?

. . . .

. . . .

. . . .

. . . .

FURTHER ACTIVITY

Think back to the last very ill person you met.

* What did you do to try to make the meeting easier?

* What did the patient do to try to make the meeting easier?

FURTHER READING

Journal articles

Booth K, Maguire P and Hillier VF (1999) Measurement of communication skills in cancer care: myth or reality? *Journal of Advanced Nursing.* 30(5): 1073–9.

Heaven CM and Maguire P (1997) Disclosure of concerns by hospice patients and their identification by nurses. *Palliative Medicine.* 11(4): 283–90.

Heaven CM and Maguire P (1998) The relationship between patients' concerns and psychological distress in a hospice setting. *Psycho-Oncology.* 7(6): 502–7.

Hurny C (2000) Communicating about cancer: Patients' needs and caregivers' skills. *Supportive Care in Cancer.* 8(6): 437–8.

Maguire P (1999) Improving communication with cancer patients. *European Journal of Cancer.* 35(14): 2058–65.

Maguire P (1999) Improving communication with cancer patients. *European Journal of Cancer.* 35(10): 1415–22.

Maguire P, Faulkner A and Booth K (1996) Helping cancer patients disclose their concerns. *European Journal of Cancer.* 32A(1): 78–81.

Maguire P, Walsh S, Jeacock J *et al.* (1999) Physical and psychological needs of patients dying from colo-rectal cancer. *Palliative Medicine.* 13(1): 45–50.

Ong LML, Visser MRM, Lammes FB *et al.* (2000) Doctor-patient communication and cancer patients' quality of life and satisfaction. *Patient Education and Counselling.* 41(2): 145–56.

Wright EP, Selby PJ, Gould A *et al.* (2001) Detecting social problems in cancer patients. *Psycho-Oncology.* 10(3): 242–50.

Resource books

Faulkner A and Maguire P (1994) *Talking to Cancer Patients and Their Relatives.* Oxford University Press, Oxford.

Lichter I (1987) *Communication in Cancer Care.* Churchill Livingstone, Edinburgh.

Stedeford A (1984) *Facing Death: patients, families and professionals.* Heinemann Medical Books, London.

University of York, NHS Centre for Reviews and Dissemination (2000) *Informing, Communicating and Sharing Decisions with People Who Have Cancer.* Centre for Reviews and Dissemination in association with the Royal Society of Medicine Press, York.

INTRODUCTION TO PALLIATIVE CARE

3 Making sensible decisions

Claud Regnard
Margaret Kindlen

INTRODUCTORY LEVEL

Aim of this worksheet

To understand that sensible decisions just need common sense – don't panic!

How to use this worksheet

- You can work through this worksheet by yourself, or with a tutor.

- Read the case study below, then work on the questions overleaf.

- The work page is on the right side, the information page is on the left.

- Work any way you want: you can try answering from your own knowledge (in which case, fold over the information page), you can use the information page (this is not cheating – you learn as you find the information) or you can use other sources of information.

- It should take you about 15 minutes. If anything is unclear, discuss it with a colleague.

- If you think any information is wrong or out of date, let us know.

- Use the activity on the back page and take this learning into your workplace.

Case study

Mary is a 29-year-old lady, married with two young children. Eight months ago she was found to have an advanced pelvic tumour which was inoperable. She received radiotherapy but the tumour persisted. She has been admitted with severe abdominal pain.

   The family are around her bed. Her husband is holding her hand and looks very worried, while the oldest child is clinging to dad. The youngest child is playing happily with a doll.

INFORMATION PAGE

Helping the distressed patient

What you need are care and common sense – don't panic!

Psychological things that may help:
- Smile, light touch, introduce yourself. **(Be polite)**
- Explain that you're there to help. **(Be informative)**
- Acknowledge that she looks distressed. **(Be sensitive)**

Other things that may help:
- Get information about her pain, e.g. Where, Character, Radiation, Precipitating and Relieving Factors (*see* CLIP worksheet *Diagnosing the cause of pain*). **(Be accurate)**
- Get help if you can't deal with the pain yourself. **(Be sensible)**
- While waiting for help or medication to work, sit with her, and ask how she feels. **(Be compassionate)**

Making decisions: dealing with 'The Fog'

In most situations, professional carers make sensitive, sensible and logical decisions, but in very advanced disease, these decisions can become insensitive, irrational and unhelpful. This has been described by Robert Twycross as the 'Cancer fog', but it could equally be the 'AIDS fog' or the 'Multiple Sclerosis fog'. This 'fog' is caused by too many emotive and unfamiliar demands coming together at one time. This drives many professionals to rely on automatic behaviour that they learnt last time they were in a similar situation. (An irreverent example would be Noah telling his workers to 'Have a break until the rain's finished!' It seems sensible at the time, but in the overall context of The Flood it makes no sense.)

'The Fog' catches everyone out from time to time, so it's worth knowing what makes it worse and what makes it easier.

Things that may make 'The Fog' worse:
- a patient in acute distress
- a distressed or angry relative
- the presence of children, especially if they seem vulnerable
- a tired professional
- training that relies too much on 'surviving'
- using a standard routine to treat an unusual problem
- lack of recognition that when we are stressed we all fall back on routines that are familiar, but that these routines were learnt under stress and may not be helpful.

Things that may make 'The Fog' clearer:
- using the skills and knowledge you already have
- using common sense
- being sensitive to what the patient and partner are saying to you
- acknowledging the distress of the patient and partner
- accepting that there are some situations that need alternative approaches.

Some principles

There are probably many principles, but we suggest that whatever you do you should be:
- **P**ragmatic
- **A**ccessible
- **S**uitable
- **S**imple.

WORK PAGE

Mary is clearly distressed, going pale every few minutes with abdominal pain, whimpering when it is at its most severe.

Don't Panic What can you do to ease Mary's pain and distress?

Psychological help   Physical help

. . . .

. . . .

. . . .

. . . .

. . . .

. . . .

Why are making decisions in this situation difficult? What would make it easier?

These make it difficult   These would make it easier

. . . .

. . . .

. . . .

. . . .

. . . .

. . . .

Write down some principles that would make it easier for you to help a very ill person.

. . . .

. . . .

. . . .

. . . .

. . . .

. . . .

FURTHER ACTIVITY

Think back to the last distressed person you met.

- What made 'the fog' more difficult?

- What made it easier?

FURTHER READING

Journal article

Tierney WM (2001) Improving clinical decisions and outcomes with information: a review. *International Journal of Medical Informatics*. **62**(1): 1–9.

Resource book

Regnard C and Hockley J (2004) *A Guide to Symptom Relief in Palliative Care* (5e). Radcliffe Medical Press, Oxford.

HELPING THE PATIENT WITH PAIN

1 What is pain?

Claud Regnard
Margaret Kindlen

INTRODUCTORY LEVEL

Aim of this worksheet

To consider general aspects of pain and pain relief.

How to use this worksheet

- You can work through this worksheet by yourself, or with a tutor.

- The work page is on the right side, the information page is on the left.

- Work any way you want: you can try answering from your own knowledge (in which case, fold over the information page), you can use the information page (this is not cheating – you learn as you find the information) or you can use other sources of information.

- It should take you about 15 minutes. If anything is unclear, discuss it with a colleague.

- If you think any information is wrong or out of date, let us know.

- Use the activity on the back page and take this learning into your workplace.

INFORMATION PAGE

What is pain?

Here are three definitions:
- Pain is perceived along a spectrum from peripheral pain receptors to the cerebral cortex, and is modified at every step along its path.
- Pain is an unpleasant, complex, sensory and emotional experience.
- Pain is what the patient says it is.

The first definition sounds authoritative, while the last sounds simplistic (and ungrammatical!). In practice, the last definition is probably the most helpful since only the patient can really know what their pain is really like. The second definition is a compromise between the two and might be preferred by those who prefer a 'proper' definition!

Causes of failure to relieve pain

Pain may remain untreated or inadequately treated for many reasons. Here are some of the reasons, with their consequences (you may have thought of some more):

Reasons	Consequences
Belief that pain is inevitable	Unnecessary pain
Inaccurate diagnosis of the cause	Inappropriate treatment
Lack of understanding of analgesics	Use of inappropriate, insufficient or infrequent analgesics
Unrealistic objectives	Dissatisfaction with treatment
Infrequent review	Rejection of treatment by patient
Insufficient attention to mood and morale	Lowered pain threshold

(Adapted from Twycross RG (1972) *Update*. **5**: 115–21.)

Pain in cancer and non-cancer diseases

Pain in cancer is often overestimated, while it is often underestimated in other conditions.

In reality, around 60% of patients with advanced disease get troublesome pain, and this figure is similar for AIDS, cardiac disease and neurological disorders. The scandal for people with advanced, non-cancer disease is that they are much less likely to be treated for their pain.

Acute versus chronic pain

During their training most professionals meet patients with acute pain (e.g. a fracture) and are much less likely to meet a patient with chronic pain (e.g. neuralgia), let alone be taught how to manage such pain. Consequently, it can be difficult to appreciate the differences in the effect of these different pains on the patient and their carer:

	Acute pain (e.g. fracture)	Chronic pain (e.g. neuralgia)
Patient	Obviously in pain	May only seem depressed
	Complains loudly of pain	May only complain of discomfort
	Understands why they have pain	May see pain as unending and meaningless
	Primarily affects the patient	Pain overflows to affect family and carers
Carer	Treatment is straightforward	Treatment may be complex
	Parenteral analgesics acceptable	Oral analgesics preferable
	Analgesic effects acceptable	Adverse effects unacceptable

Principles

There are many possible principles arising from this page of information. Here are three (you may have more):
- Pain is what the patient says it is.
- Most causes of unrelieved pain are unrelated to analgesics.
- Chronic pain cannot be treated the same as acute pain.

WORK PAGE

We have all experienced pain, but there are some rare people who cannot perceive pain. How would you tell them about pain?

Think   How would you describe and define pain?

. . . .

. . . .

. . . .

. . . .

In one survey, 88% of patients with advanced disease had pain in the last year of life; 66% found this pain 'very distressing'.

Talk it over   Talk to a colleague and write down reasons why you think there is so much unrelieved pain.

. . . .

. . . .

. . . .

. . . .

Ring the percentage closest to the correct amount of distressing pain in the following conditions?

Cancer	10%	30%	60%	80%	Motor neurone diseases	10%	30%	60%	80%
AIDS	10%	30%	60%	80%	End-stage cardiac disease	10%	30%	60%	80%

Most people have seen or treated acute pain (e.g. any injury), but many people have much less experience of persistent, long-term pain.

What are the differences between acute and chronic pain for the patient and carer?

Acute pain (e.g. fracture)	Chronic pain (e.g. neuralgia)
Patient	
Carer	

FURTHER ACTIVITY

Think back to a pain you have experienced:

• How would you describe it in a letter to a friend?

FURTHER READING

Journal articles

Davies J and McVicar A (2000) Issues in effective pain control. 1: Assessment and education. *International Journal of Palliative Nursing.* **6**(2): 58–65.

Davies J and McVicar A (2000) Issues in effective pain control. 2: From assessment to management. *International Journal of Palliative Nursing.* **6**(4): 162–9.

Mayer DM, Torma L and Byock I (2000) Speaking the language of pain. *American Journal of Nursing.* **101**(2): 44–9.

Twycross RG (1994) The fight against cancer pain. *Annals of Oncology.* **5**(2): 111–12.

Twycross RG (1999) Palliative care in the past decade and today. *European Journal of Pain.* 3(Suppl. A): 23–9.

Resource books and website

Calman K, Doyle D and Hanks GWC (eds) (2003) *The Oxford Textbook of Palliative Medicine* (3e). Oxford University Publications, Oxford.

Cancer Pain Relief and Palliative Care. (1990) WHO, Geneva.

Melzack R (1996) *The Challenge of Pain.* Updated (2e). Penguin Books, London.

Melzack R and Wall PD (1999) *Textbook of Pain* (4e). Churchill Livingstone, Edinburgh.

Regnard C and Hockley J (2004) *A Guide to Symptom Relief in Palliative Care* (5e). Radcliffe Medical Press, Oxford.

Twycross R and Lack SA (1988) *Oral Morphine, Information for Patients, Families and Friends.* Beaconsfield Publishers, Beaconsfield.

Twycross RG and Wilcock A (2001) *Symptom Management in Advanced Cancer* (3e). Radcliffe Medical Press, Oxford.

Twycross RG, Wilcock A and Charlesworth S (2003) *PCF2 – Palliative Care Formulary* (2e). Radcliffe Medical Press, Oxford.

www.palliativedrugs.com – Updated website for the *Palliative Care Formulary.*

HELPING THE PATIENT WITH PAIN

2 Issues in assessing pain

Claud Regnard
Margaret Kindlen
Sylvia Dryden

INTRODUCTORY LEVEL

Aim of this worksheet

To consider further issues relating to the assessment of pain.

How to use this worksheet

- You can work through this worksheet by yourself, or with a tutor.

- Read the case study below, then work on the questions overleaf.

- The work page is on the right side, the information page is on the left.

- Work any way you want: you can try answering from your own knowledge (in which case, fold over the information page), you can use the information page (this is not cheating – you learn as you find the information) or you can use other sources of information.

- It should take you about 15 minutes. If anything is unclear, discuss it with a colleague.

- If you think any information is wrong or out of date, let us know.

- Use the activity on the back page and take this learning into your workplace.

Case study

Pat is a 36-year-old woman, married, with two sons aged 12 and 9 years. She had problems with her bowels for several months before some rectal bleeding made her see her GP. Investigations revealed a carcinoma of the sigmoid colon with liver metastases. She copes by maintaining a level of denial and refuses to tell her sons. She tends not to complain of pain, but grimaces whenever she sits down. She looks anxious.

INFORMATION PAGE

Assessing pain

You need to ask Pat:
- How long has it been present?
- How is it affecting her daily activities?
- Is it affecting her relationships?
- How is the pain making her feel?
- How severe is the pain?
- What goals does she have for the pain?

Of all of these, severity is the *least* important in deciding treatment, with two exceptions:
- pain of such severity that it demands an immediate response
- when you need to convince a colleague that a patient has pain!

It is important to know Pat's goals at this stage.
- If they are unrealistic, we need to negotiate some shorter term goals.
- If they are too pessimistic, we need to negotiate some longer term goals.

Problems in assessing pain

- The number of different pains (50% of patients have three or more different pains) (Twycross RG *et al.* (1996) *Journal of Pain and Symptom Management.* **12**: 273–82).
- Not all pains respond to morphine.
- Patients underplaying their pain.
- Beware the stoic: 'I think there's a pain somewhere in the room, but I could not positively say that I have got it.' (Mrs Gradgrind from *Hard Times* by Charles Dickens.)

- Patients reacting markedly to their pain (usually anxiety, anger or depression are present).
- Staff or partners assessing a patient's pain. 'Your own pain is certainty: another person's pain is uncertainty.'
- The patient with poor or absent communication (coma, confusion, dysphasia, learning disability) (*see* CLIP worksheet *Identifying distress*).

Help with assessing pain

Tool	Advantages	Disadvantages
Asking the patient	Highly accurate and reproducible!	Almost none
Asking the partner or a colleague	Useful when communication with the patient is difficult	Strongly subject to bias
Body chart	Simple to use, involves the patient, helps with diagnosis	Almost none
Visual analogue scale (VAS)	Very useful, simple research tool that includes the patient's subjective view about their pain	Some patients have difficulty understanding the concept
Categorical scale	Simple to use, especially to convince other professionals of a patient's pain! Useful in research (? more consistent than VAS)	May be less sensitive than VAS
Pain diary	Provides qualitative information for care and research use	Difficult for patients to complete over long periods
Pain questionnaire	Useful research tool, provides some qualitative data	Not suitable for daily use

Principles

- Set realistic goals.
- Understand the problems of assessment.
- Know which pain assessment tools are best in which situations.

WORK PAGE

Talk *it* over Talk to a colleague and write down what else you would want to know about Pat's pain. (Ring) the ones you think are *most* important in deciding treatment.

. . . .

. . . .

. . . .

. . . .

. . . .

Think Think about *two* problems that could make it difficult to assess someone's pain.

1

2

What are the advantages and disadvantages of the following pain assessment tools?

Tool	Description	Advantages	Disadvantages
Asking the patient	Good communication and listening		
Asking the partner or a colleague	Good communication and listening		
Body chart	Body diagram allowing patient or professional to mark pain distribution		
Visual analogue scale (VAS)	Plain, 100 mm line marked 'No pain' at one end, and 'Severe pain' at the other. The patient puts a mark corresponding to the severity of the pain		
Categorical scale	5-point scale marked No pain, Mild, Moderate, Severe and Excruciating pain		
Pain diary	A daily diary written by the patient describing severity, feelings etc.		
Pain questionnaire	e.g. McGill-Melzack: sets of words describing pain (e.g. pricking, stabbing). Results in an overall score		

FURTHER ACTIVITY

Discuss the use of pain assessment tools in your team.

FURTHER READING

Journal articles

Davies J and McVicar A (2000) Issues in effective pain control. 1: Assessment and education. *International Journal of Palliative Nursing.* **6**(2): 58–65.

Davies J and McVicar A (2000) Issues in effective pain control. 2: From assessment to management. *International Journal of Palliative Nursing.* **6**(4): 162–9.

Mayer DM, Torma L and Byock I (2000) Speaking the language of pain. *American Journal of Nursing.* **101**(2): 44–9.

Twycross RG (1999) Palliative care in the past decade and today. *European Journal of Pain.* **3**(Suppl. A): 23–9.

Twycross RG (1994) The fight against cancer pain. *Annals of Oncology.* **5**(2): 111–12.

Resource books and website

Calman K, Doyle D and Hanks GWC (eds) (2003) *The Oxford Textbook of Palliative Medicine* (3e). Oxford University Publications, Oxford.

Cancer Pain Relief and Palliative Care. (1990) WHO, Geneva.

Melzack R and Wall PD (1996) *The Challenge of Pain.* Updated (2e). Penguin Books, London.

Melzack R and Wall PD (1999) *Textbook of Pain* (4e). Churchill Livingstone, Edinburgh.

Regnard C and Hockley J (2004) *A Guide to Symptom Relief in Palliative Care* (5e). Radcliffe Medical Press, Oxford.

Twycross R and Lack SA (1988) *Oral Morphine, Information for Patients, Families and Friends.* Beaconsfield Publishers, Beaconsfield.

Twycross RG and Wilcock A (2001) *Symptom Management in Advanced Cancer* (3e). Radcliffe Medical Press, Oxford.

Twycross RG, Wilcock A and Charlesworth S (2002) *PCF2 – Palliative Care Formulary.* Radcliffe Medical Press, Oxford.

www.palliativedrugs.com – Updated website for the *Palliative Care Formulary.*

HELPING THE PATIENT WITH PAIN

3 Diagnosing the cause of pain

Claud Regnard
John W Thompson
Margaret Kindlen
Dorothy Matthews
Lynn Gibson

INTERMEDIATE LEVEL

Aim of this worksheet

To understand the key clinical decisions in diagnosing pain.

How to use this worksheet

- You can work through this worksheet by yourself, or with a tutor.

- Read the case study below, then work on the questions overleaf.

- The work page is on the right side, the information page is on the left.

- Work any way you want: you can try answering from your own knowledge (in which case, fold over the information page), you can use the information page (this is not cheating – you learn as you find the information) or you can use other sources of information.

- It should take you about 15 minutes. If anything is unclear, discuss it with a colleague.

- If you think any information is wrong or out of date, let us know.

- Use the activity on the back page and take this learning into your workplace.

Case study

Pat is a 36-year-old woman, married, with two sons aged 12 and 9 years. She had problems with her bowels for several months before some rectal bleeding made her see her GP. Investigations revealed a carcinoma of the sigmoid colon with liver metastases. She copes by maintaining a level of denial and refuses to tell her sons. She tends not to complain of pain, but grimaces whenever she sits down. She looks anxious. She asks to see you because of several pains.

INFORMATION PAGE

Diagnosing pain

There is no single treatment that treats all pains. Some treatments are better for some pains than for others. Consequently, it is essential to attempt to diagnose the cause of the pain.

The checklist below helps you to do this in a systematic manner. For example:

- *bone metastases* produce pain that is worsened by movement and straining the bone on examination

- *muscle pain* produces pain on active movement (i.e. when the muscle contracts) and may have a tender spot
- *chest infection* causes pain that is worsened by inspiration
- *constipation* causes a pain at rest in the abdomen that comes and goes every few minutes (i.e. it is periodic)
- *neuropathic pain* causes an unpleasant sensory change at rest, sometimes with pain on touching.

Pain behaviours and signs in people with communication difficulties, e.g. coma, confusion, learning difficulty

Pain can cause a variety of behaviours and signs. The key issue is a *change* in behaviour and/or signs. This can only be identified by documenting the baseline behaviour and signs before the change, or by interviewing carers about previous behaviour and signs. Examples of pain behaviours and signs:

- *Expressive:* grimacing, clenched teeth, shut eyes, wide open eyes, frowning, pupil dilatation, grunting, language (descriptive or associated words), non-language (crying, screaming, sighing, moaning)

- *Adaptive:* rubbing or holding area, keeping area still, approaching staff, avoiding stimulation, reduced or absent function (reduced movement, lying or sitting)
- *Distractive:* rocking (or other rhythmic movements), pacing, biting, gesturing, clenched fists
- *Postural:* increased muscle tension, altered posture, flinching, head in hands, limping
- *Autonomic:* sympathetic (PR, BP, wide pupils, pallor, sweating), parasympathetic (BP, PR).

Diagnostic checklist

- **Does movement precipitate the pain description, behaviour or sign?**
  - Does the slightest passive movement do this? Consider:
    - skeletal instability due to a fracture caused by *bone metastases* or osteoporosis
    - nerve compression/soft tissue inflammation/local infiltration by tumour.
  - Does bone strain do this (i.e. straining bone on examination)? Consider:
    - *bone metastasis*/intermittent nerve compression due to skeletal instability.
  - Is it precipitated by local pressure on muscle, and/or by active movement (i.e. movement against resistance)? Consider:
    - *myofascial muscle pain*/skeletal muscle strain or spasm.
  - Is it precipitated by joint movement? Consider:
    - arthritis (inflammation, infection, *bone metastases*).
  - Could it be another movement-related pain? Consider:
    - organ distension (tumour infiltration, haemorrhage)/inflammation or infiltration.
  - Exclude trauma: do a 'first-aid examination' (head, neck, shoulders, limbs, back, chest, abdomen).
- **Is it due to a procedure?**
- **Is the pain description, behaviour or sign present at rest?**
  - If this occurs in regular episodes lasting minutes (often normal in between), this suggests colic. Consider:
    - bowel (*constipation*/obstruction/bowel irritation due to drugs, radiotherapy, chemotherapy, bile, or infection), bladder (infection/outflow obstruction/

unstable bladder/irritation by tumour), ureter (infection/obstruction).
- Is it in time with inspiration (or is breathing more shallow)? Consider:
  - *rib metastasis/pleuritic pain* (inflammation, tumour, infection, embolus)/peritoneal inflammation/liver capsule stretch or inflammation/distended abdomen.
- Is posture abnormal? Consider:
  - increased flexor or extensor tone/muscle spasm.
- If skin changes are present, consider:
  - trauma/skin pressure damage/infiltration/infection/irritation/skin disease.
- Is the pain an unpleasant sensory change at rest (or is the pain worsened by touch)? Consider:
  - *neuropathic pain* (deafferentation pain, sympathetically maintained pain, painful peripheral neuropathies, peripheral neuralgias)/soft tissue inflammation.
- If numbness or weakness is present, consider:
  - dermatomal nerve compression, peripheral neuropathy (e.g. compression, B12 neuropathy, paraneoplastic), cord compression, cranial nerve damage or compression.
- **Does the pain description, behaviour or sign occur during or after eating (or are feeds being refused)?** Consider:
  - dental problems/mucosal problems in GI tract/distension of stomach or bowel.
- **Is the cause of pain still uncertain?** Consider:
  - vascular disease/infection.

Pat's pains

These are probably muscle tension, colic, skin pressure and neuropathic pain.

WORK PAGE

 List the behaviours and sign associated with the following pains. The checklist opposite will give you some help.

Pain due to: **Characteristics of the pain**

- bone metastasis

- muscle strain or spasm

- chest infection

- constipation

- neuropathic pain

 Now have a go at assessing Pat's pain shown on the body diagram below:

	Behaviour, sign or description	What makes it worse	What makes it better	Cause of pain
A: neck	Holds neck still when present	Turning head. Local pressure on muscle	Rest, local massage	
B: abdomen	When present: grimacing every few minutes	Nothing	Nothing	
C: sacrum	Grimacing during day when sitting. Red skin over sacrum	Sitting	Lying on the side	
D: thigh	Grimaces occasionally. Burning feeling	Sitting. Touch	Nothing	

Observation suggests Pat has pain in the marked areas:

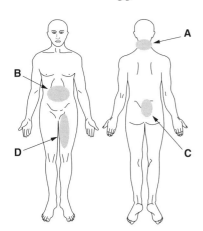

FURTHER ACTIVITY

When you next see a patient with pain:

• use the diagnostic checklist to assess the cause of the pain.

FURTHER READING

Journal articles

Davies J and McVicar A (2000) Issues in effective pain control. 1: Assessment and education. *International Journal of Palliative Nursing.* **6**(2): 58–65.

Davies J and McVicar A (2000) Issues in effective pain control. 2: From assessment to management. *International Journal of Palliative Nursing.* **6**(4): 162–9.

Mayer DM, Torma L and Byock I (2000) Speaking the language of pain. *American Journal of Nursing.* **101**(2): 44–9.

Twycross RG (1999) Palliative care in the past decade and today. *European Journal of Pain.* **3**(Suppl. A): 23–9.

Twycross RG (1994) The fight against cancer pain. *Annals of Oncology.* **5**(2): 111–12.

Resource books and website

Calman K, Doyle D and Hanks GWC (eds) (2003) *The Oxford Textbook of Palliative Medicine* (3e). Oxford University Publications, Oxford.

Cancer Pain Relief and Palliative Care. (1990) WHO, Geneva.

Melzack R and Wall PD (1996) *The Challenge of Pain.* Updated (2e). Penguin Books, London.

Melzack R and Wall PD (1999) *Textbook of Pain* (4e). Churchill Livingstone, Edinburgh.

Regnard C and Hockley J (2004) *A Guide to Symptom Relief in Palliative Care* (5e). Radcliffe Medical Press, Oxford.

Twycross R and Lack SA (1988) *Oral Morphine, Information for Patients, Families and Friends.* Beaconsfield Publishers, Beaconsfield.

Twycross RG and Wilcock A (2001) *Symptom Management in Advanced Cancer* (3e). Radcliffe Medical Press, Oxford.

Twycross RG, Wilcock A and Charlesworth S (2002) *PCF2 – Palliative Care Formulary.* Radcliffe Medical Press, Oxford.

www.palliativedrugs.com – Updated website for the *Palliative Care Formulary.*

HELPING THE PATIENT WITH PAIN

4 Choosing an analgesic

Claud Regnard
Margaret Kindlen
Sylvia Dryden

INTERMEDIATE LEVEL

Aim of this worksheet

To understand the principles of choosing an analgesic.

How to use this worksheet

- You can work through this worksheet by yourself, or with a tutor.

- Read the case study below, then work on the questions overleaf.

- The work page is on the right side, the information page is on the left.

- Work any way you want: you can try answering from your own knowledge (in which case, fold over the information page), you can use the information page (this is not cheating – you learn as you find the information) or you can use other sources of information.

- It should take you about 15 minutes. If anything is unclear, discuss it with a colleague.

- If you think any information is wrong or out of date, let us know.

- Use the activity on the back page and take this learning into your workplace.

Case study

Pat is a 36-year-old woman, married, with two sons aged 12 and 9 years. She had problems with her bowels for several months before some rectal bleeding made her see her GP. Investigations revealed a carcinoma of the sigmoid colon with liver metastases. She copes by maintaining a level of denial and refuses to tell her sons.

  She has colic, a skin pressure pain, a neuropathic pain and a pain due to muscle tension.

INFORMATION PAGE

Types of analgesic

Primary analgesics

Non-opioids e.g. paracetamol, nefopam
Weak opioid agonists e.g. codeine, dihydrocodeine, dextropropoxyphene
Strong opioid agonists e.g. morphine, diamorphine, hydromorphone, fentanyl, oxycodone
Opioid partial agonist/antagonists e.g. buprenorphine
Non-steroidal anti-inflammatory drugs e.g. ibuprofen
NMDA antagonists e.g. ketamine, methadone
Nitrous oxide (1:1 with oxygen as Entonox)

Co-analgesics (secondary or adjuvant analgesics)

Antidepressants e.g. amitriptyline, venlafaxine
Anticonvulsants e.g. carbamazepine, gabapentin
Membrane stabilising drugs e.g. flecainide, mexiletine, lidocaine
Adrenergic pathway modifiers e.g. clonidine
Corticosteroids e.g. dexamethasone
Antispasmodics e.g. hyoscine butylbromide
Antispastics e.g. baclofen
Antibiotics

Analgesic staircases

The WHO staircase uses non-opioids, weak opioids and strong opioids as the three steps. The most obvious limitation is that this approach only works for pain that responds to opioids:

- Opioids are not local anaesthetics and they cannot 'numb' all pain.
- Many pains respond poorly to opioids (e.g. colic, neuropathic pain, pressure sores, fracture).

There are two consequences:
1 The WHO staircase also encourages the use of co-analgesics at every stage.
2 It's necessary to think about an analgesic staircase for every person and pain, creating an individualised analgesic staircase.

Creating an individualised analgesic staircase

Pains can have many causes, and several pains can co-exist, sometimes in the same site. Each patient therefore needs an individualised analgesic staircase.
- For skin pressure pain the staircase is very different and might have these three steps:
  1 pressure-relieving aids and position changes
  2 topical ibuprofen gel, oral paracetamol or oral diclofenac
  3 oral diclofenac or, if the pain was severe, ketamine or spinal analgesia.
- In severe pain in cancer, it may be worth starting with opioids since several pains are often present together and one of these is commonly opioid-sensitive.
- If the remaining pain has a neuropathic element then start up the 'neuropathic pain staircase':

1 Amitriptyline 10 mg at night (lower if elderly or frail). Titrate the dose to pain and adverse effects. Typical dose range is 25–50 mg at night, but some people need (and tolerate) doses up to 150 mg at night.
2 Add carbamazepine 100 mg 8-hourly, or if this is not tolerated, try gabapentin 100 mg 8-hourly. Titrate the dose to pain and adverse effects. For gabapentin some people need (and tolerate) up to 1200 mg 8-hourly. *See also* the CLIP worksheet *Persisting pain.*
3 If the above fail, try the next steps of ketamine or spinal analgesia – these will need referral to a pain or palliative care specialist.

Frequent follow-up is often needed.

Principles

- Different analgesics work with different pains.
- Some analgesics work through secondary mechanisms.
- Different pains may need different analgesics.

WORK PAGE

Not all analgesics are the same – so we have to make choices. Some analgesics work directly by blocking pain pathways – these are primary analgesics. Others work through an indirect mechanism – these are secondary analgesics.

- Think of some primary analgesics (e.g. what you'd use for a headache).

- Think of analgesics that work by a secondary mechanism (e.g. what you'd use for colic). These are called co-analgesics.

Primary analgesics	Co-analgesics
. . . .	. . . .
. . . .	. . . .
. . . .	. . . .
. . . .	. . . .
. . . .	. . . .

The World Health Organization suggested you should start with simple analgesics, building up to more potent ones in several steps. They called this the **analgesic staircase**.

Write in the steps of the WHO analgesic staircase.

```
                                              Step 3
                          Step 2
        Step 1
```

Q Would all pains respond to this approach?

. . . .

. . . .

Try writing an analgesic ladder for Pat's skin pressure pain.

```
                                              Step 3
                          Step 2
        Step 1
```

FURTHER ACTIVITY

Review the analgesics of a patient with pain.

- Identify which are primary analgesics and which are co-analgesics.

FURTHER READING

Journal articles

Hanks GW, Conno F, Cherny N *et al.* (2001) Expert Working Group of the Research Network of the European Association for Palliative Care. Morphine and alternative opioids in cancer pain: the EAPC recommendations. *British Journal of Cancer.* 84(5): 587–93.

Hawkins C and Hanks GW (2000) The gastroduodenal toxicity of nonsteroidal anti-inflammatory drugs: a review of the literature. *Journal of Pain and Symptom Management.* 20(2): 140–51.

Hawley P, Forbes K and Hanks GW (1998) Opioid rotation: Does it have a role? *Palliative Medicine.* 12(1): 60–4.

Hanks GW and Forbes K (1997) Opioid responsiveness. *Acta Anaesthesiologica Scandinavica.* 41: 154–8.

Twycross RG (1999) Palliative care in the past decade and today. *European Journal of Pain.* 3(Suppl. A): 23–9.

Twycross RG (1994) The fight against cancer pain. *Annals of Oncology.* 5(2): 111–12.

Resource books and website

Calman K, Doyle D and Hanks GWC (eds) (2003) *The Oxford Textbook of Palliative Medicine* (3e). Oxford University Publications, Oxford.

Cancer Pain Relief and Palliative Care. (1990) WHO, Geneva.

Melzack R and Wall PD (1996) *The Challenge of Pain.* Updated (2e). Penguin Books, London.

Melzack R and Wall PD (1999) *Textbook of Pain* (4e). Churchill Livingstone, Edinburgh.

Regnard C and Hockley J (2004) *A Guide to Symptom Relief in Palliative Care* (5e). Radcliffe Medical Press, Oxford.

Twycross R and Lack SA (1988) *Oral Morphine, Information for Patients, Families and Friends.* Beaconsfield Publishers, Beaconsfield.

Twycross RG and Wilcock A (2001) *Symptom Management in Advanced Cancer* (3e). Radcliffe Medical Press, Oxford.

Twycross RG, Wilcock A and Charlesworth S (2002) *PCF2 – Palliative Care Formulary.* Radcliffe Medical Press, Oxford.

www.palliativedrugs.com – Updated website for the *Palliative Care Formulary.*

HELPING THE PATIENT WITH PAIN

5 Using morphine

Claud Regnard
Margaret Kindlen
Sylvia Dryden

INTERMEDIATE LEVEL

Aim of this worksheet

To understand the use and side effects of morphine.

How to use this worksheet

- You can work through this worksheet by yourself, or with a tutor.

- Read the case study below, then work on the questions overleaf.

- The work page is on the right side, the information page is on the left.

- Work any way you want: you can try answering from your own knowledge (in which case, fold over the information page), you can use the information page (this is not cheating – you learn as you find the information) or you can use other sources of information.

- It should take you about 15 minutes. If anything is unclear, discuss it with a colleague.

- If you think any information is wrong or out of date, let us know.

- Use the activity on the back page and take this learning into your workplace.

Case study

Pat is a 36-year-old woman, married, with two sons aged 12 and 9 years. She had problems with her bowels for several months before some rectal bleeding made her see her GP. Investigations revealed a carcinoma of the sigmoid colon with liver metastases. She copes by maintaining a level of denial and refuses to tell her sons.

She has several pains and it is decided to start her on morphine.

INFORMATION PAGE

Opioid of choice

Morphine given
Orally and
Regularly
Prevents pain.
Haloperidol treats nausea,
Injections are unnecessary,
No addiction is seen and
Early use should be considered

Starting dose:
- if previously on non-opioid = 2.5–5 mg 4-hourly
- if previously on weak opioid = 5–10 mg 4-hourly

Titration:
As a general rule: increase by half every alternate day.
Some need more rapid titration (e.g. in severe pain).
Others need slower titration (e.g. poor renal function).
The dose range for morphine is 5–>5000 mg per day (median is 100 mg/day).
90% of patients are managed on less than 600 mg per day.

The indications for injections

Inability to tolerate other routes (e.g. nausea and vomiting, exhaustion); or urgent pain control. But NOT because of poor pain control.

Giving it by injection means you need less drug to have the same effect (i.e. it is more potent) but it CANNOT be more effective because it is the same drug (i.e. the dose–response curve is the same shape)!

Metabolism

Morphine is absorbed from the small bowel, then metabolised in the liver to an active metabolite (morphine-6-glucuronide, M6G) which is excreted through the kidney. Liver impairment has little impact on how the body handles morphine. In contrast, any reduction in renal function results in accumulation of M6G.

Another metabolite, M3G, may be the cause of myoclonic jerks and agitation in some patients.

Morphine worries

Will I be drugged? Will I get addicted? Shouldn't we save it until the pain's really bad? Is this the end?
- Withdrawal symptoms on suddenly stopping can occur (usually colic and diarrhoea), but this is not seen if the morphine is reduced slowly over 5 days.
- Addiction to morphine is rare. It is very unusual for pain patients taking morphine to develop a craving for the drug. The circumstances in which they take morphine do not encourage addictive behaviour, and patients have no difficulty stopping morphine if their pain is relieved by other means.
- Tolerance to many side effects is rapid (i.e. the effects wear off quickly). **But** tolerance to analgesia is not seen (i.e. pain relief does not wear off with time). **And** constipation doesn't wear off – so prescribe a laxative!
- Confusion, hallucinations and nightmares are uncommon.

Morphine dose timing

For continuous pain, analgesia should be continuous. Regular administration should enable good pain control between doses so that the aim is no longer treatment of the pain, but preventing it from returning. The exact timing depends on experience with the length of action of the analgesic.

Reliance on 'PRN' (as required) prescribing alone is a recipe for a vicious circle of pain, anxiety/fear with reduced tolerance to pain, and so more pain.

PRN = 'Pain Relief Nil'!

Morphine intolerance

Real intolerance	• Poor renal function • Low threshold to CNS stimulation • Fear of opioids
Apparent intolerance	• Titration too rapid • Conversion ratio incorrect • Other cause of confusion • Constipation

Constipation (usually, 95%) – little or no tolerance
Dry mouth (often, 40%) – probably no tolerance
Nausea and vomiting (sometimes, 30%) – tolerance 5–10 days
Sedation (sometimes, 25%) – tolerance 3–5 days
Confusion (rare, 1–2%) – little or no tolerance
Other (rare) Urinary retention/anti-diuretic effect/asthma/urticaria/ multifocal myoclonus/respiratory depression

Treatment of opioid adverse effects

- *Constipation:* Start a stimulant laxative (e.g. senna) plus a softener (e.g. docusate or lactulose).
- *Nausea and vomiting (area postrema stimulation):* Start low dose haloperidol (1–3 mg at night).
- *Vomiting caused by gastric stasis:* Start a prokinetic agent, e.g. metoclopramide, domperidone.
- *Drowsiness:* This usually wears off by itself within 5 days, but if it persists consider using a different opioid.
- *Hallucinations:* It is usually necessary to switch to another opioid or find other means of pain relief.
- *Confusion* due to drowsiness will wear off, but with CNS stimulation switch to another opioid or use other analgesia.
- *Itch and urine retention* are in all the books, but in practice they are rare.

WORK PAGE

MCQ Having assessed Pat's pain she is started on oral morphine.

1	It should be doubled every day until the pain is controlled	True	False
2	It should be given regularly, even if she is pain-free	True	False
3	It would be more effective by injection	True	False
4	The dose should be reduced if her kidney function is poor	True	False
5	She might eventually need anything between 5–5000 mg per day	True	False

What fears about morphine might Pat have?

Fear about morphine	Is fear justified – yes or no?
. . . .	. . . .
. . . .	. . . .
. . . .	. . . .
. . . .	. . . .
. . . .	. . . .

Pat starts morphine, but her husband telephones you to say her pain is better, but she's feeling sick, she hasn't moved her bowels and she keeps nodding off in front of the television.

These are all possible side effects of morphine: complete the details.

Side effect	Usually, often, sometimes or rare?	Does it wear off?
Constipation		
Nausea and vomiting		
Sedation		
Poor gastric emptying		
Dry mouth		
Confusion		
Urine retention		
Hallucinations		
Itch		

FURTHER ACTIVITY

Find a patient who is taking morphine and find out from the care team:

- if the patient is having any troublesome side effects

- if the patient has any concerns about being on morphine.

Review the protocols used by your team for prescribing and assessing the effects of morphine.

FURTHER READING

Journal articles

Hanks GW, Conno F, Cherny N *et al.* (2001) Expert Working Group of the Research Network of the European Association for Palliative Care. Morphine and alternative opioids in cancer pain: the EAPC recommendations. *British Journal of Cancer.* 84(5): 587–93.

Hanks GW and Forbes K (1997) Opioid responsiveness. *Acta Anaesthesiologica Scandinavica.* 41: 154–8.

Hawkins C and Hanks GW (2000) The gastroduodenal toxicity of nonsteroidal anti-inflammatory drugs: a review of the literature. *Journal of Pain and Symptom Management.* 20(2): 140–51.

Hawley P, Forbes K and Hanks GW (1998) Opioid rotation: Does it have a role? *Palliative Medicine.* 12(1): 60–4.

Resource books and website

Calman K, Doyle D and Hanks GWC (eds) (2003) *The Oxford Textbook of Palliative Medicine* (3e). Oxford University Publications, Oxford.

Cancer Pain Relief and Palliative Care. (1990) WHO, Geneva.

Melzack R and Wall PD (1996) *The Challenge of Pain.* Updated (2e). Penguin Books, London.

Melzack R and Wall PD (1999) *Textbook of Pain* (4e). Churchill Livingstone, Edinburgh.

Regnard C and Hockley J (2004) *A Guide to Symptom Relief in Palliative Care* (5e). Radcliffe Medical Press, Oxford.

Twycross R and Lack SA (1988) *Oral Morphine, Information for Patients, Families and Friends.* Beaconsfield Publishers, Beaconsfield.

Twycross RG and Wilcock A (2001) *Symptom Management in Advanced Cancer* (3e). Radcliffe Medical Press, Oxford.

Twycross RG, Wilcock A and Charlesworth S (2002) *PCF2 – Palliative Care Formulary.* Radcliffe Medical Press, Oxford.

www.palliativedrugs.com – Updated website for the *Palliative Care Formulary.*

HELPING THE PATIENT WITH PAIN

6 Alternatives to morphine

Claud Regnard
Margaret Kindlen
Sarah Alport
Paul McNamara

ADVANCED LEVEL

Aim of this worksheet

To understand what other opioids can be used instead of morphine.

How to use this worksheet

- You can work through this worksheet by yourself, or with a tutor.

- Read the case study below, then work on the questions overleaf.

- The work page is on the right side, the information page is on the left.

- Work any way you want: you can try answering from your own knowledge (in which case, fold over the information page), you can use the information page (this is not cheating – you learn as you find the information) or you can use other sources of information.

- It should take you about 15 minutes. If anything is unclear, discuss it with a colleague.

- If you think any information is wrong or out of date, let us know.

- Use the activity on the back page and take this learning into your workplace.

Case study

Linda is a 43-year-old lady with myeloma. Despite some poor renal function initially, she did well with chemotherapy. Two months ago she relapsed and developed lytic bone lesions. While she was waiting for the treatment to take effect she was started on morphine for pain. This worked very well, and she has been on the same dose for several weeks and continued to work. Over the past week, however, she has become increasingly drowsy, with pin-point pupils, but remains pain-free.

INFORMATION PAGE

Deterioration on a stable dose of opioid

There are four broad possibilities:
- The disease is advancing (unusual over a short time scale, having been relatively well beforehand).
- There is a concurrent cause of drowsiness such as hypercalcaemia (common in myeloma).
- She has taken a higher dose than usual (an error would be the likeliest, as suicide attempts with morphine are rare).
- She is not eliminating her morphine as efficiently as previously.

The pin-point pupils and the circumstances of her illness suggest the last cause. One of the active metabolites of morphine is morphine-6-glucuronide (M6G) which is water soluble and excreted by the kidneys. Any change in renal function will make the M6G accumulate. Renal impairment can occur in myeloma (indeed Linda had this problem originally), and a deterioration in renal function with an accumulation of M6G is a likely cause.

Alternative opioids

Morphine, diamorphine and hydromorphone have renally excreted metabolites, methadone and fentanyl do not. Hydromorphone has fewer renally excreted active metabolites than morphine and may be safe in mild to moderate renal impairment, but in severe renal failure fentanyl is the opioid of choice.

Diamorphine is converted to morphine, and apart from greater solubility for injection it has no advantages.

Methadone has a prolonged action and should only be used by specialist teams.

1 F: IV fentanyl has a short half-life, but transdermally it can take up to 14 hours to reach steady blood levels.
2 T: Neither of these two opioids are known to have active metabolites that are renally excreted.
3 F: A pain unresponsive to morphine is unlikely to respond to these strong opioids.
4 F: Fentanyl in the body fat disappears slowly – it can take up to 30 hours for the effects to wear off.
5 T: Fentanyl produces less sedation and patients may need lower laxative doses.
6 F: The pharmacokinetics of both make them very difficult to adjust in an ill patient. In addition, diamorphine is converted to morphine, so would be unsuitable for Linda while she has renal impairment.

Steps in starting an alternative opioid

Dose conversion from morphine:
- Hydromorphone: dose ÷ 5.
- Oxycodone: dose ÷ 1.5.
- Fentanyl: a quick and safe conversion is daily oral morphine dose in mg ÷ 3 = fentanyl dose in microg/hour.

Last dose of morphine:
- Hydromorphone: give the first dose of hydromorphone in place of the next morphine dose.
- Oxycodone: give the first dose of oxycodone in place of the next morphine dose.
- Transdermal fentanyl: morphine should be continued on an 'as required' basis for at least 12 hours after starting fentanyl to cover the slow onset of fentanyl and to prevent a morphine withdrawal syndrome which can occur in some patients changing to fentanyl (most commonly sweats, feeling shivery, colic and diarrhoea).

Laxatives:
- Hydromorphone and oxycodone: continue the laxatives but adjust the dose to produce a comfortable stool.

- Fentanyl: laxatives should be reduced or stopped for 24 hours before starting fentanyl and then retitrated.

Minimum delay between dose increases:
- Hydromorphone and oxycodone: can be increased twice daily but are usually increased every other day to allow tolerance to develop to adverse effects.
- Transdermal fentanyl: at least 24 hours are needed before the dose can be adjusted.

Influences on the blood levels of the opioid:
- Hydromorphone: active metabolites are increased in severe renal failure.
- Oxycodone: oxycodone itself is increased in renal or liver impairment.
- Fentanyl:
  - increased by thin skin, pyrexia or local heat
  - decreased by thick skin or factors causing poor adhesion of patches (e.g. hair, sweating).

Choosing the right opioid

- *Subcutaneous infusion:* diamorphine
- *Mild to moderate renal impairment:* hydromorphone
- *Stable pain, unable to swallow:* SC diamorphine or transdermal fentanyl
- *Severe renal failure:* fentanyl

- *Liver impairment:* morphine (with care)
- *Afraid of using morphine:* oxycodone or fentanyl
- *Infection with pyrexia:* any can be used except transdermal fentanyl

Principles

- Alternative opioids do not give better pain relief than morphine.
- Different opioids have different adverse effect profiles.
- Each opioid has its place

WORK PAGE

  What could have caused her present problems? Could the morphine be the cause?

 Since her pain is still responsive to a strong opioid, an alternative opioid could help.

1 Transdermal fentanyl has a fast onset of action	T	F
2 Fentanyl and methadone are safe in renal failure	T	F
3 Hydromorphone, oxycodone and fentanyl could be used for morphine-resistant pains	T	F
4 In overdose, transdermal fentanyl is easier to treat than morphine	T	F
5 Transdermal fentanyl causes less sedation and constipation	T	F
6 Methadone and transdermal fentanyl are alternatives to diamorphine SC infusions in the last days of life	T	F

 What steps would you take to convert Linda to an alternative opioid?

	Hydromorphone	Oxycodone	Transdermal fentanyl
Dose conversion from oral morphine?			
When do you give the last dose of morphine?			
Do you continue laxatives?			
What is the minimum delay before increasing dose?			
What might affect the blood levels of the opioid?			

Which opioid(s) would you choose in the following situations?

Subcutaneous infusion =   Renal impairment =

Stable pain, unable to swallow =   Liver impairment =

Afraid of taking morphine =   Infection with pyrexia =

FURTHER ACTIVITY

Consider an audit in your practice setting to establish the frequency of problems related to morphine.

FURTHER READING

Journal articles

Ashby M, Fleming B, Wood M *et al.* (1997) Plasma morphine and glucuronide (M3G and M6G) concentrations in hospice patients. *Journal of Pain and Symptom Management.* 14: 157–67.

Hanks GW and Forbes K (1997) Opioid responsiveness. *Acta Anaesthesiologica Scandinavica.* 41: 154–8.

Hanks GW, Conno F, Cherny N *et al.* (2001) Expert Working Group of the Research Network of the European Association for Palliative Care. Morphine and alternative opioids in cancer pain: the EAPC recommendations. *British Journal of Cancer.* 84(5): 587–93.

Hawley P, Forbes K and Hanks GW (1998) Opioid rotation: Does it have a role? *Palliative Medicine.* 12(1): 60–4.

Kirvela M, Lindgren L, Seppala T *et al.* (1996) The pharmacokinetics of oxycodone in uremic patients undergoing renal transplantation. *Journal of Clinical Anesthesia.* 8(1): 13–18.

Lee MA, Leng ME and Tiernan EJ (2001) Retrospective study of the use of hydromorphone in palliative care patients with normal and abnormal urea and creatinine. *Palliative Medicine.* 15(1): 26–34.

Mazoit JX, Sardouk P, Zetlaoui P *et al.* (1987) Pharmacokinetics of unchanged morphine in normal and cirrhotic patients. *Anaesthesia and Analgesia.* 66: 293–8.

Nugent M, Davis C, Brooks D *et al.* (2001) Long-term observations of patients receiving transdermal fentanyl after a randomized trial. *Journal of Pain and Symptom Management.* 21(5): 385–91.

Portenoy RK, Thaler HT, Inturrisi CE *et al.* (1992) The metabolite morphine-6-glucuronide contributes to the analgesia produced by morphine infusion in patients with pain and normal renal function. *Clinical Pharmacology and Therapeutics.* 51: 422–31.

Sarhill N, Walsh D and Nelson KA (2001) Hydromorphone, pharmacology and clinical applications in cancer patients. *Supportive Care in Cancer.* 9(2): 84–96.

Resource books and website

Calman K, Doyle D and Hanks GWC (eds) (2003) *The Oxford Textbook of Palliative Medicine* (3e). Oxford University Publications, Oxford.

Cancer Pain Relief and Palliative Care. (1990) WHO, Geneva.

Melzack R and Wall PD (1999) *Textbook of Pain* (4e). Churchill Livingstone, Edinburgh.

Regnard C and Hockley J (2004) *A Guide to Symptom Relief in Palliative Care* (5e). Radcliffe Medical Press, Oxford.

Twycross R and Lack SA (1988) *Oral Morphine, Information for Patients, Families and Friends.* Beaconsfield Publishers, Beaconsfield.

Twycross RG and Wilcock A (2001) *Symptom Management in Advanced Cancer* (3e). Radcliffe Medical Press, Oxford.

Twycross RG, Wilcock A and Charlesworth S (2002) *PCF2 – Palliative Care Formulary.* Radcliffe Medical Press, Oxford.

www.palliativedrugs.com – Updated website for the *Palliative Care Formulary.*

HELPING THE PATIENT WITH PAIN

7 Changing opioids

Claud Regnard
Margaret Kindlen
Sarah Alport

ADVANCED LEVEL

Aim of this worksheet

To understand how to convert from one opioid to the other, looking at dose conversions and routes of administration.

How to use this worksheet

- You can work through this worksheet by yourself, or with a tutor.

- Read the case study below, then work on the questions overleaf.

- The work page is on the right side, the information page is on the left.

- Work any way you want: you can try answering from your own knowledge (in which case, fold over the information page), you can use the information page (this is not cheating – you learn as you find the information) or you can use other sources of information.

- It should take you about 15 minutes. If anything is unclear, discuss it with a colleague.

- If you think any information is wrong or out of date, let us know.

- Use the activity on the back page and take this learning into your workplace.

Case study

Pat is a 36-year-old woman, married, with two sons aged 12 and 9 years. She had problems with her bowels for several months before some rectal bleeding made her see her GP. Investigations revealed a carcinoma of the sigmoid colon with liver metastases. She has begun to deteriorate and is finding it hard to swallow. She has been on oral morphine for several months, but is asking if it can be given in any other way.

INFORMATION PAGE

Potency

The potency of a drug tells you how strong the drug is in comparison with other similar drugs. A potent opioid will need less drug to give the same pain relief as higher doses of a weak opioid.

The opioids listed vary considerably in their potency:
- 3 strongest: fentanyl, buprenorphine and hydromorphone
- 3 weakest: dihydrocodeine, pethidine and codeine.

3 steps for conversion

1 Find the current opioid and route at the TOP of the table.
2 Find the new opioid and route you are changing to on the RIGHT of the table.
3 Where the lines cross, read the conversion factor.
$\times$ = multiply current opioid by this factor
$\div$ = divide current opioid by this factor
nr = not recommended
Important: These conversions are approximations and the dose of the new opioid may have to be adjusted.

120 mg/24 hours
$\equiv$ 1200 mg oral codeine/24 hours [$\times$ 10]
$\equiv$ 40 mg subcutaneous diamorphine/24 hours [$\div$ 3]
$\equiv$ 600 mg oral dihydrocodeine/24 hours [$\times$ 5]
$\equiv$ 24 mg oral hydromorphone/24 hours [$\div$ 5]

For *fentanyl*, use the manufacturer's tables but the following can be used as a quick check:
- daily dose of oral morphine/day [$\div$ 3] = dose of fentanyl in microg/hour.

For Pat, this works out as the equivalent of 40 microg/hour transdermal fentanyl, but since the nearest patch size to this is 50 microg/hour, this size patch would be chosen.

Each preparation can be given in different ways:
- oral (swallowed): codeine, pethidine, dihydrocodeine, morphine, dextromoramide, diamorphine, hydromorphone
- sublingual: dextromoramide, buprenorphine, fentanyl
- injection: morphine, diamorphine, buprenorphine, fentanyl
- transdermal: fentanyl, buprenorphine.

Current opioid and route ►	Oral codeine	Oral dihydrocodeine	Oral morphine	Oral oxycodone	Diamorphine infusion	Oral hydromorphone	New opioid and route ▼
	▨	nr	x 10	x 15	x 30	nr	Oral codeine
	nr	▨	x 5	x 15	x 30	nr	Oral dihydrocodeine
	÷ 10	÷ 10	▨	x 1.5	x 3	x 5	Oral morphine
	÷ 15	÷ 15	÷ 1.5	▨	x 2	x 3	Oral oxycodone
	÷ 30	÷ 30	÷ 3	÷ 2	▨	x 2.5	Diamorphine infusion
	nr	nr	÷ 5	÷ 3	÷ 2.5	▨	Oral hydromorphone

Choice of opioids for Pat

Pat needs an opioid by a non-oral route that is at least as potent (since weaker opioids mean she would have to take a lot of the drug to have the same effect, e.g. 120 mg morphine = 1200 mg codeine!).

There are several opioids you might choose: morphine, diamorphine, buprenorphine and fentanyl. Diamorphine is the opioid of choice since it is widely available and can be given as a subcutaneous infusion. Transdermal fentanyl can take up to 14 hours to give a steady blood level, so pain control could be lost, but it is an alternative when pumps are unavailable.

Efficacy of opioids

This defines how effective a drug is, regardless of dose. It is not the same as potency. It is possible to have a potent drug such as buprenorphine which is 60 times more potent than oral morphine, but less effective at high doses. So, Pat's pain would *not* be better relieved by changing to a more potent opioid or route.

WORK PAGE

Changing opioids would be easy IF all opioids had the same potency, range of adverse effects and were available for the same routes of administration. **Life is never that simple!**

We will now look at changing doses and routes (for issues about different adverse effects, *see* CLIP worksheet *Alternatives to morphine*).

 From this list of opioids, choose the three strongest, and the three weakest (the list is in alphabetical order, so no clue there).

buprenorphine   3 strongest

codeine

dextromoramide

diamorphine

dihydrocodeine   3 weakest

fentanyl

hydromorphone

morphine

pethidine

 Next to the left hand list, write the routes of administration available (O = oral, SL = sublingual, I = injection (subcutaneous, intravenous, or intramuscular) D = transdermal).

 Pat is on 120 mg of morphine daily. Check the table opposite and write in the equivalent daily dose of other opioids. If the chart says 'nr', write in 'not recommended'

Opioid	Dose per day
codeine (oral)	mg
diamorphine (subcutaneous)	mg
dihydrocodeine (oral)	mg
hydromorphone (oral)	mg
	Dose in microg/hour
fentanyl (transdermal)	microg/hr

Now think about the available routes of administration for these opioids. Which opioids could you give Pat?

. . . .

. . . .

Ask a
colleague   Finally, if you gave Pat a more potent (stronger) opioid, would her pain be better relieved?

. . . .

. . . .

FURTHER ACTIVITY

- Find a patient on dihydrocodeine. Using the conversion chart on the information page, calculate how much daily morphine they would need.

- Find a patient on morphine. Using the conversion chart on the information page, calculate how much daily subcutaneous diamorphine they would need.

FURTHER READING

Journal articles

Ashby M, Fleming B, Wood M *et al.* (1997) Plasma morphine and glucuronide (M3G and M6G) concentrations in hospice patients. *Journal of Pain and Symptom Management.* **14**: 157–67.

Hanks GW and Forbes K (1997) Opioid responsiveness. *Acta Anaesthesiologica Scandinavica.* **41**: 154–8.

Hanks GW, Conno F, Cherny N *et al.* (2001) Expert Working Group of the Research Network of the European Association for Palliative Care. Morphine and alternative opioids in cancer pain: the EAPC recommendations. *British Journal of Cancer.* **84**(5): 587–93.

Hawley P, Forbes K and Hanks GW (1998) Opioid rotation: Does it have a role? *Palliative Medicine.* **12**(1): 60–4.

Kirvela M, Lindgren L, Seppala T *et al.* (1996) The pharmacokinetics of oxycodone in uremic patients undergoing renal transplantation. *Journal of Clinical Anesthesia.* **8**(1): 13–18.

Lee MA, Leng ME and Tiernan EJ (2001) Retrospective study of the use of hydromorphone in palliative care patients with normal and abnormal urea and creatinine. *Palliative Medicine.* **15**(1): 26–34.

Mazoit JX, Sardouk P, Zetlaoui P *et al.* (1987) Pharmacokinetics of unchanged morphine in normal and cirrhotic patients. *Anaesthesia and Analgesia.* **66**: 293–8.

Nugent M, Davis C, Brooks D *et al.* (2001) Long-term observations of patients receiving transdermal fentanyl after a randomized trial. *Journal of Pain and Symptom Management.* **21**(5): 385–91.

Portenoy RK, Thaler HT, Inturrisi CE *et al.* (1992) The metabolite morphine-6-glucuronide contributes to the analgesia produced by morphine infusion in patients with pain and normal renal function. *Clinical Pharmacology and Therapeutics.* **51**: 422–31.

Sarhill N, Walsh D and Nelson KA (2001) Hydromorphone, pharmacology and clinical applications in cancer patients. *Supportive Care in Cancer.* **9**(2): 84–96.

Resource books and website

Calman K, Doyle D and Hanks GWC (eds) (2003) *The Oxford Textbook of Palliative Medicine* (3e). Oxford University Publications, Oxford.

Cancer Pain Relief and Palliative Care. (1990) WHO, Geneva.

Melzack R and Wall PD (1999) *Textbook of Pain* (4e). Churchill Livingstone, Edinburgh.

Regnard C and Hockley J (2004) *A Guide to Symptom Relief in Palliative Care* (5e). Radcliffe Medical Press, Oxford.

Twycross R and Lack SA (1988) *Oral Morphine, Information for Patients, Families and Friends.* Beaconsfield Publishers, Beaconsfield.

Twycross RG and Wilcock A (2001) *Symptom Management in Advanced Cancer* (3e). Radcliffe Medical Press, Oxford.

Twycross RG, Wilcock A and Charlesworth S (2002) *PCF2 – Palliative Care Formulary.* Radcliffe Medical Press, Oxford.

www.palliativedrugs.com – Updated website for the *Palliative Care Formulary.*

HELPING THE PATIENT WITH PAIN

8 Persisting pain

Claud Regnard

ADVANCED LEVEL

Aim of this worksheet

To understand the principles in managing persisting pain.

How to use this worksheet

- You can work through this worksheet by yourself, or with a tutor.

- Read the case study below, then work on the questions overleaf.

- The work page is on the right side, the information page is on the left.

- Work any way you want: you can try answering from your own knowledge (in which case, fold over the information page), you can use the information page (this is not cheating – you learn as you find the information) or you can use other sources of information.

- It should take you about 15 minutes. If anything is unclear, discuss it with a colleague.

- If you think any information is wrong or out of date, let us know.

- Use the activity on the back page and take this learning into your workplace.

Case study

Pat is a 36-year-old woman, married, with two sons aged 12 and 9 years. She had problems with her bowels for several months before some rectal bleeding made her see her GP. Investigations revealed a carcinoma of the sigmoid colon with liver metastases. She copes by maintaining a level of denial and refuses to tell her sons.

   She has been troubled with a persistent, burning perineal pain which has not responded to increased opioid doses. Pat's perineal pain is getting steadily worse. It is still burning and the area is so sensitive she can't sit down. She is still adamant the boys should not be told and she has been getting increasingly unsettled.

INFORMATION PAGE

Dealing with persistent pain

- Is the diagnosis correct?
- Are the analgesics appropriate?
- Is there a new pain?
- Is the patient taking the drugs correctly?
- Have you asked your local palliative care team?

- Have the basic principles been followed?
- Has a secondary analgesic been used?
- Have other treatment options been considered (surgery, radiotherapy etc.)?
- Is the patient anxious, frightened or depressed?

Do opioids always work?

When opioid doses are increased without any effect on the pain, the pain should be reassessed.

There are several types of pain that respond poorly to opioids: skeletal instability, colic (bowel, ureter, bladder), skin damage, muscle/ligament strain or damage, neuropathic pain (e.g. neuralgia) and pain associated with inflammation (e.g. infection). In cancer, pains have several causes and several types of pain are present at the same time. So it is often worth trying an opioid as a first step in cancer pain.

Pain associated with unpleasant sensory change

Neuropathic pain does not rely on pain receptors and is due to nerve damage. This is thought to cause persisting changes in the chemical neurotransmitters in the spinal cord. Typical descriptions of the pain by patients are 'burning', 'shooting', 'sandpaper' and 'pins and needles'. There is usually altered sensation such as hypersensitivity or pain on light touch (allodynia). Trigeminal neuralgia and post-shingles neuralgia are two examples. Neuropathic pain responds poorly to morphine and often needs co-analgesic drugs.

You can create an 'analgesic staircase' for this pain:
1 amitriptyline
2 amitriptyline plus carbamazepine or gabapentin
3 ketamine
4 spinal analgesia.
NB: Steps 3 and 4 need input from a specialist pain or palliative care team.

An analgesic staircase must be specific to the individual's pain.

Co-analgesics (also called secondary or adjuvant analgesics)

- *Action understood:* antibiotics, antispasmodics (drugs that relax smooth muscle), antispastics (drugs that relax skeletal muscle), corticosteroids.
- *Action poorly understood:* adrenergic pathway modifiers (e.g. clonidine), anticonvulsants, membrane stabilising drugs (flecainide), antidepressants. These drugs may work by restoring the amount of spinal cord neurotransmitters altered as a consequence of nerve destruction.

Examples:
- *Bowel colic* is stopped by an antispasmodic which relaxes the smooth muscle of the bowel, e.g. hyoscine butylbromide.

- *Neuropathic pain* can be helped by antidepressants of which amitriptyline is the first choice.
- *Muscle spasm* is seen in conditions such as multiple sclerosis and can be eased by an antispastic (e.g. baclofen) which relaxes the skeletal muscles involved.
- *Cellulitis* is a skin infection which can cause local pain – it needs an antibiotic and flucloxacillin is first choice.
- *Nerve compression pain* caused by tumour can be eased by reducing the swelling (oedema) around the tumour using corticosteroids – dexamethasone is usually the first choice.

The effects of persisting pain on Pat

Pain is not just a sensation but is also an unpleasant experience. When it persists it can become increasingly distressing with many effects:
- *Pat's feelings:* Frustration or anger may be a response, but as it continues Pat may become troubled by anxiety, fear, low mood or even depression.
- *Pat's social life:* Severe, persistent pain often restricts activity, but the feelings Pat has may also reduce social contact because she has less wish to socialise or meet new people – even friends may be turned away. This increases her isolation.

- *Pat's family:* The stress of persistent pain spreads to partners and relatives, making relationships difficult. She has already refused to tell her sons about her illness and they will be even more frightened and worried by her pain problems which she will not be able to hide.
- *Professionals:* Failure to relieve a problem may result in a sense of failure and inadequacy at the persistence of the pain despite all their efforts. This results in reduced contact with the professionals or the 'side-room syndrome' where patients are placed in a single room (ostensibly for themselves, but as much because the problem is less visible).

WORK PAGE

 Write an analgesic staircase for Pat's perineal pain (include anything you think could help, not just drugs).

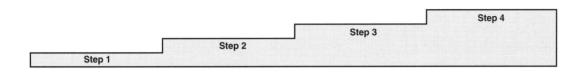

 Some pains need drugs other than primary analgesics. What would work best for the following – link up the pair (the first has been done for you).

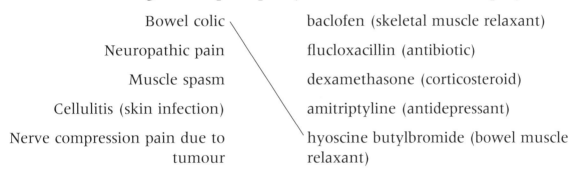

Bowel colic   baclofen (skeletal muscle relaxant)

Neuropathic pain   flucloxacillin (antibiotic)

Muscle spasm   dexamethasone (corticosteroid)

Cellulitis (skin infection)   amitriptyline (antidepressant)

Nerve compression pain due to tumour   hyoscine butylbromide (bowel muscle relaxant)

 Think about the effects of Pat's persistent pain.

Effects on Pat's feelings	Effects on Pat's social life	Effects on Pat's family	Effects on professionals

FURTHER ACTIVITY

For a patient with persistent pain:

- observe the effects on the patient and on you.

FURTHER READING

Journal articles

Attal N (2000) Chronic neuropathic pain: mechanisms and treatment. *Clinical Journal of Pain*. 16(Suppl. 3): S118–30.

Dellemijn P (1999) Are opioids effective in relieving neuropathic pain? *Pain*. 80(3): 453–62.

Enarson MC, Hays H and Woodroffe MA (1999) Clinical experience with oral ketamine. *Journal of Pain and Symptom Management*. 17(5): 384–6.

Hanks GW and Forbes K (1997) Opioid responsiveness. *Acta Anaesthesiologica Scandinavica*. 41: 154–8.

Hanks GW, Conno F, Cherny N *et al.* (2001) Expert Working Group of the Research Network of the European Association for Palliative Care.

Morphine and alternative opioids in cancer pain: the EAPC recommendations. *British Journal of Cancer*. 84(5): 587–93.

Rabben T, Skjelbred P and Oye I (1999) Prolonged analgesic effect of ketamine, an N-methyl-D-aspartate receptor inhibitor, in patients with chronic pain. *Journal of Pharmacology and Experimental Therapeutics*. 289(2): 1060–6.

Rice ASC, Maton S, Postherpetic Neuralgia Study Group (2001) Gabapentin in postherpetic neuralgia: a randomised, double blind, placebo controlled trial. *Pain*. 94: 215–24.

Watson CP (2000) The treatment of neuropathic pain: antidepressants and opioids. *Clinical Journal of Pain*. 16(Suppl. 2): S49–55.

Resource books and website

Calman K, Doyle D and Hanks GWC (eds) (2003) *The Oxford Textbook of Palliative Medicine* (3e). Oxford University Publications, Oxford.

Melzack R and Wall PD (1999) *Textbook of Pain* (4e). Churchill Livingstone, Edinburgh.

Regnard C and Hockley J (2004) *A Guide to Symptom Relief in Palliative Care* (5e). Radcliffe Medical Press, Oxford.

Twycross RG and Wilcock A (2001) *Symptom Management in Advanced Cancer* (3e). Radcliffe Medical Press, Oxford.

Twycross RG, Wilcock A and Charlesworth S (2002) *PCF2 – Palliative Care Formulary*. Radcliffe Medical Press, Oxford.

www.palliativedrugs.com – Updated website for the *Palliative Care Formulary*.

HELPING THE PATIENT WITH PAIN

9 Managing severe pain

Claud Regnard

ADVANCED LEVEL

Aim of this worksheet

To understand the principles in managing severe pain.

How to use this worksheet

- You can work through this worksheet by yourself, or with a tutor.

- Read the case study below, then work on the questions overleaf.

- The work page is on the right side, the information page is on the left.

- Work any way you want: you can try answering from your own knowledge (in which case, fold over the information page), you can use the information page (this is not cheating – you learn as you find the information) or you can use other sources of information.

- It should take you about 15 minutes. If anything is unclear, discuss it with a colleague.

- If you think any information is wrong or out of date, let us know.

- Use the activity on the back page and take this learning into your workplace.

Case study

Pat is a 36-year-old woman, married, with two sons aged 12 and 9 years. Investigations revealed a carcinoma of the sigmoid colon with liver metastases. She copes by maintaining a level of denial and refuses to tell her sons. She has a persistent, burning perineal pain which has not responded to increased opioid doses and is getting steadily worse. One evening you are asked to see her urgently and find her very distressed. She is on the bed, on her knees rocking to and fro, saying the pain is 'all over'.

INFORMATION PAGE

What can cause severe pain?

There are many reasons why pain may become suddenly severe:

- *A change in the analgesia:* this may be due to a recent change in opioid (opioid conversion ratios are only approximations), not taking an analgesic (e.g. because of vomiting or adverse effects) or a change in the uptake or elimination of an analgesic (e.g. loss of adhesion of a fentanyl patch).
- *Inflammation:* due to infection (e.g. pleurisy due to a chest infection), irritation (e.g. pleurisy due to a pulmonary embolus or peritonitis due to a bowel perforation) or chemical damage (e.g. drug-induced gastrointestinal mucosal damage or a perianal skin burn caused by dantron).
- *Ischaemia:* due to peripheral vascular disease, or myocardial ischaemia.

- *Tissue distension:* e.g. a bleed into a liver metastasis causing liver capsule pain.
- *Muscle spasm:* e.g. colic or skeletal muscular spasms.
- *Tissue rupture:* e.g. bone fractures due to metastatic disease or fistula formation.
- *Reduced ability to cope:* due to fear, depression or past experiences.

In Pat, there is nothing to suggest a new pain. Her comment that the pain is 'all over' is typical of so-called 'overwhelming pain'. This is when pain is accompanied by marked fear and the whole experience becomes too intense to make sense of it all. Her persisting pain may have steadily reduced her ability to cope until no coping skills were left and the situation became overwhelming.

A plan of action

Immediately: To achieve sufficient comfort to allow an initial assessment you need to:

- find a comfortable position for Pat
- give Pat her usual 'as required' dose of analgesic. This may be best by injection for speed of onset
- try and reduce her fear with reassurance, company and distraction. In overwhelming pain this is usually insufficient and the level of fear needs medication such as lorazepam 0.5 mg sublingually or midazolam 2.5 mg SC or sublingually. She needs to get enough to relax her, but not so much that she falls asleep and cannot tell you about her pain.

Within 1 hour: Exclude causes that need urgent management or can be treated simply. Examples that need urgent management are myocardial infarction, pulmonary embolus, bone fracture, spinal cord compression and peritonitis. An example of a severe pain that can be treated simply is colic.

Within 4 hours: Achieve comfort at rest by:

- increasing the regular analgesia by 50%
- checking whether this is a new pain (*see* CLIP worksheet *Diagnosing the cause of pain*)
- contacting a palliative care or pain specialist to advise on planning the next step. This is essential if the pain is unchanged at this stage.

Within 24 hours: plan for stable pain control by:

- ensuring a good night's sleep for Pat
- reviewing the support and treatment she will need to cope with any anxiety or low mood. Persistence of psychological problems will delay the resolution of the pain for several weeks and to avoid disappointment this needs to be understood by patient, partner and staff. *See* the CLIP worksheets *Helping the anxious person* and *Helping the withdrawn patient*.

An analgesic staircase for the drugs used in severe pain

This should include many of the approaches you have already written down in the plan of action above:

- *Step 1:* Give usual 'as required' dose. Give a benzodiazepine if fear is prominent.
- *Step 2:* Give any simple treatments (e.g. hyoscine butylbromide for colic), otherwise increase regular analgesia by 50%.

- *Step 3:* Refer to pain or palliative care specialist to:
  - review pain
  - consider the use of ketamine.
- *Step 4:* Consider spinal analgesia or a nerve block. If the pain remains severe, sedation may be needed until the procedure can be organised.

WORK PAGE

 Think about:

- Why Pat is saying her pain is 'all over'

- What could have caused her pain to go out of control.

 Write a plan of action for helping Pat.

- *Immediately:* Goal: to achieve sufficient comfort to allow an initial assessment.
  Your action:

  . . . .

  . . . .

- *Within 1 hour:* Goal: to exclude causes requiring urgent management.
  Your action:

  . . . .

  . . . .

- *Within 4 hours:* Goal: to achieve comfort at rest.
  Your action:

  . . . .

  . . . .

- *Within 24 hours:* Goal: to plan for stable pain control.
  Your action:

  . . . .

  . . . .

 Write an analgesic staircase for the drugs you might have to use for Pat's severe pain.

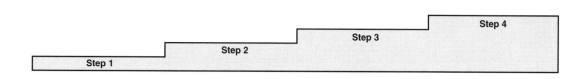

FURTHER ACTIVITY

Think back to a patient with severe pain:

- How frightened was the patient?

- How quickly was the pain brought under control?

FURTHER READING

Journal articles

Attal N (2000) Chronic neuropathic pain: mechanisms and treatment. *Clinical Journal of Pain.* 16(Suppl. 3): S118–30.

Dellemijn P (1999) Are opioids effective in relieving neuropathic pain? *Pain.* 80(3): 453–62.

Enarson MC, Hays H and Woodroffe MA (1999) Clinical experience with oral ketamine. *Journal of Pain and Symptom Management.* 17(5): 384–6.

Hanks GW and Forbes K (1997) Opioid responsiveness. *Acta Anaesthesiologica Scandinavica.* 41: 154–8.

Hanks GW, Conno F, Cherny N *et al.* (2001) Expert Working Group of the Research Network of the European Association for Palliative Care. Morphine and alternative opioids in cancer pain: the EAPC recommendations. *British Journal of Cancer.* 84(5): 587–93.

Rabben T, Skjelbred P and Oye I (1999) Prolonged analgesic effect of ketamine, an N-methyl-D-aspartate receptor inhibitor, in patients with chronic pain. *Journal of Pharmacology and Experimental Therapeutics.* 289(2): 1060–6.

Rice ASC, Maton S, Postherpetic Neuralgia Study Group (2001) Gabapentin in postherpetic neuralgia: a randomised, double blind, placebo controlled trial. *Pain.* 94: 215–24.

Watson CP (2000) The treatment of neuropathic pain: antidepressants and opioids. *Clinical Journal of Pain.* 16(Suppl. 2): S49–55.

Resource books and website

Calman K, Doyle D and Hanks GWC (eds) (2003) *The Oxford Textbook of Palliative Medicine* (3e). Oxford University Publications, Oxford.

Melzack R and Wall PD (1999) *Textbook of Pain* (4e). Churchill Livingstone, Edinburgh.

Regnard C and Hockley J (2004) *A Guide to Symptom Relief in Palliative Care* (5e). Radcliffe Medical Press, Oxford.

Twycross RG and Wilcock A (2001) *Symptom Management in Advanced Cancer* (3e). Radcliffe Medical Press, Oxford.

Twycross RG, Wilcock A and Charlesworth S (2002) *PCF2 – Palliative Care Formulary.* Radcliffe Medical Press, Oxford.

www.palliativedrugs.com – Updated website for the *Palliative Care Formulary.*

HELPING THE PATIENT WITH SYMPTOMS OTHER THAN PAIN

1 Constipation

Claud Regnard
Margaret Kindlen

INTRODUCTORY LEVEL

Aim of this worksheet

To learn how to assess and manage constipation.

How to use this worksheet

- You can work through this worksheet by yourself, or with a tutor.

- Read the case study below, then work on the questions overleaf.

- The work page is on the right side, the information page is on the left.

- Work any way you want: you can try answering from your own knowledge (in which case, fold over the information page), you can use the information page (this is not cheating – you learn as you find the information) or you can use other sources of information.

- It should take you about 15 minutes. If anything is unclear, discuss it with a colleague.

- If you think any information is wrong or out of date, let us know.

- Use the activity on the back page and take this learning into your workplace.

Case study

John is a 54-year-old man who had a surgery for a carcinoma of the colon. Despite liver metastases he has been managing well. He asks to see you because for the past few weeks he has been 'having trouble with the bowels'.

INFORMATION PAGE

Constipation

There are many symptoms that suggest constipation:

• infrequent stool • *uncomfortable stool* • *hard stool* • small volume • *sensation of an incomplete evacuation* • diarrhoea (yes, diarrhoea) • abdominal discomfort • nausea • vomiting • colic • anorexia.

Whilst all of these give useful information, the best identifiers are the ones in italics. For example:
• daily motion that is uncomfortable = constipation
• motion every 6 days that is comfortable = no constipation
So it's about quality, not quantity (just like palliative care!).

Causes of constipation

When you realise that a hard stool is a dry stool, you only have to think of what might cause a stool to lose more water than usual. There are three broad causes:

1 *Dehydration* will cause more water to be absorbed from the small bowel and colon.
2 *Factors causing the stool to stay longer in the colon:* This gives the colon more time to extract water:
  • Endogenous (from within the body):
    – reduced mobility (exercise increases bowel motility)
    – depression.

  • Exogenous (from outside the body) – drugs are the commonest:
    – those that reduce secretions into the gut (opioids and antimuscarinic drugs like hyoscine)
    – those that increase 'mixing' movements at the expense of forward movement (opioids)
    – those that reduce all bowel movements (antimuscarinic drugs like hyoscine)
    – those that set hard in the colon (barium).
3 *Factors which reduce the ability of the stool to hold on to water:* reduced dietary fibre.

Laxatives

• *Senna tablets or syrup:* Senna stimulates the colon when in contact with the lining of the colon.
• *Docusate capsules:* Docusate is a wetting agent which reduces water loss from the stool and is also a mild contact colonic stimulant. A syrup is available but it has an unpleasant, bitter taste.
• *Polyethylene glycol (Movicol):* When taken with the correct amount of water (125 ml) this produces an isotonic solution which stays in the bowel and helps soften any stool in the bowel.
• *Lactulose syrup:* Lactulose is an osmotic agent which draws water into the gut throughout the bowel, but also is

converted to organic acids in the colon, where they act as stimulants.
• *Curry supper:* A bowel irritant!
Note that:
1 Commercial combinations (e.g. co-danthramer, co-danthrusate) are expensive and contain dantron which can colour the urine red (causing anxiety) and can cause skin burns around the anus.
2 Lactulose is best used in combination with senna as, used alone, larger doses are needed, which cause abdominal bloating, and can cause fluid shifts resulting in postural hypotension.

Helping the patient: clinical decisions

Ideally, constipation should be prevented – a need to treat constipation suggests a failure in prevention. If constipation is present, then follow these clinical decisions and actions:
• **Exclude**
  – an ileus (a slowing or paralysis of the bowel caused by surgery, drugs or infection)
  – obstruction (a blockage caused by tumour or scarring).
• **Have the faeces been easy and comfortable to pass?**
  – If John's stool is infrequent this may be a normal response to reduced intake and only reassurance is needed.
  – If this is diarrhoea, this may be overflow due to severe constipation. An abdominal X-ray may help the diagnosis.
• **Ensure privacy:** try to help John get to a toilet, or if bed bound ask John if he would prefer a single room.

• **Is there a treatable cause?** Examples include hypercalcaemia, dehydration, and constipating drugs.
• **Is the rectum or stoma full?**
  – If the faeces are hard, encourage fluids and start laxatives. Stimulate rectal emptying with a bisacodyl suppository.
  – If the faeces are soft, start a stimulant laxative.
  – If there is no success, consider a manual evacuation if necessary (under sedation if possible).
• **Is the colon full?**
  – If colic is present, start regular docusate and consider a high arachis oil enema.
  – If colic is absent, start a stimulant laxative (e.g. senna) plus a softener (docusate or lactulose).
• **Is the constipation persisting?** Consider using polyethylene glycol with a prokinetic agent (e.g. metoclopramide).

A treatment plan

1 Ensure the basics: fibre intake (but not in bowel cancers or ill patients), keep up hydration.
2 Clear the rectum, start a laxative combination.
3 Enema or manual evacuation as a last resort.

WORK PAGE

Think 'What's constipation?' Easy isn't it? Think of a definition that is clear to you *and* the patient.

Your definition

Constipation is: . . . .

. . . .

. . . .

. . . .

 What factors might cause constipation?

. . . .

. . . .

. . . .

. . . .

. . . .

. . . .

Think What is the action of these laxatives?

Laxative   Action

senna

lactulose

polyethylene glycol (Movicol)

docusate

Madras curry supper

What would be your plan for John?

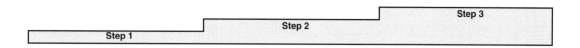

FURTHER ACTIVITY

In the next month, and using the definition of 'quality, not quantity':

- identify how many patients in your care are constipated

- what action is taken.

FURTHER READING

Journal articles

Agra Y, Sacristan A, Gonzalez M *et al.* (1998) Efficacy of senna versus lactulose in terminal cancer patients treated with opioids. *Journal of Pain and Symptom Management.* 15(1): 1–7.

Bruera E, Suarez-Almanzor M, Velasco A *et al.* (1994) The assessment of constipation in terminal cancer patients admitted to a palliative care unit: a retrospective review. *Journal of Pain and Symptom Management.* 9(8): 515–19.

Cleveland MV, Flavin DP, Ruben RA *et al.* (2001) New polyethylene glycol laxative for treatment of constipation in adults: a randomized, double-blind, placebo-controlled study. *Southern Medical Journal.* 94(5): 478–81.

Fallon M and O'Neill B (1997) ABC of palliative care: constipation and diarrhoea. *BMJ.* 315: 1293–6.

Fallon MT and Hanks GW (1999) Morphine, constipation and performance status in advanced cancer patients. *Palliative Medicine.* 13(2): 159–60.

Mancini I and Bruera E (1998) Constipation in advanced cancer patients. *Supportive Care in Cancer.* 6(4): 356–64.

Nugent M, Davis C, Brooks D *et al.* (2001) Long-term observations of patients receiving transdermal fentanyl after a randomized trial. *Journal of Pain and Symptom Management.* 21(5): 385–91.

O'Mahony S, Coyle N and Payne R (2001) Current management of opioid-related side effects. *Oncology (Huntington).* 15(1): 61–73, 77.

Prather CM and Ortiz-Camacho CP (1998) Evaluation and treatment of constipation and fecal impaction in adults. *Mayo Clinic Proceedings.* 73(9): 881–6.

Sykes NP (1996) A volunteer model for the comparison of laxatives in opioid-related constipation. *Journal of Pain and Symptom Management.* 11(6): 363–9.

Sykes NP (1998) The relationship between opioid use and laxative use in terminally ill cancer patients. *Palliative Medicine.* 12(5): 375–82.

Thorpe DM (2001) Management of opioid-induced constipation. *Current Pain and Headache Reports.* 5(3): 237–40.

Wiesel PH, Norton C and Brazzelli M (2002) Management of faecal incontinence and constipation in adults with central neurological diseases. *The Cochrane Database of Systematic Reviews.* 2.

Xing JH and Soffer EE (2001) Adverse effects of laxatives. *Diseases of the Colon and Rectum.* 44(8): 1201–9.

Resource books and website

Calman K, Doyle D and Hanks GWC (eds) (2003) *The Oxford Textbook of Palliative Medicine* (3e). Oxford University Publications, Oxford.

Regnard C and Hockley J (2004) *A Guide to Symptom Relief in Palliative Care* (5e). Radcliffe Medical Press, Oxford.

Twycross RG and Wilcock A (2001) *Symptom Management in Advanced Cancer* (3e). Radcliffe Medical Press, Oxford.

Twycross RG, Wilcock A and Charlesworth S (2002) *PCF2 – Palliative Care Formulary.* Radcliffe Medical Press, Oxford.

www.palliativedrugs.com – Updated website for the *Palliative Care Formulary.*

HELPING THE PATIENT WITH SYMPTOMS OTHER THAN PAIN

2 Fatigue, lethargy, drowsiness and weakness

Claud Regnard

INTERMEDIATE LEVEL

Aim of this worksheet

To understand some principles about fatigue and weakness in advanced disease.

How to use this worksheet

- You can work through this worksheet by yourself, or with a tutor.

- Read the case study below, then work on the questions overleaf.

- The work page is on the right side, the information page is on the left.

- Work any way you want: you can try answering from your own knowledge (in which case, fold over the information page), you can use the information page (this is not cheating – you learn as you find the information) or you can use other sources of information.

- It should take you about 15 minutes. If anything is unclear, discuss it with a colleague.

- If you think any information is wrong or out of date, let us know.

- Use the activity on the back page and take this learning into your workplace.

Case study

John is a 54-year-old man who had a surgery for a carcinoma of the colon. Despite liver metastases he has been managing well. In recent months he has noticed that he has less energy and finds taking his Irish setter dog for a walk is becoming more difficult.

INFORMATION PAGE

Definitions

Drowsiness, tiredness, lethargy, fatigue and weakness have different meanings for different patients. Many people use some of these terms interchangeably. Strict definitions are therefore difficult but the following may help.

- *Drowsiness:* Patients usually link this to a sensation of wanting to sleep.
- *Tiredness:* This seems to be linked to mild energy loss and is commonly experienced by everyone, although any illness (even a mild viral infection) can result in tiredness. Some people use the term tiredness to describe drowsiness.
- *Lethargy:* Patients seem to link this to psychological aspects such as, 'I can't be bothered'. Lethargy is a feature of feeling low in mood and of a clinical depression.

- *Fatigue:* Fatigue is perceived by patients as more severe and persistent than tiredness. Patients describe a number of accompanying sensations: lack of energy, exhaustion, restlessness, boredom, lack of interest in activities, weakness, dyspnoea, pain, altered taste and itching. The concept of fatigue seems to be a combination of physical sensations (e.g. slowing up), feelings (e.g. irritability, loss of interest) and cognitive sensations (e.g. loss of concentration).
- *Weakness:* Although this term can be used by patients to describe lethargy or fatigue, it is usually used to describe a loss of physical strength. This can be localised (e.g. paralysis) or generalised (when it is more likely to suggest fatigue).

Causes of fatigue, lethargy, drowsiness and weakness

1 *Generalised fatigue and lethargy:* possibilities include infection, anaemia, severe breathlessness, nutritional deficiency, drugs, recent surgery, recent radiotherapy, recent chemotherapy, low sodium (IADH syndrome, chest infection, diuretics), low potassium (diuretics, corticosteroids), high calcium (due to cancer), low magnesium (poor nutrition or chemotherapy), low oxygen levels (chest infection, pleural effusion, lung metastases), psychological causes (severe anxiety, clinical depression) or cachexia.
2 *Drowsiness:*
   - Sudden onset: drowsiness occurring in minutes, hours or days needs urgent review. Possible causes are drugs (sedation, respiratory depression), severe infection, hypoglycaemia, hypercalcaemia, haemorrhage and

hypoadrenalism (adrenal insufficiency or steroid withdrawal).
   - Slow onset: drowsiness occurring over days or weeks may be due to drug accumulation (e.g. diazepam), hyperglycaemia or organ failure (e.g. liver or kidney).
3 *Localised weakness:*
   - Proximal weakness (weakness of muscles closest to the trunk): corticosteroids, low potassium, thyroid abnormalities, motor neurone disease, osteomalacia, Lambert-Eaton myaesthenic syndrome.
   - Localised muscle weakness: think of intracerebral causes (CVA, brain metastases), localised nerve compression or damage, spinal cord compression or peripheral neuropathy.

The effects of fatigue on John, his family and professionals

- *Reduced mobility and function:* This will start to restrict his activities and ability to carry out daily activities.
- *Loss of control:* Many patients see the physical limitations and increasing reliance on others as a further loss of independence and control. Some are accepting of this and are willing to receive help, and may even see the dignity inherent in receiving this help. Others see themselves becoming a burden to others, causing frustration, anger, anxiety or low mood.
- *Reminder of the illness:* John and his family will see the fatigue as a clear outward sign that the illness is still present

and advancing. For some, denial or a determination to fight will be an effective way of coping with this fact, others will accept what is happening, while some will struggle with the deterioration.
- *Missed opportunities:* John and his family may feel there is no point in planning ahead (e.g. for holidays), while professionals may assume the fatigue is due to the illness and cannot be changed. Although fatigue and tiredness may indicate that the illness is progressing, there are many other causes and some causes due to the cancer may be fully or partly reversible.

Helping John cope

- *Treat coexisting physical symptoms:* e.g. anaemia, pain, dyspnoea, nausea, vomiting.
- *Exclude depression or an anxiety state:* See CLIP worksheets *Helping the anxious person* and *Helping the withdrawn patient.*
- *Modify activities that cause fatigue:* Use rest periods between activities, re-time activities to a time of day when energy is highest, plan regular gentle exercise, arrange help for low-priority activities, review sleep behaviours and sleep environment. Ask a physiotherapist for advice.

- *Ensure food presentation encourages sufficient nutritional intake:* See CLIP worksheet series *Helping the patient with reduced hydration and nutrition.*
- *Drugs:* These may have a limited role – ask for advice from a palliative care specialist. Dexamethasone 2–4 mg daily can give short-term improvement for up to 4 weeks. Psycho-stimulants are occasionally used.

WORK PAGE

 Link the symptoms on the left with those phrases you think best describe those symptoms (some may link to more than one phrase). The first is suggested for you.

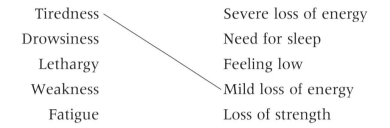

Tiredness — Severe loss of energy

Drowsiness — Need for sleep

Lethargy — Feeling low

Weakness — Mild loss of energy

Fatigue — Loss of strength

 Write down possible causes of John's fatigue in the following categories:

Category	Possible causes
Drowsiness	
Generalised tiredness	
Localised weakness	

Think How could fatigue and tiredness show in John, his family and his professional carers? Think of some examples.

Effect	How might this affect John, family and professionals?
Reduced mobility	
Loss of control	
Reminder of the illness	
Missed opportunities	

Think What treatments for fatigue and tiredness can you think of?

. . . .

. . . .

FURTHER ACTIVITY

The next time you feel tired:

- Consider whether you are experiencing drowsiness, fatigue or weakness.

FURTHER READING

Journal articles

Aapro MS, Cella D and Zagari M (2002) Age, anemia, and fatigue. *Seminars in Oncology.* 29(Suppl. 8): 55–9.

Dimeo F (2002) Radiotherapy-related fatigue and exercise for cancer patients: a review of the literature and suggestions for future research. *Frontiers of Radiation Therapy and Oncology.* 37. 49–56.

Fulton C and Knowles G (2000) Cancer fatigue. *European Journal of Cancer Care.* 9(3): 167–71.

Gall H (1996) The basis of fatigue: where does it come from? *European Journal of Cancer Care.* 5: 31–4.

Glaus A, Crow R and Hammond S (1996) A qualitative study to explore the concept of fatigue/tiredness in cancer patients and healthy individuals. *European Journal of Cancer Care.* 5: 8–23.

Håvard Loge J (2003) Unpacking fatigue. *European Journal of Palliative Care.* 10(Suppl. 2): 14–20.

Kirsh KL, Passik S and Holtsclaw E (2001) I get tired for no reason: a single item screening for cancer-related fatigue. *Journal of Pain and Symptom Management.* 22(5): 931–7.

Mock V, Dow KH, Meares CJ *et al.* (1997) Effects of exercise on fatigue, physical functioning, and emotional distress during radiation therapy for breast cancer. *Oncology Nursing Forum.* 24(6): 991–1000.

Nail LM (2002) Fatigue in patients with cancer. *Oncology Nursing Forum.* 29(3): 537.

Richardson A (1995) Fatigue in cancer patients: a review of the literature. *European Journal of Cancer Care.* 4: 20–32.

Richardson A and Ream E (1996) The experience of fatigue and other symptoms in patients receiving chemotherapy. *European Journal of Cancer Care.* 5: 24–30.

Stone P (2002) The measurement, causes and effective management of cancer-related fatigue. *International Journal of Palliative Nursing.* 8(3): 120–8.

Winningham ML, Nail LM, Burke MB *et al.* (1994) Fatigue and the cancer experience: the state of the knowledge. *Oncology Nursing Forum.* 21(1): 23–36.

Yarbro CH (1996) Interventions for fatigue. *European Journal of Cancer Care.* 5: 35–8.

Resource books and websites

Calman K, Doyle D and Hanks GWC (eds) (2003) *The Oxford Textbook of Palliative Medicine* (3e). Oxford University Publications, Oxford.

Regnard C and Hockley J (2004) *A Guide to Symptom Relief in Palliative Care* (5e). Radcliffe Medical Press, Oxford.

Twycross RG and Wilcock A (2001) *Symptom Management in Advanced Cancer* (3e). Radcliffe Medical Press, Oxford.

Twycross RG, Wilcock A and Charlesworth S (2002) *PCF2 – Palliative Care Formulary*. Radcliffe Medical Press, Oxford.

Winningham ML and Barton-Burke M (2000) *Fatigue in Cancer: a multidimensional approach.* Jones and Bartlett, Boston.

www.cancerbacup.org.uk/info/fatigue.htm – Online version of patient information booklet on fatigue.

www.cancerfatigue.org – Information on fatigue set up by the Oncology Nursing Society, USA.

www.oncolink.upenn.edu/support/fatigue – Tips on managing fatigue and anaemia.

www.palliativedrugs.com – Updated website for the *Palliative Care Formulary*.

HELPING THE PATIENT WITH SYMPTOMS OTHER THAN PAIN

3 Breathlessness

Claud Regnard
Margaret Kindlen
Kathryn Mannix

INTRODUCTORY LEVEL

Aim of this worksheet

To learn to assess and manage breathlessness.

How to use this worksheet

- You can work through this worksheet by yourself, or with a tutor.

- Read the case study below, then work on the questions overleaf.

- The work page is on the right side, the information page is on the left.

- Work any way you want: you can try answering from your own knowledge (in which case, fold over the information page), you can use the information page (this is not cheating – you learn as you find the information) or you can use other sources of information.

- It should take you about 15 minutes. If anything is unclear, discuss it with a colleague.

- If you think any information is wrong or out of date, let us know.

- Use the activity on the back page and take this learning into your workplace.

Case study

John is a 54-year-old man who had a surgery for a carcinoma of the colon. Despite liver metastases he has been managing well until he was found to have a pleural effusion. He has become increasingly breathless over the past few weeks and contacts you because his breathing has got worse.

INFORMATION PAGE

Getting started

- You need to know when his breathing started to get worse because breathlessness of sudden onset (seconds or minutes) has different causes (e.g. pulmonary embolus) from those that build up over days or longer (e.g. pleural effusion).
- You need to check if he is pale (anaemia will worsen the situation), and observe if he is confused, agitated or frightened. You also need to observe if he is peripherally cyanosed (bluish tinge to fingers and toes) or centrally cyanosed (an additional blue tinge to the lips). Both suggest that the oxygen level in his blood is low (i.e. he is hypoxic). Remember, however, that some patients can be hypoxic and yet look pink. A pulse oximeter can tell if these patients are hypoxic.
- Listening to the chest would give information on the presence of a chest infection, pleural effusion or a pleural rub due to inflammation of the pleura (e.g. infection, pulmonary embolus, tumour).

Simple measures

Some simple measures are worth trying. The simplest is increasing the movement of air over the patient's face using a fan or opening a window. Sitting John upright may also help. Don't forget to explain what you are doing and, if you know, explain why he is more breathless. Relaxing the shoulders may help (*see Breathing retraining* below).

A trial with oxygen may help. Initially the source will be an oxygen cylinder, but an oxygen concentrator can be prescribed if oxygen is going to be used for 15 hours or more each day. Initially a patient should have no more than 28% oxygen until a doctor who knows the patient's history can confirm that it is safe to use higher levels for more than a few days. Nasal cannulae are better tolerated than a mask.

Make sure John has company, and also has a distraction like a television because loneliness and boredom make it harder to cope with breathlessness.

Tackling persistent breathlessness

- *Antibiotics* are important in treating breathlessness caused by a chest infection.
- *Steroids* may reduce enough oedema around lung metastases to free up more normal lung for gas exchange.
- *Strong opioids* are also used, initially orally in low doses. Contact your local palliative care specialists for advice.
- *Nabilone* is a derivative of cannabis and is a bronchodilator with central effects that together can ease breathlessness in some patients. The usual dose is 200–500 microg 8-hourly.
- *Acupuncture* can be useful using points in the upper sternum and the L14 points in the hands.

- *Benzodiazepines* have been used, e.g. lorazepam (diazepam is too sedating and long-acting).
- *Breathing retraining:* Patients have been shown to benefit from breathing retraining and breathlessness clinics are beginning to be established. One useful exercise is to teach the patient to relax their shoulders when they are breathless, since they are often tensed up during breathless episodes and letting the shoulders relax down increases the lung capacity to take in air. Massage can help the shoulders relax.

Managing severe breathlessness

The key here is to manage John's agitation, which is probably being caused by hypoxia.

1 Ensure that the simple measures above are in use.
2 If possible use midazolam IV, titrating 2–10 mg over several minutes.
   - alternatives are to give the midazolam sublingually (absorption 2–5 mins), IM into deltoid (absorption 10 mins) or subcutaneous (absorption 20 mins)
   - you could give diazepam IV or PR, but its effect is long lasting and it can accumulate and complicate the situation (John may not wish to be fully asleep)

   - for minimal sedation you could try lorazepam 0.5 mg or 1 mg, which can be taken sublingually.
3 You could also give him something for his secretions:
   - hyoscine butylbromide is effective in 50% of cases in a dose of 20 mg SC repeated as necessary, but is short acting (2–3 hours).
   - hyoscine hydrobromide is as effective and longer acting than hyoscine butylbromide, but more sedating in a dose of 200–400 microg SC.
   - diuretics can help clear secretions in some patients with cardiac problems.

WORK PAGE

When you arrive, John is able to tell you he is breathless at rest, and gets much more breathless as he walks from his chair to the bed.

Think   As John slowly gets into bed think about:

* What do you want to ask him?

* What will you want to check?

. . . .

. . . .

. . . .

. . . .

What could you do straight away that might help him?

What other arrangements could you make that might help?

. . . .

. . . .

. . . .

. . . .

Think   Despite your initial efforts, John is still breathless. Investigations have shown multiple lung metastases and a small effusion. What could help John?

. . . .

. . . .

. . . .

. . . .

Initially John improves, but one night you're called to see him urgently. This time he's so breathless he can't speak, he looks very frightened and he's coughing up loose sputum.

Write down what you can do to help John.

. . . .

. . . .

. . . .

FURTHER ACTIVITY

When you next care for a breathless patient:

• Check through the list of simple measures the team could use.

FURTHER READING

Journal articles

Back IN, Jenkins K and Blower A (2001) A study comparing hyoscine hydrobromide and glycopyrrolate in the treatment of death rattle. *Palliative Medicine*. **15**(4): 329–36.

Bailey C (1995) Nursing as therapy in the management of breathlessness in lung cancer. *European Journal of Cancer Care*. **4**: 184–90.

Bredin M, Corner J, Krishnasamy M *et al.* (1999) Multicentre randomised controlled trial of nursing intervention for breathlessness in patients with lung cancer. *BMJ*. **318**(7188): 901–4.

Corner J and O'Driscoll M (1999) Development of a breathlessness assessment guide for use in palliative care. *Palliative Medicine*. **13**(5): 375–84.

Cox C (2002) Non-pharmacological treatment of breathlessness. *Nursing Standard*. **16**(24): 33–6.

Davis C (1997) ABC of palliative care: Breathlessness, cough, and other respiratory problems. *BMJ*. **315**: 931–4.

Davis CL (1999) Palliation of breathlessness. *Cancer Treatment and Research*. **100**: 59–73.

Edmonds P, Karlsen S, Khan S *et al.* (2001) A comparison of the palliative care needs of patients dying from chronic respiratory diseases and lung cancer. *Palliative Medicine*. **15**(4): 287–95.

Flowers B (2003) Palliative care for patients with end-stage heart failure. *Nursing Times*. **99**: 30–2.

Janssens JP, de Muralt B and Titelion V (2000) Management of dyspnea in severe chronic obstructive pulmonary disease. *Journal of Pain and Symptom Management*. **19**(5): 378–92.

LeGrand SB and Walsh D (1999) Palliative management of dyspnea in advanced cancer. *Current Opinion in Oncology*. **11**(4): 250–4.

Mancini I and Body JJ (1999) Assessment of dyspnea in advanced cancer patients. *Supportive Care in Cancer*. **7**(4): 229–32.

O'Driscoll M, Corner J and Bailey C (1999) The experience of breathlessness in lung cancer. *European Journal of Cancer Care*. **8**(1): 37–43.

Ripamonti C (1999) Management of dyspnea in advanced cancer patients. *Supportive Care in Cancer*. **7**(4): 233–43.

Shee CD (1995) Palliation in chronic respiratory disease. *Palliative Medicine*. **9**(1): 3–12.

Wilcock A, Crosby V, Hughes A *et al.* (2002) Descriptors of breathlessness in patients with cancer and other cardiorespiratory diseases. *Journal of Pain and Symptom Management*. **23**(3): 182–9.

Zeppetella G (1998) The palliation of dyspnea in terminal disease. *American Journal of Hospice and Palliative Care*. **15**(6): 322–30.

Resource books and website

Calman K, Doyle D and Hanks GWC (eds) (2003) *The Oxford Textbook of Palliative Medicine* (3e). Oxford University Publications, Oxford.

Regnard C and Hockley J (2004) *A Guide to Symptom Relief in Palliative Care* (5e). Radcliffe Medical Press, Oxford.

Twycross RG and Wilcock A (2001) *Symptom Management in Advanced Cancer* (3e). Radcliffe Medical Press, Oxford.

Twycross RG, Wilcock A and Charlesworth S (2002) *PCF2 – Palliative Care Formulary*. Radcliffe Medical Press, Oxford.

www.palliativedrugs.com – Updated website for the *Palliative Care Formulary*.

HELPING THE PATIENT WITH SYMPTOMS OTHER THAN PAIN

4 Oral problems

Lynn Gibson
Dorothy Matthews
Claud Regnard

INTRODUCTORY LEVEL

Aim of this worksheet

To learn to assess and manage oral problems.

How to use this worksheet

- You can work through this worksheet by yourself, or with a tutor.

- Read the case study below, then work on the questions overleaf.

- The work page is on the right side, the information page is on the left.

- Work any way you want: you can try answering from your own knowledge (in which case, fold over the information page), you can use the information page (this is not cheating – you learn as you find the information) or you can use other sources of information.

- It should take you about 15 minutes. If anything is unclear, discuss it with a colleague.

- If you think any information is wrong or out of date, let us know.

- Use the activity on the back page and take this learning into your workplace.

Case study

John is a 54-year-old man who had a surgery for a carcinoma of the colon. For the past week he has been eating less and less and now has swallowing problems. Today John is complaining of a sore mouth.

INFORMATION PAGE

Principles of oral hygiene

We take oral health for granted because we live with a mouth that is moist and pain-free. But consider the opposite – a mouth that is full of oral debris, ulcerated, dry or painful.

- Regular mouth care is essential and the objective of such care is simple, i.e. to achieve a clean, moist, pain-free, non-infected mouth.

- Oral assessment can identify sites of infection and chronic irritations in the mouth, which is important, as oral dysfunction significantly affects the client's quality of life.
- Frequent mechanical cleansing of the mouth is more important in oral care than the antiseptic qualities of mouthwash.

Four phases of oral status

	Healthy phase	Early warning (mild dysfunction)	Problem present (moderate dysfunction)	Serious problem (severe dysfunction)
Saliva	Adequate	Decreased	Scant, with taste alteration	Thick or absent
Mucosa	Pink, moist, intact and comfortable	Pale and dry, with uncomfortable red areas	Dry, inflamed, blistered and sore	Red and shiny, with blisters, ulcers and pain
Tongue	Pink, moist and comfortable	Dry, with prominent papillae	Dry and swollen, white coating at base, sore, inflammatory lines of demarcation	Dry and thick, coated and blistered, painful, red and demarcated
Lips	Smooth, pink, moist and comfortable	Dry and wrinkled	Dry, cracked and uncomfortable	Dry, cracked, painful with ulcerated areas and bleeding
Teeth	Clean, without debris and comfortable. Patient able to wear dentures	Dull, with localised areas of debris	Dull, debris on half of the enamel, areas of irritation, intermittent pain	Dull, with debris generalised along gum line or denture area. Patient unable to wear dentures. Frequent dental pain

Risk factors and prevention

Risk factors
- Debility
- Reduced oral intake
- Unable to brush teeth
- Dehydration
- Saliva-reducing drugs
- Chemotherapy
- Radiotherapy
- Mouth breathing
- Oxygen therapy

Prevention is a priority
To establish a healthy mouth regime the following are recommended:
- regular tooth and denture brushing twice daily
- regular use of anti-bacterial and anti-fungal mouthwash
- check fit of dentures, remembering nightly soak
- regular dental checks
- regular mouth care: frequency dictated following assessment, e.g. for general care, treat 6–12-hourly, for at-risk patients treat 2-hourly, for high-risk patients and for serious problems treat hourly.

Possible problems and solutions

- *Dry mouth:* Frequent sips or sprays of water, use of artificial saliva (but avoid acidic preparations), ensure frequent mouth care, vaseline to lips, iced drinks, ice cubes, pineapple juice. Chewing gum helps some patients. Pilocarpine 5 mg 8-hourly helps some patients.
- *Dirty mouth:* Remove dentures if used and soak/clean accordingly. If patients have their own teeth, regular brushing is important. Alternatively, clean the mouth with sponge swabs or gauze over a gloved finger.
- *Candida (candidiasis, thrush):* Ketoconazole (200 mg once daily for 5 days), fluconazole (150 mg as single dose), nystatin (2 ml 6-hourly for at least 10 days).
- *Ulceration and infection:*
  - Virus infections: acyclovir 200 mg 4-hourly for 1 week (400 mg if immunosuppressed).
  - Apthous ulcers: topical corticosteroid (triamcinalone in Orabase or betamethasone tablets), or tetracycline suspension mouthwash (disperse a 250 mg capsule in water and rinse in the mouth for 2 minutes then swallow 6-hourly).
  - Malignant ulcers: if anaerobic infection present (i.e. foul smell) use systemic metronidazole 12-hourly 500 mg PO or 1g PR, or use 1% topical gel if not tolerated systemically (topical gel is expensive).
- *Sore mouth:* Benzydamine (Difflam) spray or mouthwash, sucralfate suspension mouthwash, choline salicylate gel (Bonjela), benzocaine lozenges (100 mg sucked as required) or a lidocaine spray.

WORK PAGE

Think   Think about what actions might reduce the chance of John getting a sore mouth?

. . . .

. . . .

. . . .

What would 'ring an alarm' that something is wrong with John's mouth?

Area affected	Early warning	Serious problem
Saliva		
Mucosa		
Tongue		
Lips		
Teeth		

Think   Think about what factors would increase the risk of oral problems.

. . . .

. . . .

. . . .

. . . .

Write down treatments for these problems.

Problem	Treatments
Dry mouth	
Dirty mouth	
Candida (thrush)	
Sore or painful mouth	

FURTHER ACTIVITY

- What do you think should be involved in establishing a healthy mouth regime?

- Taste a variety of fluids, e.g. coffee, soda water, pineapple juice etc. and consider which is the most refreshing.

FURTHER READING

Journal articles

Bagg J (2003) Oral candidosis: how to treat a common problem. *European Journal of Palliative Care.* **10**(2): 54–6.

Coleman P (2002) Improving oral health care for the frail elderly: A review of widespread problems and best practices. *Geriatric Nursing.* **23**(4): 189–99.

Fiske J and Shafik HH (2001) Down's syndrome and oral care. *Dental Update.* **28**(3): 148–56.

Freer SK (2000) Use of oral assessment tool to improve practice. *Professional Nurse.* **15**: 635–7.

Haddad P and Karimi M (2002) A randomized, double-blind, placebo-controlled trial of concomitant pilocarpine with head and neck irradiation for prevention of radiation-induced xerostomia. *Radiotherapy and Oncology.* **64**(1): 29.

Lee L, White V and Ball J (2001) An audit of oral care practice and staff knowledge in hospital palliative care. *International Journal of Palliative Nursing.* **7**(8): 395–400.

Mercadante S (2002) Dry mouth and palliative care. *European Journal of Palliative Care.* **9**(5): 182–5.

Milligan S, McGill M and Sweeney MP (2001) Oral care for people with advanced cancer: an evidence-based protocol. *International Journal of Palliative Nursing.* **7**(9): 418–26.

Miller M and Kearney N (2001) Oral care for patients with cancer: a review of the literature. *Cancer Nursing.* **24**(4): 241–54.

Rawlins CA and Trueman IW (2001) Effective mouth care for seriously ill patients. *Professional Nurse.* **16**(4): 1025–8.

Regnard CFB, Gillham L and Fitton S (1997) Mouth care, skin care, lymphoedema. In: WM O'Neill and G Hanks (eds) ABC series of palliative care. *BMJ.* **315**: 1002–5.

Roberts H (1990) Mouthcare in oral cavity cancer. *Nursing Standard.* **4**(19): 26–9.

Scully C and Shotts R (2000) ABC of oral health: mouth ulcers and other causes of orofacial soreness and pain. *BMJ.* **321**: 162–5.

Xavier G (2000) The importance of mouth care in preventing infection. *Nursing Standard.* **14**(18): 47–51.

Resource books and website

Calman K, Doyle D and Hanks GWC (eds) (2003) *The Oxford Textbook of Palliative Medicine* (3e). Oxford University Publications, Oxford.

Regnard C and Hockley J (2004) *A Guide to Symptom Relief in Palliative Care* (5e). Radcliffe Medical Press, Oxford.

Twycross RG and Wilcock A (2001) *Symptom Management in Advanced Cancer* (3e). Radcliffe Medical Press, Oxford.

Twycross RG, Wilcock A and Charlesworth S (2002) *PCF2 – Palliative Care Formulary.* Radcliffe Medical Press, Oxford.

www.palliativedrugs.com – Updated website for the *Palliative Care Formulary.*

HELPING THE PATIENT WITH SYMPTOMS OTHER THAN PAIN

5 Nausea and vomiting

Claud Regnard
Margaret Kindlen
Sylvia Dryden
Kathryn Mannix
Sarah Alport

INTERMEDIATE LEVEL

Aim of this worksheet

To learn how to assess and manage nausea and vomiting.

How to use this worksheet

- You can work through this worksheet by yourself, or with a tutor.

- Read the case study below, then work on the questions overleaf.

- The work page is on the right side, the information page is on the left.

- Work any way you want: you can try answering from your own knowledge (in which case, fold over the information page), you can use the information page (this is not cheating – you learn as you find the information) or you can use other sources of information.

- It should take you about 15 minutes. If anything is unclear, discuss it with a colleague.

- If you think any information is wrong or out of date, let us know.

- Use the activity on the back page and take this learning into your workplace.

Case study

John is a 54-year-old man who had a surgery for a carcinoma of the colon. He asks to see you because he has started to feel nauseated with occasional vomiting.

INFORMATION PAGE

Nausea and vomiting

This is common, occurring in 62% of patients with advanced cancer. You need to ask the patient about the following:

- *Nausea:* How often, how long, precipitating and relieving factors, whether it is accompanied by vomiting.

- *Vomiting:* How often, how long, how much, content, precipitating/relieving factors, whether it is accompanied by nausea.

Current treatment

Treatment is based on blocking the effects of specific neurotransmitters:

- *Haloperidol* blocks *central dopamine* receptors (D_2) in the chemoreceptor trigger zone (CTZ), i.e. haloperidol is a dopamine antagonist.
- *Cyclizine* blocks *histamine* receptors (H_1) and *muscarinic* receptors (Ach_m) in the brainstem, i.e. cyclizine is an antihistamine and an antimuscarinic drug.
- *Domperidone* and *metoclopramide* block *peripheral dopamine* receptors (D_2) in the stomach and upper small bowel. They act by restoring motility towards normal.

Other antiemetics:

- *Levomepromazine* (methotrimeprazine: Nozinan) is a useful second line antiemetic because of its broad spectrum action on a range of receptors. It blocks histamine (H_1), dopamine (D_2) and acetylcholine (Ach_m) receptors as well as $5HT_2$ receptors.
- *Ondansetron* and *granisetron* block $5HT_3$ receptors. They have been disappointing in palliative care despite their obvious success in chemotherapy vomiting and in post-operative nausea and vomiting.
- *Prochlorperazine* (Stemetil) has a weak action on the three main receptors (H_1, D_2 and Ach_m).

Drug doses and routes

Haloperidol is used in very low doses, 1–3 mg once at night SC or PO. There is no need to give it by continuous SC infusion since it has a 16-hour half-life.

Cyclizine is given as 25–50 mg 8-hourly PO or PR, or 75–150 mg per 24 hours as a continuous SC infusion.

Domperidone can be give PR or PO, metoclopramide PO or SC. Metoclopramide and domperidone are equally effective and either can be used. Domperidone is much less likely to cause movement disorders.

Levomepromazine can be given PO or SC 2.5–12.5 mg once at night.

Acupuncture and acupressure

There are 33 randomised controlled trials (12 of high quality) that support the use of the P6 acupuncture point for vomiting due to chemotherapy, morphine or post-operative nausea and vomiting. The P6 point is on the middle of the inner wrist, two finger breadths up the arm from the wrist crease. It can be stimulated with pressure or an acupuncture needle.

Clinical decisions and treatment

- *Is the patient mainly troubled by vomiting?*
  If the vomits are large volume and the patient dehydrating rapidly, consider gastric outflow obstruction as a cause.

  If the vomits are large volume but hydration is reasonable, this could be gastric stasis. It is usually accompanied by early satiation, epigastric fullness and pain, flatulence, hiccup, large volume vomiting, or heartburn. Metoclopramide or domperidone should help, but they need to start SC or PR to be effective.

  If the volume of vomit is small consider regurgitation due to dysphagia, stomach paralysis or a 'squashed stomach syndrome' (caused by external pressure on the stomach from tumour, ascites or a large liver).
- *Could the cause be drugs, toxins or biochemical?* e.g. drugs (morphine, metronidazole, trimethoprim), bacterial toxins, hypercalcaemia or uraemia. Haloperidol or levomepromazine should help.
- *Is the nausea or vomiting worse on movement?* For motion sickness try hyoscine hydrobromide, otherwise cyclizine or cinnarizine may help.
- *Is gastritis present?* Treat the cause if known. Metoclopramide may help reduce nausea and vomiting.
- *Could fear or anxiety be contributing?* See CLIP worksheet *Helping the anxious person.*
- *Is the nausea and vomiting persisting?* Start levomepromazine 3–6 mg PO or 2.5–5 mg SC at bedtime. Other antiemetics that occasionally help are ondansetron, dexamethasone and low dose olanzepine.

WORK PAGE

Consider the mechanisms involved in the vomiting reflex in the diagram below. The neuro-transmitters involved at the peripheral and central sites vary. By selectively blocking receptors with drugs, it is possible to control symptoms in most patients.

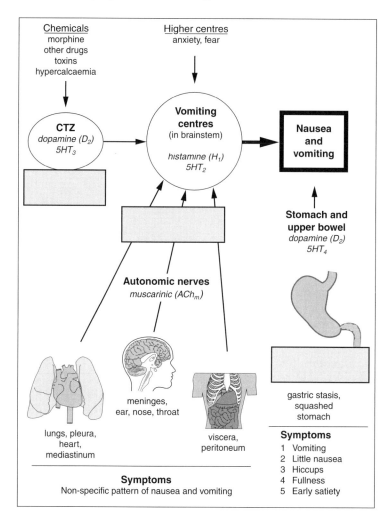

This diagram shows a simplified mechanism for nausea and vomiting.

The receptors involved are written in *italics*.
In the shaded boxes, write the site of action of:

- metoclopramide
- cyclizine
- haloperidol
- domperidone

What other antiemetics do you know?. . . . .
. . . .
What other treatments do you know? . . . .
. . . .

Q: What are the possible causes of John's vomiting?

. . . .

. . . .

FURTHER ACTIVITY

Find a patient who is troubled with nausea and/or vomiting.

- Can you identify a pattern suggesting gastric stasis?

- What possible causes are there in this patient?

FURTHER READING

Journal articles

Bentley A and Boyd K (2001) Use of clinical pictures in the management of nausea and vomiting: a prospective audit. *Palliative Medicine.* 15(3): 247–53.

Bruera E, Belzile M, Neumann C *et al.* (2000) A double-blind, crossover study of controlled-release metoclopramide and placebo for the chronic nausea and dyspepsia of advanced cancer. *Journal of Pain and Symptom Management.* 19(6): 427–35.

Critchley P, Plach N, Grantham M *et al.* (2001) Efficacy of haloperidol in the treatment of nausea and vomiting in the palliative patient: a systematic review. *Journal of Pain and Symptom Management.* 22(2): 631–4.

Currow DC, Coughlan M, Fardell B *et al.* (1997) Clinical note. Use of ondansetron in palliative medicine. *Journal of Pain and Symptom Management.* 13(5): 302–7.

Davis MP and Walsh D (2000) Treatment of nausea and vomiting in advanced cancer. *Supportive Care in Cancer.* 8(6): 444–52.

Han P and Arnold B (2001) The challenge of chronic AIDS-related nausea and vomiting. *Journal of Palliative Medicine.* 4(1): 65–8.

Herrstedt J (2002) Nausea and emesis: still an unsolved problem in cancer patients? *Supportive Care in Cancer.* 10(2): 85–7.

Johnstone PA, Polston GR, Niemtzow RC *et al.* (2002) Integration of acupuncture into the oncology clinic. *Palliative Medicine.* 16(3): 235–9.

Lichter I (1993) Which antiemetic? *Journal of Palliative Care.* 9: 42–50.

Quigley EM, Hasler WL and Parkman HP (2001) AGA technical review on nausea and vomiting. *Gastroenterology.* 120(1): 263–86.

Rhodes VA and McDaniel RW (2001) Nausea, vomiting, and retching: complex problems in palliative care. *Ca: a Cancer Journal for Clinicians.* 51(4): 232–48.

Skinner J and Skinner A (1999) Levomepromazine for nausea and vomiting in advanced cancer. *Hospital Medicine (London).* 60(8): 568–70.

Watson M, Meyer L, Thomson A *et al.* (1998) Psychological factors predicting nausea and vomiting in breast cancer patients on chemotherapy. *European Journal of Cancer.* 34(6): 831–7.

Resource books and website

Calman K, Doyle D and Hanks GWC (eds) (2003) *The Oxford Textbook of Palliative Medicine* (3e). Oxford University Publications, Oxford.

Regnard C and Hockley J (2004) *A Guide to Symptom Relief in Palliative Care* (5e). Radcliffe Medical Press, Oxford.

Twycross RG and Wilcock A (2001) *Symptom Management in Advanced Cancer* (3e). Radcliffe Medical Press, Oxford.

Twycross RG, Wilcock A and Charlesworth S (2002) *PCF2 – Palliative Care Formulary.* Radcliffe Medical Press, Oxford.

www.palliativedrugs.com – Updated website for the *Palliative Care Formulary.*

HELPING THE PATIENT WITH SYMPTOMS OTHER THAN PAIN

6 Bowel obstruction

Claud Regnard

INTERMEDIATE LEVEL

Aim of this worksheet

To learn how to assess and manage bowel obstruction due to cancer.

How to use this worksheet

- You can work through this worksheet by yourself, or with a tutor.

- Read the case study below, then work on the questions overleaf.

- The work page is on the right side, the information page is on the left.

- Work any way you want: you can try answering from your own knowledge (in which case, fold over the information page), you can use the information page (this is not cheating – you learn as you find the information) or you can use other sources of information.

- It should take you about 15 minutes. If anything is unclear, discuss it with a colleague.

- If you think any information is wrong or out of date, let us know.

- Use the activity on the back page and take this learning into your workplace.

Case study

John is a 54-year-old man who had a surgery for a carcinoma of the colon. He has been having problems with nausea and vomiting. At first this responded to cyclizine, but he calls you because the nausea has returned and he has started having bouts of colic. He normally opens his bowels every few days but has not opened his bowels for nearly a week. He has noticed that his abdomen is swollen today.

INFORMATION PAGE

Is this bowel obstruction?

It may seem strange to ask this question, but many of John's symptoms could have other causes:

- other causes of nausea and vomiting (*see* CLIP worksheet *Nausea and vomiting*)
- colic due to infection or stimulant laxatives
- constipation, which can reduce the frequency of opening

bowels, causes nausea and vomiting and may even cause a physical obstruction if severe enough.

- ascites, which can cause abdominal swelling.

Obviously reversible causes (such as constipation) need to be treated. However, it can be difficult to decide the cause and it may be necessary to use investigations (ultrasound, abdominal X-ray) or to keep John under observation.

Clinical decisions

- *Is a physical blockage absent or unlikely?* A bowel obstruction is not always due to a physical blockage. If the bowel slows or stops working (an 'ileus') this will have a similar effect to a bowel obstruction (absent bowel sounds, distension, no bowel motions). Several conditions can cause ileus such as peritonitis, septicaemia or recent cord compression. Drugs that slow the bowel can be a cause, such as antimuscarinics (e.g. amitriptyline, hyoscine).
- *Is thirst present?* In bowel obstruction fluid is secreted into the bowel lumen. This fluid is effectively lost and makes the patient dehydrated. If a patient feels thirsty they will have lost at least 1 litre and this needs to be replaced.
- *Is surgery or stenting possible?* This should always be considered. It may only require a loop colostomy or dividing adhesions, but surgery can have significant mortality and morbidity. An understanding surgical opinion can be helpful, although it can be difficult to decide if there is a single level obstruction that is amenable to surgery. Stenting of duodenal or colonic obstructions can be an easier alternative.
- *Is nausea or vomiting present?* Patients find that the most

distressing problem is nausea. Vomiting may remain but at a reduced volume or frequency and patients perceive it as much less distressing than constant nausea. Vomiting is less of a problem in more distal obstructions. Patients with distended colons may later restart with nausea, possibly since bacterial toxins are now adding to the nausea.

- *Is pain present?* The commonest cause of pain is colic caused by the bowel trying to push bowel contents against the obstruction. It usually comes in regular waves, each lasting several minutes. Colic does not respond well to opioids and needs a drug to relax the bowel such as hyoscine butylbromide (Buscopan).
- *Is this complete or partial bowel obstruction?* In partial obstruction it is important to keep the bowel moving with laxatives while avoiding colic – drugs such as hyoscine have to be used sparingly to avoid slowing the bowel too much. With a complete obstruction that is inoperable, any bowel movements have no benefit and laxatives should be stopped, while colic can be safely treated with hyoscine butylbromide.

Treatment

- *Ileus:* Stop antiperistaltic drugs (e.g. antimuscarinics) and osmotic laxatives. A stimulant laxative such as senna may help to stimulate the bowel. Metoclopramide SC infusion 30–90 mg per 24 hours may also encourage the bowel to function.
- *Feeding and hydration:* In advanced disease there is no advantage in restricting fluids or snacks. Cups of tea when wanted are preferable to 25 ml water each hour! Troublesome dehydration is best treated orally, but if the patient is nauseated or vomiting it will need to be replaced intravenously or subcutaneously.
- *Surgery:* Surgery is possible if the patient agrees and they are in good or reasonable nutritional and medical condition. The prognosis is poor if there are abdominal masses or ascites, multiple blockages, a small bowel blockage, or there has been previous abdominal radiotherapy.
- *Nausea and vomiting:* Cyclizine 25–50 mg PO 8-hourly (or SC infusion 75–150 mg/24 hours) is the first choice. Some patients need to have haloperidol added 1.5–3 mg SC at night. If this is ineffective, replace both antiemetics with levomepromazine 5 mg SC at night. If the vomiting persists then antisecretory drugs such as hyoscine butylbromide or

octreotide can be used. Nasogastric tubes are very inefficient at easing the symptoms of bowel obstruction, but can help in reducing distress due to faeculant vomiting caused by infected small bowel contents.

- *Pain:* If this is colic give hyoscine butylbromide 20 mg SC (it is ineffective given orally). In inoperable complete obstruction, this can be given as a continuous SC infusion 30–90 mg/24 hours. Some patients have abdominal distension pain which usually responds to analgesics on the WHO analgesic ladder. Coeliac plexus pain will need gabapentin 100 mg 8-hourly and then titrated to achieve a response.
- *Laxatives:* In partial obstruction a gentle laxative such as docusate can be continued – lactulose may cause bloating while senna or danthron can cause colic. In inoperable complete obstruction, all laxatives should be stopped.

With medical management, it is possible to manage inoperable bowel obstruction at home.

Questions: (1) T; (2) F; (3) T; (4) F; (5) F; (6) T.

Treatment–symptom links: colic – hyoscine; nausea – cyclizine; vomiting – bucket; dehydration – IV or SC fluids; thirst – cup of tea; faeculant vomiting – nasogastric tube.

WORK PAGE

Q: What are the features of bowel obstruction? Think of other possible causes for these features.

Feature of bowel obstruction   Alternative causes

. . . .

. . . .

. . . .

. . . .

. . . .

. . . .

. . . .

MCQ Consider the following statements about bowel obstruction.

1	A physical obstruction does not have to be present to cause bowel obstruction	True	False
2	The pain of bowel obstruction usually responds to morphine	True	False
3	Laxatives should be continued in partial bowel obstruction	True	False
4	Restricted oral fluids are a key part of treatment	True	False
5	Nasogastric tubes are an effective treatment for vomiting	True	False
6	Patients with inoperable bowel obstruction can be managed at home	True	False

Match the following treatments to the symptoms they can treat. The first has been done for you.

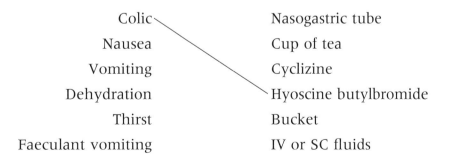

Colic   Nasogastric tube

Nausea   Cup of tea

Vomiting   Cyclizine

Dehydration   Hyoscine butylbromide

Thirst   Bucket

Faeculant vomiting   IV or SC fluids

FURTHER ACTIVITY

Find a patient who is troubled with nausea and/or vomiting:

• Can you identify a pattern suggesting gastric stasis?

• What possible causes are there in this patient?

FURTHER READING

Journal articles

Agra Y, Sacristan A, Gonzalez M *et al.* (1998) Efficacy of senna versus lactulose in terminal cancer patients treated with opioids. *Journal of Pain and Symptom Management.* 15(1): 1–7.

Bruera E, Suarez-Almanzor M, Velasco A *et al.* (1994) The assessment of constipation in terminal cancer patients admitted to a palliative care unit: a retrospective review. *Journal of Pain and Symptom Management.* 9(8): 515–19.

Cleveland MV, Flavin DP, Ruben RA *et al.* (2001) New polyethylene glycol laxative for treatment of constipation in adults: a randomized, double-blind, placebo-controlled study. *Southern Medical Journal.* 94(5): 478–81.

Davis MP and Nouneh C (2000) Modern management of cancer-related intestinal obstruction. *Current Oncology Reports.* 2(4): 343–50.

Davis MP and Walsh D (2000) Treatment of nausea and vomiting in advanced cancer. *Supportive Care in Cancer.* 8(6): 444–52.

Dean A (2001) The palliative effects of octreotide in cancer patients. *Chemotherapy.* 47(Suppl. 2): 54–61.

Gamlin R (2001) Successful management of malignant bowel obstruction. *International Journal of Palliative Nursing.* 7(11): 565.

Gwilliam B and Bailey C (2001) The nature of terminal malignant bowel obstruction and its impact on patients with advanced cancer. *International Journal of Palliative Nursing.* 7(10): 474–81.

Miller G, Boman J, Shrier I and Gordon PH (2000) Small-bowel obstruction secondary to malignant disease: an 11-year audit. *Canadian Journal of Surgery.* 43(5): 353–8.

Nugent M, Davis C, Brooks D *et al.* (2001) Long-term observations of patients receiving transdermal fentanyl after a randomized trial. *Journal of Pain and Symptom Management.* 21(5): 385–91.

Platt V (2001) Malignant bowel obstruction: so much more than symptom control. *International Journal of Palliative Nursing.* 7(11): 547–54.

Ripamonti C, Twycross R, Baines M *et al.* (2001) Working Group of the European Association for Palliative Care. Clinical-practice recommendations for the management of bowel obstruction in patients with end-stage cancer. *Supportive Care in Cancer.* 9(4): 223–33.

Sykes NP (1996) A volunteer model for the comparison of laxatives in opioid-related constipation. *Journal of Pain and Symptom Management.* 11(6): 363–9.

Sykes NP (1998) The relationship between opioid use and laxative use in terminally ill cancer patients. *Palliative Medicine.* 12(5): 375–82.

Wiesel PH, Norton C and Brazzelli M (2002) Management of faecal incontinence and constipation in adults with central neurological diseases. *The Cochrane Database of Systematic Reviews.* 2.

Resource books and website

Calman K, Doyle D and Hanks GWC (eds) (2003) *The Oxford Textbook of Palliative Medicine* (3e). Oxford University Publications, Oxford.

Regnard C and Hockley J (2004) *A Guide to Symptom Relief in Palliative Care* (5e). Radcliffe Medical Press, Oxford.

Twycross RG and Wilcock A (2001) *Symptom Management in Advanced Cancer* (3e). Radcliffe Medical Press, Oxford.

Twycross RG, Wilcock A and Charlesworth S (2002) *PCF2 – Palliative Care Formulary.* Radcliffe Medical Press, Oxford.

www.palliativedrugs.com – Updated website for the *Palliative Care Formulary.*

HELPING THE PATIENT WITH SYMPTOMS OTHER THAN PAIN

7 Oedema

Claud Regnard
Andrew Hughes

INTERMEDIATE LEVEL

Aim of this worksheet

To review the causes of oedema, and identify features that should prompt concern.

How to use this worksheet

- You can work through this worksheet by yourself, or with a tutor.

- Read the case study below, then work on the questions overleaf.

- The work page is on the right side, the information page is on the left.

- Work any way you want: you can try answering from your own knowledge (in which case, fold over the information page), you can use the information page (this is not cheating – you learn as you find the information) or you can use other sources of information.

- It should take you about 15 minutes. If anything is unclear, discuss it with a colleague.

- If you think any information is wrong or out of date, let us know.

- Use the activity on the back page and take this learning into your workplace.

Case study

John is a 54-year-old man who had surgery for a carcinoma of the colon. Despite liver metastases he has been managing well. He has been troubled with some ankle swelling for the past two months. One week ago he woke up in the morning with a swollen left leg. Any discomfort has now settled, but the leg is still very swollen.

INFORMATION PAGE

What is oedema?

Fluid normally leaks from blood capillaries into the tissues. Some returns to the capillaries, while the rest is removed by a drainage system called the lymphatics.

The build-up of excess fluid in the tissues that causes oedema can have many causes:

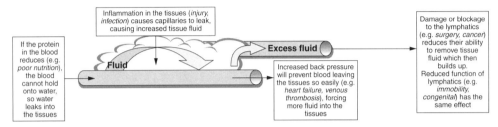

Why bother identifying different causes of oedema?

Some causes of oedema need urgent treatment (e.g. venous thrombosis). In 106 referrals to a lymphoedema clinic the causes were:

Lymphoedema only	70%	(of which 2/3 obstructive, 1/3 other)
Mixed causes	19%	(of which 1/3 heart failure)
Other causes of oedema	11%	(of which 1/3 venous)

In advanced disease, problems in multiple systems cause multiple symptoms.

Signs and symptoms of oedema

In causes below **bold** indicates 'alarm' signs and symptoms.

Many causes of oedema just cause swelling in the affected area without clear clues as to the problem. However, some causes have patterns of signs and symptoms that are typical.

Causes that need urgent investigation or treatment

- *Vena caval obstruction* (blockage of main veins draining upper or lower body):
  - Acute type: **sudden onset** (hours to days)/bilateral limb oedema/pits easily/midline oedema of head or genitals/**dusky, purplish hue** to skin/headache if superior vena cava obstructed (SVCO).
  - Chronic type: prominent, **distended veins over trunk**/± mild oedema/distended veins on elevation.
- *Venous thrombosis* (blood clot in vein): **sudden onset** (hours to days)/localised, tense oedema/local pain/**dusky, purplish hue** to skin/distended veins on elevation.
- *Heart failure:* **very soft oedema/breathlessness** on exercise ± on lying down/tiredness.
- *Local malignancy:* dusky, purplish hue to skin with demarcated, often raised edge/satellite lesions/advances within time (occasionally days to weeks)/local **ulceration** may occur.
- *Infection:* warmer than other limb/**pink skin** (pinker than surrounding skin)/**pain**/pyrexia ± systemic illness.

Other causes

- *Venous incompetence:* usually in legs/may be a **dusky, purplish hue** to the skin/warmer than surrounding skin/± distended veins/skin ulceration if long-term/distended veins/veins collapse on elevation/with tourniquet applied, on standing: if veins stay empty = superficial incompetence; if veins fill = deep incompetence.
- *Lipoedema:* large, soft skin folds in proximal limb/dimpled appearance to skin/stops at ankles in 'pantaloon effect/avoids feet and ankles.
- *Dependency oedema:* invariably lower legs/usually soft/skin is initially healthy.

Alarm signs and symptoms

These suggest that further investigation and treatment is needed urgently:
- midline oedema (head or genitals)
- rapid onset (hours – days)
- dusky or purplish hue
- ulceration
- breathlessness
- distended veins.

What about John's swelling?

The rapid appearance of John's swelling overnight suggests a blood clot. This needs urgent investigation and treatment.

WORK PAGE

 Oedema is caused by a build up of fluid in the tissues. Write down some causes of the following types of oedema.

Types of oedema	Examples of causes
Reduced protein in the blood (prevents blood holding onto water)	
Inflammation in tissues (causes capillaries to leak)	
Increased pressure in veins (forces more fluid out of capillaries)	
Blocked or damaged lymphatics (reduced ability to remove tissue fluid)	

 Match the causes of swelling on the left with the signs or symptoms on the right. NB: some have several causes or several signs and symptoms. The first one has been done for you.

Cause of oedema	Signs or symptoms
Venous thrombosis (DVT)	Dusky, purplish hue to skin
Infection (cellulitis)	Distended veins over the trunk
Lipoedema (abnormal fat deposition)	Skin ulceration
Heart failure	Sudden onset of oedema (within hours)
Chronic vena caval obstruction	'Pantaloon' effect
Local malignancy	Breathlessness
Venous incompetence	Pink skin
	Midline oedema (i.e. genitals or head)
	Pain
	Very soft oedema

Think Think about what signs and symptoms would prompt you to seek out further advice, investigation or treatment.

. . . .

. . . .

. . . .

. . . .

Think Think about what might have caused John's swelling.

. . . .

. . . .

FURTHER ACTIVITY

Find a patient in your practice with oedema of the legs.

• List the possible cause of oedema in that patient.

FURTHER READING

Journal articles

Anonymous (2000) Arm oedema following breast cancer treatment. *Drug and Therapeutics Bulletin.* **38**(6): 41–3.

Badger CM, Peacock JL and Mortimer PS (2000) A randomized, controlled, parallel-group clinical trial comparing multilayer bandaging followed by hosiery versus hosiery alone in the treatment of patients with lymphedema of the limb. *Cancer.* **88**(12): 2832–7.

Hofman D (1998) Oedema and the management of venous ulcers. *Journal of Wound Care.* **7**(7): 345–8.

Jeffs E (1998) Management of chronic oedema. *Journal of Wound Care.* **7**(Suppl. 9): 1–4.

Leung AK and Robson WL (2000) Oedema in childhood. *Journal of the Royal Society of Health.* **120**(4): 212–19.

Mulvenna P, Gillham L and Regnard CFB (1995) Lymphangiosarcoma – experience in a lymphoedema clinic. *Palliative Medicine.* **9**: 55–9.

Topham EJ and Mortimer PS (2002) Chronic lower limb oedema. *Clinical Medicine.* **2**(1): 28–31.

Young GL and Jewell D (2000) Interventions for varicosities and leg oedema in pregnancy. *Cochrane Database of Systematic Reviews.* **2**: CD001066.

Resource books and website

Calman K, Doyle D and Hanks GWC (eds) (2003) *The Oxford Textbook of Palliative Medicine* (3e). Oxford University Publications, Oxford.

Regnard C and Hockley J (2004) *A Guide to Symptom Relief in Palliative Care* (5e). Radcliffe Medical Press, Oxford.

Regnard C, Badger C and Mortimer P (2003) *Lymphoedema: advice on treatment* (3e). Beaconsfield Publishers, Beaconsfield.

Twycross RG, Todd J and Jenns K (eds) (2000) *Lymphoedema.* Radcliffe Medical Press, Oxford.

Twycross RG and Wilcock A (2001) *Symptom Management in Advanced Cancer* (3e). Radcliffe Medical Press, Oxford.

Twycross RG, Wilcock A and Charlesworth S (2002) *PCF2 – Palliative Care Formulary.* Radcliffe Medical Press, Oxford.

www.palliativedrugs.com – Updated website for the *Palliative Care Formulary.*

HELPING THE PATIENT WITH SYMPTOMS OTHER THAN PAIN

8 Lymphoedema

Claud Regnard
Andrew Hughes

ADVANCED LEVEL

Aim of this worksheet

To review the features of lymphoedema and to consider how to help.

How to use this worksheet

- You can work through this worksheet by yourself, or with a tutor.

- Read the case study below, then work on the questions overleaf.

- The work page is on the right side, the information page is on the left.

- Work any way you want: you can try answering from your own knowledge (in which case, fold over the information page), you can use the information page (this is not cheating – you learn as you find the information) or you can use other sources of information.

- It should take you about 15 minutes. If anything is unclear, discuss it with a colleague.

- If you think any information is wrong or out of date, let us know.

- Use the activity on the back page and take this learning into your workplace.

Case study

John is a 54-year-old man who had surgery for a carcinoma of the colon. Despite liver metastases he has been managing well. Two months ago he had a venous thrombosis which caused some swelling in his left leg. The thrombosis was successfully treated but the leg is still swollen and hard and occasionally becomes red and painful. It is preventing him from going out because walking is difficult due to stiffness and he cannot fit a shoe on the left foot.

INFORMATION PAGE

What is lymphoedema?

It is normal for fluid to leak from the blood capillaries into the tissues. Most of this fluid returns to the capillaries, but the excess is taken away by drainage channels called the lymphatics. The fluid in the lymphatics is called lymph. Lymphoedema is swelling, usually of a leg or arm, caused by the build-up of lymph in the tissues because of lymphatics that are damaged, missing or working inefficiently.

Lymphoedema is part of a range of causes of oedema. *See* CLIP worksheet *Oedema* for a summary of the mechanisms and causes of oedema.

If other causes of oedema are present for long enough, the lymphatics become damaged and lymph builds up in the tissues causing lymphoedema.

Causes of lymphoedema

- *Damaged or blocked lymphatics:* This is the commonest cause. It may be due to any cause of long-term oedema, especially if infection occurs. Other causes are surgery, radiotherapy, cancer and local injury.

- *Absent, insufficient or poorly functioning lymphatics:* If the lymphatics are severely affected the lymphoedema may occur in a baby, but if it is mild there may never be much swelling. This type of lymphoedema is probably inherited.

Identifying lymphoedema

Features in **bold** are specific for lymphoedema.

Physical problems: Weight of limb, loss of function, difficulty fitting garments, joint and muscle strain, recurrent local infection, reduced venous drainage, lymphangiosarcoma (rare)

Symptoms: Swelling, joint stiffness, reduced function. Lymphoedema itself is not painful, but may cause pain because of infection or the weight of a limb

Psychosocial problems: Altered body and sexual image, increased anxiety and depression, reduced adjustment to illness, reduced social contacts. In cancer: fear of recurrence or reminder of the disease

Signs: Cool and pale skin, increased volume, **hardness**, **deep skin folds**, **thickened skin** (hyperkeratosis), inability to pinch up a skin fold over the 2nd toe (**Stemmer's sign**), leakage of lymph through the skin (lymphorrhoea)

Treating lymphoedema

Lymphoedema is a progressive condition that does not resolve by itself, produces physical and psychosocial morbidity and becomes more difficult to treat the longer it is left untreated. Treatment is therefore important.

The key to treatment is a patient-centred, not a therapist-centred approach. There are four treatments (SETS):
- *Support:* This limits the reaccumulation of fluid and provides resistance to muscle contraction. The bandaging or hosiery must be graduated, high pressure, well fitting and comfortable.
- *Exercise and movement:* This stimulates lymphatic drainage and should be part of normal activity, gentle, done whilst wearing support and active (rather than just passive movement).
- *Truncal massage:* This stimulates lymphatic drainage and encourages removal of large molecules such as protein in

the lymph. It needs to be started at a site furthest away from the oedema. Firm, gentle, stroking movements are used on bare, dry skin (no talc or oil). The patient can do this by hand or with an electrical massager. Specialist massage (Manual Lymph Drainage – MLD) is helpful in severe lymphoedema.
- *Skin care:* This prevents infection, and keeps skin supple and healthy. Usually moisturising oil or cream is rubbed into the skin every day. Any infection needs to be treated promptly.

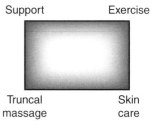

Where to get advice and treatment

For moderate to severe lymphoedema, specialist clinics are now available in most areas in the UK. Many are attached to hospices, but others are based in NHS hospitals. Contact the British Lymphology Society for more information (*see* Further

reading). Local palliative care teams often know the site of local lymphoedema clinics (*see* www.stchristophers.org/hic for the location and contact numbers for all UK palliative care teams).

WORK PAGE

Think   Lymphatics are channels that drain fluid from tissues. Think about ways that lymphatics might not be able to do their job.

. . . .

. . . .

. . . .

. . . .

. . . .

. . . .

Ring the features which separate lymphoedema from other causes of oedema.

Difficulty fitting clothes	Increase in limb volume	Thickened skin
Hard tissues	Anxiety	Infection
Joint stiffness	Deep skin folds	Difficulty pinching up a skin fold

Think   Think about ways you know of using the following treatments for lymphoedema.

Treatment	How could this be done?
Support to the tissues	
Exercise	
Massage	
Skin care	

Think   Do you know where to get advice on lymphoedema?

FURTHER ACTIVITY

Find out where your nearest lymphoedema clinic is based.

FURTHER READING

Journal articles

Badger CM, Peacock JL and Mortimer PS (2000) A randomized, controlled, parallel-group clinical trial comparing multilayer bandaging followed by hosiery versus hosiery alone in the treatment of patients with lymphedema of the limb. *Cancer*. **88**(12): 2832–7.

Bernas MJ, Witte CL and Witte MH (2001) International Society of Lymphology Executive Committee. The diagnosis and treatment of peripheral lymphedema: draft revision of the 1995 Consensus Document of the International Society of Lymphology Executive Committee for discussion at the September 3–7, 2001, XVIII International Congress of Lymphology in Genoa, Italy. *Lymphology*. **34**(2): 84–91.

Board J and Harlow W (2002) Lymphoedema 1: components and function of the lymphatic system. *British Journal of Nursing*. **11**(5): 304–9.

Board J and Harlow W (2002) Lymphoedema 2: classification, signs, symptoms and diagnosis. *British Journal of Nursing*. **11**(6): 389.

Board J and Harlow W (2002) Lymphoedema 3: the available treatments for lymphoedema. *British Journal of Nursing*. **11**(7): 438–50.

Hofman D (1998) Oedema and the management of venous ulcers. *Journal of Wound Care*. **7**(7): 345–8.

Jeffs E (1998) Management of chronic oedema. *Journal of Wound Care*. **7**(Suppl. 9): 1–4.

Leung AK and Robson WL (2000) Oedema in childhood. *Journal of the Royal Society of Health*. **120**(4): 212–19.

MacLaren JA (2001) Lymphoedema. *Professional Nurse*. **17**(2): 93–4.

Mason M (2001) Bandaging and subsequent elastic hosiery is more effective than elastic hosiery alone in reducing lymphoedema. *Australian Journal of Physiotherapy*. **47**(2): 153.

Mortimer PS (1998) The pathophysiology of lymphedema. *Cancer*. **83**(12 Suppl. American): 2798–802.

Mortimer PS (2000) Swollen lower limb 2: lymphoedema. *BMJ*. **320**: 1527–9.

Mulvenna P, Gillham L and Regnard CFB (1995) Lymphangiosarcoma – experience in a lymphoedema clinic. *Palliative Medicine*. **9**: 55–9.

Regnard C, Allport S and Stephenson L (1997) ABC of palliative care. Mouth care, skin care, and lymphoedema. *BMJ*. **315**: 1002–5.

Sitzia J and Harlow W (2002) Lymphoedema 4: research priorities in lymphoedema care. *British Journal of Nursing*. **11**(8): 531–41.

Sitzia J, Woods M, Hine P *et al.* (1998) Characteristics of new referrals to twenty-seven lymphoedema treatment units. *European Journal of Cancer Care (English Language Edition)*. **7**(4): 255–62.

Stanton AW, Levick JR and Mortimer PS (1996) Current puzzles presented by postmastectomy oedema (breast cancer related lymphoedema). *Vascular Medicine*. **1**(3): 213–25.

Topham EJ and Mortimer PS (2002) Chronic lower limb oedema. *Clinical Medicine*. **2**(1): 28–31.

Williams A (1997) Lymphoedema. *Professional Nurse*. **12**(9): 645–8.

Williams A and Venables J (1996) Skin care in patients with uncomplicated lymphoedema. *Journal of Wound Care*. **5**(5): 223–6.

Woo PC, Lum PN, Wong SS *et al.* (2000) Cellulitis complicating lymphoedema. *European Journal of Clinical Microbiology and Infectious Diseases*. **19**(4): 294–7.

Resource books and website

Calman K, Doyle D and Hanks GWC (eds) (2003) *The Oxford Textbook of Palliative Medicine* (3e). Oxford University Publications, Oxford.

Regnard C and Hockley J (2004) *A Guide to Symptom Relief in Palliative Care* (5e). Radcliffe Medical Press, Oxford.

Regnard C, Badger C and Mortimer P (1994) *Lymphoedema: advice for patients*. Beaconsfield Publishers, Beaconsfield.

Twycross RG, Todd J and Jenns K (eds) (2000) *Lymphoedema*. Radcliffe Medical Press, Oxford.

Twycross RG and Wilcock A (2001) *Symptom Management in Advanced Cancer* (3e). Radcliffe Medical Press, Oxford.

Twycross RG, Wilcock A and Charlesworth S (2002) *PCF2 – Palliative Care Formulary*. Radcliffe Medical Press, Oxford.

www.lymphoedema.org/bls – British Lymphology Society.

CURRENT LEARNING IN PALLIATIVE CARE

HELPING THE PATIENT WITH SYMPTOMS OTHER THAN PAIN

9 Confusion

Claud Regnard
Margaret Kindlen

INTERMEDIATE LEVEL

Aim of this worksheet

To review the features and causes of confusional states, and to consider how to help.

How to use this worksheet

- You can work through this worksheet by yourself, or with a tutor.

- Read the case study below, then work on the questions overleaf.

- The work page is on the right side, the information page is on the left.

- Work any way you want: you can try answering from your own knowledge (in which case, fold over the information page), you can use the information page (this is not cheating – you learn as you find the information) or you can use other sources of information.

- It should take you about 15 minutes. If anything is unclear, discuss it with a colleague.

- If you think any information is wrong or out of date, let us know.

- Use the activity on the back page and take this learning into your workplace.

Case study

John is a 54-year-old man who had surgery for a carcinoma of the colon. Two weeks ago his wife noticed he seemed vague on occasions. Over the past week he has become increasingly disorientated. At times he has been agitated and suspicious of anyone visiting.

INFORMATION PAGE

Confusional states

Acute confusional states are the commonest form of confusion in advanced disease. It is present if there are four or more typical features. Six are highly specific: acute onset, fluctuating course, disorganised thinking, inattention, memory impairment, and disorientation. Five are less specific: altered sleep-awake cycle, abnormal psychomotor activity, altered level of consciousness, and perceptual disturbance.

Chronic confusional states are seen in the dementias. They can have similar features to acute states, but the history is longer, the symptoms fluctuate less, and the patient's alertness is unlikely to have changed.

Features of confusion

- *Memory failure:* This is common in confusional states and is usually due to a reversible failure to take in information. In the dementias there is a failure to retain information because of irreversible cortical damage.
- *Alteration in alertness:* In acute confusional states this can be either an increase or decrease in alertness. In chronic confusional states alertness is usually unchanged.
- *Impaired concentration:* This can occur independently of any change in alertness. An extreme form is seen in 'frozen terror' where severe anxiety produces a state of immobility and withdrawal.
- *Abnormal experiences:* Misperceptions and hallucinations need to be differentiated. *Misperceptions* have an external stimulus and occur with reduced alertness or concentration. A patient may think they see someone to one side, only to turn and find no one is there. *Hallucinations* are much less common, have no outside stimulus and persist in being real to the patient. This differentiation is important with morphine since misperceptions will usually disappear as tolerance to drowsiness occurs, whereas hallucinations require a change in dose or opioid. It is probable that misperceptions and hallucinations are at opposite ends of the same spectrum of abnormal experiences.

Clinical decisions and causes of confusion

- *Is memory failure present?* If the history suggests several months of problems with no change in alertness and slow deterioration then this suggests dementia. Otherwise, suspect organic failure of memory, e.g. cerebral tumour (an unusual cause of confusion).
- *Has alertness changed?* Check for: dehydration; drug started recently; chemical withdrawal (drugs, alcohol, tobacco); infection; biochemical cause (hypercalcaemia, uraemia, inappropriate ADH secretion); cardiac disease; respiratory disease (infection, pulmonary embolus, pleural effusion, pulmonary metastases); recent trauma (long bone fracture, subdural haematoma). Infections, drugs and biochemical causes are the commonest causes. Hypercalcaemia should always be suspected in patients with cancer who have unexpected confusion.

- *Is concentration impaired?*
  - *In the presence of anxiety:* Fear, depression, communication problems or social problems may be the cause.
  - *In the absence of anxiety:* Consider distraction as a cause (e.g. pain).
- *Is the patient experiencing unusual sights or sounds?*
  - *If misinterpreting an external stimulus:* Consider the causes of altered alertness above.
  - *If hallucinating (i.e. no external stimulus):* Consider causes such as drugs, chemical withdrawal or psychiatric illness.
- *Has behaviour altered?* Consider causes such as memory failure (*see* above), drugs and psychiatric illness.

Simple approaches

- *Explanation:* Confusional states can be frightening for all involved: the patients fear they are 'losing their mind', while carers feel uneasy at the unpredictability of the patient's words and actions. Confused patients can understand explanations, although if their concentration is impaired this explanation may have to repeated several times.

- *Stable environment:* It helps to keep the environment quiet and light, while keeping staff changes to a minimum.
- *Re-orientation:* Repeated, gentle reminders of place, time and people provide 'hooks on which to hang their reality'.

Urgent control of disturbance

Occasionally the behaviour risks harm to the patient or others. Because escape and paranoia are two common features, it may take a great deal of explanation and a calm, well-lit environment. If medication is unavoidable, it is best to start with drugs with minimal sedation unless the disturbance is severe. In the absence of abnormal behaviour, anxiety and fear are prominent and benzodiazepines will help suppress the anxiety to a level that is manageable for the patient. When abnormal behaviour is present, antipsychotic medication is needed, although a few patients need both.

- *In absence of abnormal experience or behaviour:*
  - *for minimal sedation:* lorazepam 0.5–1 mg PO or sublingually
  - *if sedation is required:* midazolam 2–10 mg SC or sublingually 1-hourly as required (or as a continuous infusion).
- *In the presence of abnormal experience or behaviour:*
  - *for minimal sedation:* haloperidol 2.5–10 mg once at night PO or SC, or risperidone 0.5–2 mg at bedtime
  - *if sedation is required:* olanzepine PO 5–10 mg daily or levomepromazine (methotrimeprazine) 12.5–100 mg 8-hourly PO or SC (or as a SC infusion 25–300 mg per 24 hours).
- *In the presence of aggression:*
  - haloperidol 2.5–10 mg PO or SC at bedtime, or risperidone 0.5–2 mg at bedtime.

WORK PAGE

Ring the features which are typical of these two types of confusional state.

Acute confusional state, e.g. infection	Chronic confusional state, e.g. dementia
acute onset	acute onset
long history	long history
slow deterioration	slow deterioration
poor concentration	poor concentration
memory failure	memory failure
disorientation	disorientation
altered sleep-awake cycle	altered sleep-awake cycle
changes in alertness	changes in alertness
alertness unchanged	alertness unchanged

Think about possible causes of John's confusion.

• Most likely:

. . . .

. . . .

. . . .

• Less likely:

. . . .

. . . .

. . . .

List some simple approaches you could take to help John.

. . . .

. . . .

. . . .

Think – what would make you feel that urgent control of the confusion with drugs was needed?

. . . .

. . . .

. . . .

FURTHER ACTIVITY

Think back to the last confused patient you met:

*   What simple measures were used to help?

FURTHER READING

Journal articles

Brown S and Degner L (2001) Delirium in the terminally-ill cancer patient: aetiology, symptoms and management. *International Journal of Palliative Nursing*. 7(6): 266–72.

Caraceni A, Nanni O, Maltoni M *et al*. (2000) Impact of delirium on the short term prognosis of advanced cancer patients. Italian Multicenter Study Group on Palliative Care. *Cancer*. 89(5): 1145–9.

Foreman MD, Wakefield B, Culp K *et al*. (2001) Delirium in elderly patients: an overview of the state of the science. *Journal of Gerontological Nursing*. 27(4): 12–20.

Hughes A (2001) Recognising the causes of delirium in older people. *Nursing Times*. 97(33): 32–3.

Inouye SK, van Dyck CH, Alesi CA *et al*. (1990) Clarifying confusion: the confusion assessment method – a new method for detection of delerium. *Annals of Internal Medicine*. 113: 941–8.

Katz IR, Jeste DV, Mintzer JE *et al*. (1999) Comparison of risperidone and placebo for psychosis and behavioral disturbances associated with dementia: a randomized, double-blind trial. Risperidone Study Group. *Journal of Clinical Psychiatry*. 60(2): 107–15.

Lawlor PG, Gagnon B, Mancini IL *et al*. (2000) Occurrence, causes, and outcome of delirium in patients with advanced cancer: a prospective study. *Archives of Internal Medicine*. 160(6): 786–94.

Lawlor PG and Bruera ED (2002) Delirium in patients with advanced cancer. *Hematology – Oncology Clinics of North America*. 16(3): 701–14.

Lawlor PG (2002) The panorama of opioid-related cognitive dysfunction in patients with cancer: a critical literature appraisal. *Cancer*. 94(6): 1836–53.

Lonergan E, Luxenberg J and Colford J (2002) Haloperidol for agitation in dementia (Cochrane Review). *The Cochrane Library; Issue 2*. Update Software Ltd, Oxford. (www.cochrane.org)

Morita T, Tsunoda J, Inoue S *et al*. (1999) Survival prediction of terminally ill cancer patients by clinical symptoms: development of a simple indicator. *Japanese Journal of Clinical Oncology*. 29(3): 156–9.

Schuurmans MJ, Duursma SA and Shortridge-Baggett LM (2001) Early recognition of delirium: review of the literature. *Journal of Clinical Nursing*. 10(6): 721–9.

Shury A (2002) Managing delirium in the palliative care of older people. *Nursing Older People*. 14(4): 16–18.

Wakefield B and Johnson JA (2001) Acute confusion in terminally ill hospitalized patients. *Journal of Gerontological Nursing*. 27(4): 49–55.

Resource books and website

Calman K, Doyle D and Hanks GWC (eds) (2003) *The Oxford Textbook of Palliative Medicine* (3e). Oxford University Publications, Oxford.

Regnard C and Hockley J (2004) *A Guide to Symptom Relief in Palliative Care* (5e). Radcliffe Medical Press, Oxford.

Stedeford A (1994) Confusion. In: *Facing Death: patients, families and professionals* (2e). Sobell Publications, Oxford.

Twycross RG and Wilcock A (2001) *Symptom Management in Advanced Cancer* (3e). Radcliffe Medical Press, Oxford.

Twycross RG, Wilcock A and Charlesworth S (2002) *PCF2 – Palliative Care Formulary*. Radcliffe Medical Press, Oxford.

www.palliativedrugs.com – Updated website for the *Palliative Care Formulary*.

HELPING THE PATIENT WITH SYMPTOMS OTHER THAN PAIN

10 Recognising emergencies

Claud Regnard

INTERMEDIATE LEVEL

Aim of this worksheet

To learn to recognise emergencies in patients with advanced disease.

How to use this worksheet

- You can work through this worksheet by yourself, or with a tutor.

- Read the case study below, then work on the questions overleaf.

- The work page is on the right side, the information page is on the left.

- Work any way you want: you can try answering from your own knowledge (in which case, fold over the information page), you can use the information page (this is not cheating – you learn as you find the information) or you can use other sources of information.

- It should take you about 15 minutes. If anything is unclear, discuss it with a colleague.

- If you think any information is wrong or out of date, let us know.

- Use the activity on the back page and take this learning into your workplace.

Case study

John is a 54-year-old man who had surgery for a carcinoma of the colon. Two weeks ago his wife noticed he seemed vague on occasions. Over the past week he has become increasingly disorientated. Overnight he has become drowsy. At times he becomes agitated and seems in pain, but is unable to describe his symptoms.

INFORMATION PAGE

Identifying emergencies in advanced disease

In someone with a progressing, advanced disease it is easy to assume that any deterioration is due to the disease and to assume that this is inevitable and irreversible. However, there are many conditions that can be treated or reversed that will improve the quality of life for such patients. This is important for John, whose confusion will be distressing for him and his family. Although treatment will not always be possible because the patient is too ill or they refuse treatment, it is important to identify the possibilities.

- *Severe pain:* Any severe pain needs treatment. Pain worsened by even the slightest movement may be due to a fracture of a long bone or a vertebral collapse. This will need analgesics and may need surgery or radiotherapy. (*See* CLIP worksheet *Managing severe pain.*)
- *Agitation:* This may be because of fear or be part of a confusional state (*see* CLIP worksheet *Confusion*).
- *Blue fingers:* This shows that the amount of oxygen in the blood is low (although it is possible to be low on oxygen (hypoxic) and still look pink). Causes of hypoxia are reduced ventilation (respiratory depression due to drugs), reduced lung capacity (infection, pleural effusion, cancer, COPD), reduced blood circulation (pulmonary embolus) or reduced gas transfer in the lungs (pulmonary oedema, lymphangitis, fibrosis).
- *Fatigue:* This is common in advanced disease and, although it needs to managed and treated if possible, it is not an emergency. *See* CLIP worksheet *Fatigue, lethargy, drowsiness and weakness.*
- *Sudden drowsiness:* This is unusual in advanced disease and suggests an urgent problem. It is unusual for someone to be up and about one day and then become bed-bound and sleepy within a few days. Possible causes are hypoxia, hypercalcaemia, steroid withdrawal, glucose abnormality (high or low), seizure, drug adverse effect, CVA, raised intracranial pressure and severe infection.
- *Swollen face:* This can be due to blockage of the main vein

draining the head, the superior vena cava (SVC) by tumour in the chest. It needs urgent treatment with steroids and radiotherapy (chemotherapy is used for SVC obstruction in patients with sensitive malignancies such as small cell lung cancer).
- *Confusion:* This is distressing for all. The commonest causes are drugs, infection and blood chemistry abnormalities (*see* CLIP worksheet *Confusion*).
- *Weak legs:* In the presence of fatigue it is tempting to put this complaint down to the general effects of the disease. In cancer, however, vertebral collapse can compress the spinal cord. If this is not treated urgently then paralysis of the legs is the result.
- *Chest pain:* This may be due to a myocardial infarction, pulmonary embolus or chest infection. All need treatment.
- *Sudden breathlessness:* This is distressing for the patient and needs urgent assessment. *See* the causes of hypoxia above and the CLIP worksheet *Breathlessness*.
- *Rasping breathing:* This is unusual in advanced disease but can be due to narrowing of the airway (usually by tumour) when it is called 'stridor'. It needs emergency treatment to stop the airway closing off altogether.
- *'Coffee-ground' vomit:* This indicates altered blood due to an ulcer or inflamed stomach lining. This may be due to the physical and psychological stress of the illness or to drugs such as non-steroidal anti-inflammatory drugs. It needs urgent treatment to prevent severe bleeding.
- *Blood in sputum:* This is common in lung cancer and is usually just streaks in the sputum. More troublesome bleeding needs drugs that reduce bleeding (e.g. tranexamic acid), radiotherapy or embolisation.
- *Swollen legs:* This is common and not usually an emergency, but sudden swelling suggests a blood clot (DVT – deep venous thrombosis) or blockage of the inferior vena cava (IVC) and this needs urgent assessment.

Decisions in unexpected deterioration

1 *Are drugs the cause?* Reduce the **drug** dose and, if necessary, partially reverse their effects (e.g. naloxone for opioid toxicity). NB: In palliative care, reversal should be titrated so the benefit of the original drugs is not lost.
2 *Is comfort only possible?* e.g. **very short prognosis** (hour by hour deterioration), **patient refusing** treatment, **irreversible problem**. Company and warmth are the most important – if sedation is needed ask advice.
3 *If treatment is clearly appropriate:* Arrange tests and treat cause.
4 *If the need for treatment is uncertain:* **Consult with the patient** if they are able to understand and discuss what is going on. Otherwise **talk to partner or family** as they may indicate what the patient has said previously. **Consult with the care**

team taking into account the history, rate of deterioration and **availability of treatment**. Judgement of the patient's previous quality of life by others is **not** helpful – there is good evidence of its subjectivity and inaccuracy.
5 *If need for treatment is still unclear:* Use the rule of 3 – if deteriorating hourly **wait** 3 hours, if deteriorating daily wait 3 days. If further deterioration has occurred then treat for comfort, otherwise consider treating.

NB: Assessment of **quality of life** by professionals should *not* be used in deciding treatment – there is good evidence to show that professionals are very inaccurate in such assessments. Only patients can estimate their own quality of life. (*See* Mencap website www.mencap.org.uk/html/campaigns/health_pubs.htm)

Where to get help

Decisions about emergencies can be clear cut, but in patients with advanced disease there are many occasions when uncertainty exists on: whether the deterioration is treatable, if it should be treated, how it should be treated. Advice can be

sought from specialist teams for the disease concerned, pain teams and palliative care (PC) teams. *See* www.st.christophers.org/hic for information on local PC teams. Some provide 24-hour advice on difficult problems.

WORK PAGE

 Ring those features which you think might indicate an emergency.

Severe pain	Agitation
Blue fingers	Fatigue
Sudden drowsiness	Swollen face
Confusion	Weak legs
Chest pain	Sudden breathlessness
Rasping breathing	Blood in sputum
'Coffee-ground' vomit	Sudden swollen legs

 Ring whichever of the following you think would be helpful in deciding if treatment should be considered.

Current treatment as a cause (e.g. drugs)	Rate of deterioration
Patient's opinion	Whether cause is treatable
Partner's opinion	Patient's previous views
Availability of treatment	Teams' view of patient's quality of life
Wait and see what happens	

Where can you get advice?

. . . .

. . . .

. . . .

. . . .

. . . .

FURTHER ACTIVITY

Think back to the last emergency you were part of and consider which factors made decisions on treatment harder and which made them easier.

FURTHER READING

Journal articles

Aurora R, Milite F and Vander Els NJ (2000) Respiratory emergencies. *Seminars in Oncology*. **27**(3): 256–69.

Brigden ML (2001) Hematologic and oncologic emergencies. Doing the most good in the least time. *Postgraduate Medicine*. **109**(3): 143–6.

Flombaum CD (2000) Metabolic emergencies in the cancer patient. *Seminars in Oncology*. **27**(3): 322–34.

Keefe DL (2000) Cardiovascular emergencies in the cancer patient. *Seminars in Oncology*. **27**(3): 244–55.

Manglani HH, Marco RA, Picciolo A *et al.* (2000) Orthopedic emergencies in cancer patients. *Seminars in Oncology*. **27**(3): 299–310.

Quinn JA and DeAngelis LM (2000) Neurologic emergencies in the cancer patient. *Seminars in Oncology*. **27**(3): 311–21.

Russo P (2000) Urologic emergencies in the cancer patient. *Seminars in Oncology*. **27**(3): 284–98.

Schnoll-Sussman F and Kurtz RC (2000) Gastrointestinal emergencies in the critically ill cancer patient. *Seminars in Oncology*. **27**(3): 270–83.

Tan SJ (2002) Recognition and treatment of oncologic emergencies. *Journal of Infusion Nursing*. **25**(3): 182–8.

Resource books and websites

Calman K, Doyle D and Hanks GWC (eds) (2003) *The Oxford Textbook of Palliative Medicine* (3e). Oxford University Publications, Oxford.

Regnard C and Hockley J (2004) *A Guide to Symptom Relief in Palliative Care* (5e). Radcliffe Medical Press, Oxford.

Twycross RG and Wilcock A (2001) *Symptom Management in Advanced Cancer* (3e). Radcliffe Medical Press, Oxford.

Twycross RG, Wilcock A and Charlesworth S (2002) *PCF2 – Palliative Care Formulary*. Radcliffe Medical Press, Oxford.

www.mencap.org.uk – Information on caring for people with mental health and learning difficulties.

www.palliativedrugs.com – Updated website for the *Palliative Care Formulary*.

See www.st.christophers.org/hic for information on local PC teams. Some provide 24-hour advice on difficult problems.

HELPING THE PATIENT WITH SYMPTOMS OTHER THAN PAIN

11 Issues around resuscitation

Claud Regnard
Bryan Vernon
Paul McNamara
Gail Nicholson

INTERMEDIATE LEVEL

Aim of this worksheet

To review the issues around resuscitation and consider when not to attempt resuscitation.

How to use this worksheet

- You can work through this worksheet by yourself, or with a tutor.

- Read the case study below, then work on the questions overleaf.

- The work page is on the right side, the information page is on the left.

- Work any way you want: you can try answering from your own knowledge (in which case, fold over the information page), you can use the information page (this is not cheating – you learn as you find the information) or you can use other sources of information.

- It should take you about 15 minutes. If anything is unclear, discuss it with a colleague.

- If you think any information is wrong or out of date, let us know.

- Use the activity on the back page and take this learning into your workplace.

Case study

John is a 54-year-old man who had surgery for a carcinoma of the colon. He has been deteriorating steadily and is now reaching the end stages of his disease. He has become increasingly disorientated, chesty and sleepy over the past week. The clinical team agree that he is within days of death as a result of his cancer. The doctor on the team feels that John is not for resuscitation and is adamant that John's wife must be asked for permission not to resuscitate. On this basis the doctor has stopped John's antibiotics that were started for his chest.

INFORMATION PAGE

What is resuscitation?

Over the past few years publicised cases of treatment withdrawal have demonstrated that different clinicians define resuscitation in different ways. In the context of palliative care (the care of people with progressive life-threatening illness), resuscitation is clearer:

- *These are resuscitation measures:* Cardiac massage, artificial respiration. These cardiopulmonary resuscitation (CPR) measures will be instituted by local staff, but would precipitate calling emergency services and admission to an acute hospital.
- *These are comfort and palliative treatment measures:* Analgesia, antibiotics, drugs for symptom control, feeding (any route), hydration (any route), oxygen, hospital admission for investigation and treatment of a reversible condition, seizure control, suction, treatment for choking. These measures would involve discussion and consideration as to their need.

When guidelines do not exist or are unclear, it is common for clinicians and carers to confuse the two types of measures. In palliative care there is little confusion between these two types of measures:

- CPR is instituted immediately and in full following an *unexpected* collapse, and if there is a reasonable chance of success.
- Comfort and treatment measures are instituted after assessment, consultation with patient and family, and on the basis of clinical need.

Who decides about resuscitation?

Ideally this results from a consensus between the patient and the clinical team. With the patient's permission, this consensus should include the partner and relatives. Occasionally the patient does not want the partner or relatives to be involved in discussions about resuscitation, in which case the patient's wishes should be respected.

When a patient like John is unable to take part in the decision, the clinical team must act in John's best interests. The partner or relatives must be asked if they are aware of John's previous views on resuscitation, and they must be kept informed of decisions, but they have no legal right to decide on John's behalf.

In the terminal stage of progressive conditions such as cancer or motor neurone disease, death is an *expected*, inevitable result of the underlying disease. In this situation, the clinical team can be 'as certain as it can be' that resuscitation would fail. Here there is no treatment decision to be made. Discussing a treatment that cannot be offered (because it would fail) causes unnecessary distress and burden on the patient, partner or relative. However, there is a need to be as open about the facts as the patient, partner and family feel able to cope with at the time (*see* CLIP worksheet *Breaking difficult news*).

MCQ answers: (1) T; (2) F; (3) F; (4) T; (5) F.

What is DNAR and how do you make decisions about DNAR?

This stands for 'Do Not Attempt Resuscitation'. It replaces terms such as 'Not for CPR', 'Not for Resuscitation' or 'Not for 350, 999' etc.

Decisions and actions

- *Decide on the competency of the patient:* Competent patients are able to understand their situation and the consequences of their decisions, are free from depression (a clinical diagnosis which is usually treatable), and are not under the influence of others (e.g. pressure from a dominant person on a passive patient). If a person is not competent for this decision, the clinical team must make a decision based on information of the patient's previous wishes. The partner or relatives can be very helpful in providing such information.
- Consider which of the following three situations apply:
  1 *The circumstances of the future arrest cannot be anticipated:* In this situation no decision can be made that would help the clinical team. If the patient arrests unexpectedly, carry out CPR if there is a reasonable possibility of success.
  2 *The person is dying naturally of their disease:* CPR would not help the patient, so there is no need to burden the patient or family with any decision, although they must be given as much information as they want at the time. The aim is to 'Allow Natural Death' (AND) while providing comfort and dignity with effective palliative care.
  3 *The circumstances of an arrest can be anticipated (e.g. following previous life-threatening events):* In this situation discuss with the patient what they would want in the future.
- In all cases, *keep the patient, partner and family informed* of the situation with information given at their pace.
- *There cannot be a 'default' position regarding DNAR:* An unexpected arrest must be assessed by the clinical team at the time.
- *Document decision in notes:* Keep a DNAR order in front of the notes. Send a copy of the form to key clinical staff. Regularly review the need for resuscitation (while this does not mean burdening the patient and family with a DNAR decision every day, it does require staff to be sensitive in picking up any change of views during discussions with the patient, partner or family). Any change in decision needs a new DNAR form.

When consensus is difficult to achieve

On occasions the decision is not unanimous and has to be made by a majority view. When one or two members of the team hold a minority view, the rest of the team should respect their view and be prepared to review the situation after a time period agreed by the whole team. Staff or family with continuing concerns should approach the senior nurse and doctor for discussion. Staff who still have concerns should approach their line manager. Staff and family who still feel dissatisfied should contact the Chief Executive of their organisation who has responsibility for clinical governance. The chair of the local ethics committee can offer advice on further action.

The Courts may to be approached for the final say. This is usually a last resort, although courts can be helpful in deciding complex cases.

WORK PAGE

Think   Think briefly about the doctor's wish to ask John's wife for permission not to resuscitate and the doctor's decision to stop antibiotics. Do you agree, disagree or are you unsure?

. . . .

. . . .

 (Ring) those words below you think are covered by the term 'resuscitation'.

antibiotics	hydration	heart massage
feeding	controlling a fit	oxygen for breathlessness
artificial respiration	analgesics	suction

MCQ

1	Relatives have no legal right to decide on John's behalf	True	False
2	Where death is expected, the patient and relative must be asked for permission not to resuscitate	True	False
3	If a decision is made not to resuscitate, then anything which might prolong life must also be stopped (e.g. antibiotics)	True	False
4	Decisions about resuscitation can change	True	False
5	Decisions about resuscitation must be unanimous	True	False

Think   Think about what could be done in these situations.

Situation	Possible solution(s)
John's wife makes it clear she does want resuscitation	
John improves and is becomes mentally clear	
The rest of the clinical team feel the antibiotics should continue	
John suddenly chokes on some food and stops breathing	

 Think   What do you think about John's situation now?

FURTHER ACTIVITY

Find out what your resuscitation policy says in your clinical setting.

* Does it address the issues of people with advanced disease?

FURTHER READING

Key documentation

Decisions relating to cardiopulmonary resuscitation: a joint statement from the British Medical Association, the Resuscitation Council (UK) and the Royal College of Nursing (2001) *Journal of Medical Ethics*. **27**: 310–16.

Decisions Relating to Cardiopulmonary Resuscitation: a joint statement from the British Medical Association, the Resuscitation Council (UK) and the Royal College of Nursing. BMA, March 2001, London. (Available in full in the guidelines section on www.bma.org.uk.)

British Medical Association (2000) *The Impact of the Human Rights Act 1998 on Medical Decision Making*. BMA, London.

British Medical Association (2001) *Withholding or Withdrawing Life-prolonging Medical Treatment* (2e). BMA Books, London. (Second edition available in full on www.bmjpg.com/withwith/ww.htm.)

Mencap (2001) Considerations of 'quality of life' in cases of medical decision making for individuals with severe learning disabilities. Mencap, London. (Summary available on www.mencap.org.uk/html/campaigns/health_pubs.htm.)

Randall F (2002) Recent guidance on resuscitation: patients' choices and doctors' duties. *Palliative Medicine*. **15**: 449–50.

Other sources

Ethical Decision-making in Palliative Care: cardiopulmonary resuscitation (CPR) for people who are terminally ill. (1997) Joint working party between the National Council for Specialist Palliative Care Services and the Ethics Committee of the Association for Palliative Medicine of Great Britain and Ireland.

Dautzenberg PLJ, Broekman TC, Hooyer C *et al.* (1993) Review: patient-related predictors of cardiopulmonary resuscitation of hospitalised patients. *Age and Ageing*. **22**: 464–75.

Ebell MH (1994) Pre-arrest predictors of survival following in-hospital cardiopulmonary resuscitation: comparison of two predictive instruments. *Resuscitation*. **28**: 21–5.

Elwell L (2000) The no-CPR decision: the ideal and the reality. *Journal of Palliative Care*. **16**: 53–6.

George AL, Folk BP, Crecelius PL *et al.* (1989) Pre-arrest morbidity and other correlates of survival after in-hospital cardiopulmonary arrest. *American Journal of Medicine*. **87**: 28–34.

Murphy DJ, Burrows D, Santilli S *et al.* (1994) The influence of the probability of survival on patients' preferences regarding cardiopulmonary resuscitation. *New England Journal of Medicine*. **330**: 545–9.

Smith S (2001) The role of the court in ethical decision making. *Clinical Medicine (Journal of the Royal College of Physicians of London)*. **5**: 371–3.

Willard C (2000) Cardiopulmonary resuscitation for palliative care patients: a discussion of ethical issues. *Palliative Medicine*. **14**: 308–12.

Further information resources

www.hospice-spc-council.org.uk/index.htm
  National Council for Hospice and Specialist Palliative Care Services.

www.resus.org.uk – Resuscitation Council.
www.rcpch.ac.uk/rcpch – Royal College of Paediatrics and Child Health.

MOVING THE ILL PATIENT

1 General principles

Lynn Gibson
Laura Lowes
Claud Regnard
Margaret Kindlen
Lisa Bushby

INTRODUCTORY LEVEL

Aim of this worksheet

To consider the general principles in moving ill patients.

How to use this worksheet

- You can work through this worksheet by yourself, or with a tutor.

- Read the case study below, then work on the questions overleaf.

- The work page is on the right side, the information page is on the left.

- Work any way you want: you can try answering from your own knowledge (in which case, fold over the information page), you can use the information page (this is not cheating – you learn as you find the information) or you can use other sources of information.

- It should take you about 15 minutes. If anything is unclear, discuss it with a colleague.

- If you think any information is wrong or out of date, let us know.

- Use the activity on the back page and take this learning into your workplace.

Case study

Margaret is a 57-year-old lady with Down's syndrome who has recently moved into a residential home. Her behaviour is unpredictable, and her cognitive skills and mobility have deteriorated. This has resulted in Margaret becoming physically slower and stiffer in moving, compounded by her weight problem (she weighs 60 kg and is 1.4 m high).

INFORMATION PAGE

Margaret's difficulties

Old age does not always cause these difficulties by itself but any of the following could cause her problems:

- *Joint problems:* **Osteoarthritis** or rheumatoid disease can cause stiff painful joints with loss of range of movement which can cause problems with function.
- *Neurological problems:* Motor neurone disease, Parkinson's disease or multiple sclerosis can all cause severe difficulties with movement, including muscle spasms. **Alzheimer's dementia** is associated with Down's syndrome and can present with a change of muscle tone plus there is a delay in stimulus of muscles from the brain causing mobility and swallowing problems.
- *Psychological:* Laziness is not a cause of reduced mobility, but lack of stimulation and encouragement will reduce

mobility. **Depression** affects the person's willingness to move, so mobility reduces.

- *Drugs:* The side effects of some drugs can slow movement or cause abnormal movements. Other **drugs** may cause drowsiness or sedation which will reduce movement.
- *Physical illness:* General fatigue and lethargy due to many illnesses can impede mobility, e.g. causes of **anaemia**. Nerve damage due to tumours can cause muscle weakness and wasting of muscle groups.
- *Trauma:* Has Margaret fallen? Undiagnosed injury such as a **hip fracture** would cause mobility problems.
- *Obesity:* Is Margaret clinically overweight? This **obesity** would effect her mobility.

Associated problems

Margaret weight is 60 kg, but she is very short (1.4 m) and she has a high Body Mass Index (BMI). This is calculated as weight in kg divided by the square of the height in metres. Margaret's BMI is 37 and therefore she is clinically obese. Her behaviour

is unpredictable in that some days she is able to move around her environment. With verbal and physical prompts she manages most daily living skills, but she is unable to transfer and needs maximum input from staff.

Caring for Margaret

Necessities:

- a moving and handling assessment leading to a care plan
- multidisciplinary team approach and a key-worker
- risk assessment policy on moving and handling with moving and handling training for staff
- appropriate equipment for the environment

- agreed dates to review the care plan in view of Margaret's changing condition
- safety at all times for Margaret and her carers
- staff need to communicate any difficulties they have in moving Margaret.

Problems with poor moving and handling

To Margaret:

- *Trauma:* Mild: bruising, nipping, scratching of Margaret. Major: joint dislocation, fractures, falls or dropping due to lack of awareness and education.
- *Shearing force:* When skin is moved with force over underlying tissues causing soft tissue damage.
- *Friction:* Where skin is roughly moved over a surface.

- *Anxiety*: If Margaret is continually moved and handled badly she will be frightened and possibly unwilling to co-operate with future situations.

To carers:

- back injuries, time off work, early retirement.

What to do and not do

Do:

- Remember the complexity of moving and handling issues in patients with complex needs.
- Follow the moving and handling care plan and reassess at agreed times.
- Use available equipment appropriately, e.g. hoists, adjustable beds, specialist baths, easy rise chairs, sliding sheets, turn tables, wheelchairs and walking aids.
- Encourage the patient's independence whenever possible and when it is safe to do so.
- Remember good posture and back care.
- Carry out your own personal risk assessment: think about

the environment, make sure there is room to manoeuvre and think out the situation before you move.

- Communicate with all carers – this is essential and needs someone to lead the process.

Don't:

- Lift the patient from a chair or bed.
- Use any holds or manoeuvres which are regarded as unsafe (e.g. Drag Lift, Australian Lift, Bear Hug, Lateral Transfer).
- Take any risk with yourself or Margaret.
- Grab out to save her if Margaret falls. Hard as it is you must try to lower her to the ground in a controlled fall.
- Attempt to lift a patient from the floor after a fall; you must use a hoist.

WORK PAGE

Think (Ring) Think about possible causes of Margaret's reduced mobility.

Old age   Osteoarthritis   Alzheimer's dementia

Depression   Laziness   Drugs

Anaemia   Hip fracture   Obesity

Write down the consequences of poor moving and handling.

- To Margaret:

. . . .

. . . .

. . . .

. . . .

- To staff:

. . . .

. . . .

. . . .

. . . .

Write a list of Dos and Don'ts in moving an ill patient.

Do these	Don't do these
. . . .	. . . .
. . . .	. . . .
. . . .	. . . .
. . . .	. . . .
. . . .	. . . .
. . . .	. . . .
. . . .	. . . .

FURTHER ACTIVITY

Consider a patient with moving and handling needs.

• What are the underlying problems and how can they be managed?

FURTHER READING

Ellis BE (1993) Moving and handling patients: An evaluation of current training for physiotherapy students. *Physiotherapy*. **79**(5): 323–6.

National Back Pain Association (1997) *The Guide to the Handling of Patients. Introducing a Safer Handling Policy* (4e). National Back Pain Association, Middlesex.

Smith S, Roberts P and Balmer S (2000) Role overlap and professional boundaries: Future implications for physiotherapy and occupational therapy in the NHS: Forum. *Physiotherapy*. **86**(8): 397–400.

Walker MF, Hawkins K, Gladman JRF *et al.* (2001) Randomised controlled trial of occupational therapy at home: Results at 1 year. *Journal of Neurology, Neurosurgery and Psychiatry*. **70**(2): 267.

MOVING THE ILL PATIENT

2 Equipment, adaptations and improving the environment

Christine Armstrong
Claud Regnard
Margaret Kindlen

INTERMEDIATE LEVEL

Aim of this worksheet

To consider the importance of maintaining patient/client skills while making the environment safer for both the patient/client and staff/carers.

How to use this worksheet

- You can work through this worksheet by yourself, or with a tutor.

- Read the case study below, then work on the questions overleaf.

- The work page is on the right side, the information page is on the left.

- Work any way you want: you can try answering from your own knowledge (in which case, fold over the information page), you can use the information page (this is not cheating – you learn as you find the information) or you can use other sources of information.

- It should take you about 15 minutes. If anything is unclear, discuss it with a colleague.

- If you think any information is wrong or out of date, let us know.

- Use the activity on the back page and take this learning into your workplace.

Case study

Margaret is a 57-year-old lady with Down's syndrome who has been living in a residential home for just over a year. During that year she has shown a considerable decline in her cognitive skills, she has difficulty in recognising people, objects and places within the home. Margaret has lost many self care skills, and has problems feeding herself. Her behaviour can be unpredictable and she has recently become incontinent. Her mobility has reduced to the extent that she is now in a wheelchair, although she is still able to manage a standing transfer with assistance from two people. An assessment has been requested from the occupational therapist.

INFORMATION PAGE

Margaret's difficulties

Physical problems:
- Physical illness could impede mobility and cause some of Margaret's symptoms. Illness can cause general **fatigue** and **lethargy** through problems such as anaemia.
- Alzheimer's disease is associated with Down's syndrome and causes behavioural changes, problems with memory and **cognitive decline**. Other features can include a **change in muscle tone** and a delay in stimulus of muscles from the brain, causing mobility and swallowing problems.
- *Hypothyroidism:* this occurs in 20–30% of people with Down's syndrome, and can result in lethargy, functional decline, dry skin, confusion, constipation, fatigue and depression.
- *Trauma:* A recent fall could cause a clot to form slowly between brain and skull (subdural haematoma) resulting in **confusion** and **memory loss**, and could cause some of Margaret's symptoms. A **fracture** would obviously limit mobility.
- Drugs can cause problems with **drowsiness** and **dizziness**.

Psychological problems:
- *Depression:* this affects self-esteem and can result in **reduced motivation** to move.
- Anxiety can make Margaret **lose her self-confidence** in walking.

Social problems:
- A **lack of support and aids** may make it hard for Margaret to function with some independence.

Improving the situation: an action plan

Following assessment of Margaret's current abilities and possible future needs the residential home agreed to act on the following recommendations:
- *Visual clues:* To reduce the demands made on Margaret. Use clear pictures to help identify which room she is going into, e.g. picture of a bath on the door of the bathroom. Use colour to help differentiate significant rooms; colours from the top end of the spectrum such as red, orange, yellow can aid recognition and help reduce disorientation.
- *Bath aids:* Examples are a support cushion which would prevent her from sliding down the bath, make the bath surface more comfortable and assist with pressure care.
- *Easy chair with integral pressure care cushion:* To provide Margaret an alternative option to her wheelchair.
- *Mealtime advice:* Supply a right angled built-up spoon and start a feeding programme with staff using hand-on-hand techniques so that Margaret's self feeding skills can be maintained as long as possible (*see* CLIP worksheet *Maintaining the environment for eating and drinking*).
- *Multisensory environment:* Give advice on the layout and potential use of sound, tactile objects, lighting effects and fibreoptic lights. This additional resource to be developed by the home, an environment where staff can use sensory experience to engage with Margaret.
- *Ceiling track hoist:* To address Margaret's deteriorating mobility and future needs, make moving and handling safer for Margaret and staff. Track to be installed in Margaret's bedroom and run from her bed into her en-suite facilities, appropriate slings to be issued. En-suite facilities mean that Margaret can be changed on the bed, and be hoisted in and out of the bathroom with her dignity maintained. A mobile hoist (a cheaper option) is unsafe in someone with unpredictable behaviour.
- *Adjustable height profiling bed:* This would allow Margaret to be changed on the bed by rolling, the height adjustable feature allows staff to find their right working height in order to maintain good back care. The profiling feature allows Margaret to adopt a variety of positions and helps prevent sliding down the bed. A standard adjustable height bed (a cheaper option) with frames may help initially, but as Margaret deteriorates she will need the profiling bed.
- *Adjustable height bath:* To replace existing arrangement to allow staff to work at an appropriate height when assisting Margaret; to address present and future needs the bath has a transfer seat which can be used while Margaret can still transfer. The seat can be removed when hoisting is required.

*These are expensive items which will need funding, e.g. through social services.

The role of the occupational therapist in Margaret's care

- To work with other healthcare professionals to maintain Margaret's skills while making the environment safer for Margaret and staff/carers.
- To demonstrate prescribed equipment and or technique/routine to staff/carers.
- Occupational therapists do not always prescribe equipment and may sometimes suggest alternative techniques or environmental changes.

WORK PAGE

List some of the problems that might reduce Margaret's mobility.

....

....

....

....

What advice could you give to Margaret's residential home to improve her situation?

• To help Margaret's memory difficulties:

....

....

....

....

• To help the staff move Margaret:

....

....

....

....

• To reduce any risk of injury to Margaret:

....

....

....

....

• To keep Margaret comfortable and healthy:

....

....

....

....

FURTHER ACTIVITY

Identify a patient with reduced mobility:

• What would be needed for this person to return home?

• How could this be funded?

FURTHER READING

Ellis BE (1993) Moving and handling patients: An evaluation of current training for physiotherapy students. *Physiotherapy.* **79**(5): 323–6.

National Back Pain Association (1997) *The Guide to the Handling of Patients. Introducing a Safer Handling Policy* (4e). National Back Pain Association, Middlesex.

Smith S, Roberts P and Balmer S (2000) Role overlap and professional boundaries: Future implications for physiotherapy and occupational therapy in the NHS: Forum. *Physiotherapy.* **86**(8): 397–400.

Walker MF, Hawkins K, Gladman JRF *et al.* (2001) Randomised controlled trial of occupational therapy at home: Results at 1 year. *Journal of Neurology, Neurosurgery and Psychiatry.* **70**(2): 267.

PSYCHOLOGICAL NEEDS

1 Fostering hope

Claud Regnard
Margaret Kindlen
Janet Jackson
Jackie Chaplin

INTRODUCTORY LEVEL

Aim of this worksheet

To consider ways of fostering hope in advanced disease.

How to use this worksheet

- You can work through this worksheet by yourself, or with a tutor.

- Read the case study below, then work on the questions overleaf.

- The work page is on the right side, the information page is on the left.

- Work any way you want: you can try answering from your own knowledge (in which case, fold over the information page), you can use the information page (this is not cheating – you learn as you find the information) or you can use other sources of information.

- It should take you about 15 minutes. If anything is unclear, discuss it with a colleague.

- If you think any information is wrong or out of date, let us know.

- Use the activity on the back page and take this learning into your workplace.

Case study

John is a 46-year-old man who initially complained of increasing weakness in his legs. As he was always an anxious man, this was at first put down to stress. When the weakness worsens, however, the suspicion turns to motor neurone disease. He is married with two teenage children. He suspects he has a serious illness and comes to see you for reassurance.

INFORMATION PAGE

What is hope?

Hope of realistically achieving something good in the future is at the heart of coping with advanced illness and enabling a good quality of life. Unlike denial or optimism, hope needs people to be realistic, since one can only successfully hope for something that is possible, not something that can never be achieved. It is about being open to possibilities.

It is not about being unrealistic or being in denial, it is different to optimism (which needs some denial and perhaps avoidance of reality), and it is not about finding the meaning of life.

It is a realistic desire for good in the face of uncertainty and it helps a person cope with tragedy and loss.

What John needs to foster hope

- A willingness to confront uncertainties, but at John's pace.
- Professionals willing to offer information at John's pace, not the pace of professionals.
- Support that John can trust, allowing him to feel safe to express his distress.
- A willingness to consider possibilities.

- Professionals who are willing to allow and help John to adapt his hope as his illness progresses.
- The ability of John to imagine his hope by seeing it as a realistic possibility, not just fantasising or wishing that something may happen.

MCQ: (1) F; (2) F; (3) T; (4) F; (5) T.

How does hope show itself?

Hope shows itself in different ways at different stages of illness:
- Early in the disease there is hope of cure.
- As the illness progresses there is hope of control and hope for comfort.
- At the end of life the hope often changes to one of peace and hope of a pain-free death.

Hope shows itself in different ways in different people:
- Some people are practical in their hope, e.g. hoping to avoid pain, tie up loose ends, or going home to die.
- Others are more generalised in their hope, e.g. the hope to be at peace, to take 'each day as it comes', hope that they are valued, and a hope of 'letting go' at the end.

How can I use this information to help?

- As an illness progresses, John needs to be allowed to change the focus of his hope, e.g. from cure to comfort.
  Action: Allowing John to talk freely about his fears and hopes will help.
- Keep a look-out for patients whose pace of change has been abrupt, e.g. being told their illness cannot be cured or treated.
  Action: These people will need extra time to mull over this new information, with a trusting ear to listen.
- John may make it clear he does not want more information at present, e.g. 'I don't want to hear any more bad news'. This shows he is in 'reality overload' and cannot take any more information right now.
  Action: Make sure the team knows of John's wishes. Avoid misinterpreting his 'reality overload' as a lack of knowledge – this can push professionals into loading even

more information onto John when he is already struggling with the knowledge he has already!
- Hope is soon damaged by persistent physical symptoms, e.g. pain, nausea, vomiting.
  Action: Make sure the team knows about the problem and deals promptly with the symptom.
- Hope is very difficult to keep going in the presence of persistent psychological symptoms, e.g. anxiety, anger or a clinical depression.
  Action: Let the team know if John seems anxious, angry, frightened or withdrawn so these symptoms can be eased.
- Hope is difficult to foster if a person's life has been one of neglect, rejection or abuse.
  Action: These people will need time to talk to mull over future possibilities. They may need specialist help.

Key points

- Hope is a realistic desire for something good in the face of uncertainty.
- Hope is not about denial or optimism.
- Hope changes as the illness progresses.
- A trusted, listening ear is the most helpful support, not someone who offers false reassurance.

WORK PAGE

Think What do you think hope means for people with incurable illness?

. . . .

. . . .

. . . .

. . . .

MCQ Consider the following about hope:

1 Hope is about being optimistic	True	False
2 You cannot be realistic and hopeful in the face of death	True	False
3 Hope is greater if information is given at the patient's pace	True	False
4 Wishing is the same as hope	True	False
5 To be hopeful, a person needs support and trust	True	False

Think Think of ways in which patients adapt their hope as the illness advances:

Early in the disease

. . . .

. . . .

. . . .

As the illness advances

. . . .

. . . .

. . . .

How could you help foster John's hope in these situations?

Situation	How you can help
Recently told bad news	
John says he wants no more information	
John is nauseated	

FURTHER ACTIVITY

Think back to the last person you met with an advanced illness.

* Did they show any signs of hope?

FURTHER READING

Journal articles

Benzein E, Norberg A and Saveman BI (2001) The meaning of the lived experience of hope in patients with cancer in palliative home care. *Palliative Medicine*. **15**(2): 117–26.

Chelf JH, Deshler AM and Hillman S (2000) Story-telling. A strategy for living and coping with cancer. *Cancer Nursing*. **23**(1): 1–5.

Clark D (2002) Between hope and acceptance: the medicalisation of dying. *BMJ*. **324**: 905–7.

Cutcliffe JR and Herth K (2002) The concept of hope in nursing 1: its origins, background and nature. *British Journal of Nursing*. **11**(12): 832–40.

Herth K (2000) Enhancing hope in people with a first recurrence of cancer. *Journal of Advanced Nursing*. **32**(6): 1431–41.

Kennett CE (2000) Participation in a creative arts project can foster hope in a hospice day centre. *Palliative Medicine*. **14**(5): 419–25.

Moadel A, Morgan C, Fatone A *et al.* (1999) Seeking meaning and hope: self-reported spiritual and existential needs among an ethnically-diverse cancer patient population. *Psycho-Oncology*. **8**(5): 378–85.

Penson J (2000) A hope is not a promise: fostering hope within palliative care. *International Journal of Palliative Nursing*. **6**(2): 94–8.

Rustoen T and Wiklund I (2000) Hope in newly diagnosed patients with cancer. *Cancer Nursing*. **23**(3): 214–19.

Warr T (1999) The physician's role in maintaining hope and spirituality. *Bioethics Forum*. **15**(1): 31–7.

Resource books

Calman K, Doyle D and Hanks GWC (eds) (2003) *The Oxford Textbook of Palliative Medicine* (3e). Oxford University Publications, Oxford.

Faulkner A (1994) *Talking to Cancer Patients and Their Relatives*. Oxford University Press, Oxford.

Faulkner A (1998) *Effective Interaction with Patients* (2e). Churchill Livingstone, New York.

Regnard C and Hockley J (2004) *A Guide to Symptom Relief in Palliative Care* (5e). Radcliffe Medical Press, Oxford.

Twycross R (2003) *Introducing Palliative Care* (4e). Radcliffe Medical Press, Oxford.

PSYCHOLOGICAL NEEDS

2 Helping the person to share their problems

Claud Regnard

INTRODUCTORY LEVEL

Aim of this worksheet

To explore the issues of the person in an initial interview.

How to use this worksheet

- You can work through this worksheet by yourself, or with a tutor.

- Read the case study below, then work on the questions overleaf.

- The work page is on the right side, the information page is on the left.

- Work any way you want: you can try answering from your own knowledge (in which case, fold over the information page), you can use the information page (this is not cheating – you learn as you find the information) or you can use other sources of information.

- It should take you about 15 minutes. If anything is unclear, discuss it with a colleague.

- If you think any information is wrong or out of date, let us know.

- Use the activity on the back page and take this learning into your workplace.

Case study

John is a 46-year-old man who initially complained of increasing weakness in his legs. Always an anxious man, at first this was put down to stress. When the weakness worsens, however, the suspicion turns to motor neurone disease. He is married with two teenage children. He comes to see you for an initial 20-minute appointment.

INFORMATION PAGE

Setting the scene

Seeing John alone will result in more disclosure of John's concerns. This needs to be balanced against the important need to include partners and relatives in the care. It is common practice in palliative care, therefore, to see patients and partners together on the first interview, and then to see individuals on their own at a later stage.

Time available for interview

It is not possible to elicit the problems of a patient involved with advanced disease in less than 30 minutes. Less time than this allows for only a few major issues to be elicited. Nevertheless, it is important to make the time available clear to the person and people disclose their problems more quickly knowing this.

Taking notes

It is essential to make notes of important cues and issues because it shows the person you are taking their problems seriously. It does not hinder disclosure and gives you a record for the future.
Your body language is important while you take notes.

Unhelpful

- sitting on the other side of the desk to the person
- hunched over the notes
- rarely looking at the person

Helpful

- sitting with the desk to one side
- no obstruction between you and the person
- keeping eye contact with the person as much as possible

Distress

Disclosure of emotions is more likely to happen if feelings have been mentioned in the first 10 minutes of an interview. Patients or partners who are distressed would like this acknowledged, together with help to understand why they are feeling this way. Professionals often feel anxious when this distress is openly expressed, fearing that they have 'upset' the person or caused psychological damage. Harm will only occur if the professional insists on talking about a problem that the individual has stated is too difficult to discuss.

Eliciting problems

This is easier if John can describe problems in his own way without interruption. Summarising what he has just said demonstrates you were listening and makes sure the problem list is correct.

- *Dealing with the facts:*
  - *Identify* each problem in turn, making sure both of you are talking about the same problem.
  - *Clarify* the precise nature of the problem, what it is like, and what effects it is having on the person.
  - *Specify* the duration of the problem, whether it is continuous or intermittent, when it started and its severity.

- *Active listening:* This is not just paying interest, but demonstrating that you are listening by:
  - *keeping eye contact*
  - *feeding back* e.g. 'So, tell me more about this pain.'
  - *reflecting* e.g. 'This seems to be making you anxious . . .'
  - *summarising* e.g. 'Let me make sure I've understood, your main problems are . . .'
  - *open body language* i.e. *not* hunched over a desk with little eye contact.
- *Deciding priorities:* This will depend mainly on what is troubling John most. At other times priorities will be influenced by what treatment is possible or available. Don't assume John will put the priorities in the same order as you!

Sharing information

Sharing information is essential to team working and makes the best use of the team's pooled expertise. It also reduces the risk of dependency on the professional, unrealistic expectations and over-dependency. Holding 'secrets' for patients is unhelpful for patients and potentially harmful to professionals. The only exceptions may be clergy in a confessorial role or professionals who regularly receive individualised professional support to fulfil their work such as social workers or trained counsellors.

Concluding the interview

This is as important as starting the interview. If the professional does not finish within the agreed time the person may think they have unlimited time and demand more time which prevents the professional spending time with other patients.

WORK PAGE

Think

- Is it best to see John alone?　　　Yes　　　No

- Is 20 minutes enough?　　　Yes　　　No

  . . . .

- Should you take notes during the interview?　　　Yes　　　No

  . . . .

- How soon in the interview should you ask about John's feelings?　5 mins　20 mins　At the end

  . . . .

John describes a number of problems. Write below how you can show John that you are doing your best for him.

Dealing with the facts

. . . .

. . . .

. . . .

Showing you are listening

. . . .

. . . .

. . . .

Deciding priorities

. . . .

. . . .

. . . .

Think During the interview, John tells you he wants to give you some information about himself that must be kept between the two of you. Think about what you could say.

. . . .

. . . .

. . . .

Q: How do you conclude the interview?

. . . .

. . . .

. . . .

FURTHER ACTIVITY

Think back to the last person who chose to tell you their problems.

*   How did you show them that you were actively listening?

FURTHER READING

Journal articles

Detmar SB, Aaronson NK, Wever LD *et al.* (2000) How are you feeling? Who wants to know? Patients' and oncologists' preferences for discussing health-related quality-of-life issues. *Journal of Clinical Oncology.* **18**: 3295–301.

Fallowfield L and Jenkins V (1999) Effective communication skills are the key to good cancer care. *European Journal of Cancer.* **35**(11): 1592–7.

Hinton J (1998) An assessment of open communication between people with terminal cancer, caring relatives, and others during home care. *Journal of Palliative Care.* **14**(3): 15–23.

Hjorleifsdottir E and Carter DE (2000) Communicating with terminally ill cancer patients and their families. *Nurse Education Today.* **20**(8): 646–53.

Kruijver IP, Kerkstra A, Bensing JM *et al.* (2000) Nurse-patient communication in cancer care. A review of the literature. *Cancer Nursing.* **23**(1): 20–31.

Maguire P (1999) Improving communication with cancer patients. *European Journal of Cancer.* **35**(14): 2058–65.

Maguire P (1999) Improving communication with cancer patients. *European Journal of Cancer.* **35**(10): 1415–22.

Ong LM, Visser MR, van Zuuren FJ *et al.* (1999) Cancer patients' coping styles: doctor-patient communication. *Psycho-Oncology.* **8**(2): 155–66.

Rogers MS and Todd CJ (2000) The 'right kind' of pain: talking about symptoms in outpatient oncology consultations. *Palliative Medicine.* **14**: 299–307.

Sapir R, Catane R, Kaufman B *et al.* (2000) Cancer patients' expectations of and communication with oncologists and oncology nurses: the experience of an integrated oncology and palliative care service. *Supportive Care in Cancer.* **8**(6): 458–63.

Sawyer H (2000) Meeting the information needs of cancer patients. *Professional Nurse.* **15**(4): 244–7.

Stark DP and House A (2000) Anxiety in cancer patients. *British Journal of Cancer.* **83**(10): 1261–7.

Resource books

Faulkner A (1998) *Effective Interaction with Patients* (2e). Churchill Livingstone, New York.

Faulkner A (1994) *Talking to Cancer Patients and Their Relatives.* Oxford University Press, Oxford.

PSYCHOLOGICAL NEEDS

3 Breaking difficult news

Claud Regnard
Margaret Kindlen
Tessa Nichol

INTERMEDIATE LEVEL

Aim of this worksheet

To offer a brief guide to breaking difficult news.

How to use this worksheet

- You can work through this worksheet by yourself, or with a tutor.

- Read the case study below, then work on the questions overleaf.

- The work page is on the right side, the information page is on the left.

- Work any way you want: you can try answering from your own knowledge (in which case, fold over the information page), you can use the information page (this is not cheating – you learn as you find the information) or you can use other sources of information.

- It should take you about 15 minutes. If anything is unclear, discuss it with a colleague.

- If you think any information is wrong or out of date, let us know.

- Use the activity on the back page and take this learning into your workplace.

Case study

John is a 46-year-old man, married with two children. He initially complained of increasing weakness in his legs. Always an anxious man, at first this was put down to stress. When the weakness worsened, however, investigations and examination suggested motor neurone disease, and subsequent progression of the signs and symptoms has confirmed the diagnosis. He has come to hear the results of the investigations.

INFORMATION PAGE

Getting started

When you ask people with considerable experience in breaking difficult news, they will tell you the same thing (if they're being honest), it feels uncomfortable and it can be distressing. Remember that difficult news *is difficult*, you can't make it less difficult!

- Introduce yourself – don't forget normal courtesies.

- Be warm and open – what does your body language convey?
- Let John remain in control of the situation – ask his permission if you can talk to him.
- Be prepared for silence – expect it, encourage it.
- Let John direct – follow behind, not in front.
- Avoid jargon – if some slips out, re-phrase it in John's words.

Three things to check

1 *Can John understand?* Make sure he can hear or that he's capable of understanding (confusion, anxiety and depression can all reduce concentration).
2 *What does John already know?* This is crucial to find out –

never assume, e.g. 'What have you understood about the tests so far?'
3 *Does John want to know more and how much?* This is not as difficult as it sounds: 'Do you want me to explain the results of the tests so far?'

Three possible reactions

Nearly all patients have some advanced warning that something might be wrong, e.g. they've had a biopsy of a suspicious lump. In most cases, therefore, you have the opportunity to ask them what more they want to know.

It is rare that patients have absolutely no idea that any difficult news is on the way. Finding an unsuspected cancer during a routine operation is such an example. In this case it will be important to give a 'warning shot' (*see* below).

John could have one of three reactions:
1 He is clear he wants to know more, i.e. communicates yes or says 'I want to know the results'.
2 He is clear he doesn't want to know, i.e. communicates no,

or says 'No, I don't want to know' or 'Oh, I'll leave all that to you, doctor'.
3 He isn't sure whether he wants to know or not, i.e. he communicates uncertainty or 'It's difficult to know, doctor'.

If John's response is equivocal you can check this with him, 'Do want to leave it for now?' or 'Are you the sort of person who likes to know everything that is happening to them?' If he's still equivocal, then acknowledge this and make it clear you are open to further discussion: 'I can see you're not sure. That's OK, you can ask me sometime in the future if you want'.

Three steps: the warn/pause/check approach (WPC)

Remember that most patients are already worried that something might be seriously wrong.
1 **Warn:** you still need to provide a warning shot: 'I'm afraid the nerve tests were more serious than we thought'.
2 **Pause:** wait for response. The conversation might then continue like this: *Person:* 'What do you mean, more serious'? *You:* 'The tests suggest a condition of the nervous system that will worsen in time, do you want me to explain'? Pause: wait for response. *Person:* 'Yes' *You:* 'This is a condition called motor neurone disease, do you want

me to explain more?' NB: this may take several more warn/pause/checks before John decides he has all the facts he needs. John may choose to do this in stages over several days.
3 **Check** that John has understood the news, and check for his reaction.

It is not the job of the professional to decide what to tell, but to find out what the person wants to know. Like drugs, information needs to be titrated to the individual.

Handling the effects of difficult news

- Check the person's reaction ('How are you feeling?').
- Acknowledge any distress (e.g. 'I can see this is distressing for you'). This may seem superfluous, but it shows the patient that you have noticed the distress.
- Is the person accepting the difficult news? Even if they are, they should be monitored for anger, anxiety, depression.
- Is the person overwhelmingly distressed?
- Is the person denying or holding unrealistic expectations?

If the person is coping well with their present feelings, do not persist in challenging the denial. If they are not coping with their feelings, gently challenge the unrealistic expectations (e.g. 'Is there ever a moment, even for a second, when you think this may be more serious?').

- Is the person ambivalent? Acknowledge the uncertainty and offer the opportunity to talk further.
- Is the relative or partner colluding? (If so, *see* CLIP worksheet *Collusion and denial*.)

WORK PAGE

Think   How do you start? (think of the simple things you need to establish communication).

. . . .

. . . .

. . . .

Before giving any news, write down three things that you need to check with John.

1   . . . .

2   . . . .

3   . . . .

How can you find out whether John wants to know more?

• What three possible responses could he give?

How can you ask?   What three possible responses could there be?

. . . .   1   . . . .

. . . .   2   . . . .

. . . .   3   . . . .

John makes it clear he wants to know what's happening.

Q: What are the next steps?

. . . .

. . . .

. . . .

Q: How might John react to any difficult news?

. . . .

. . . .

. . . .

FURTHER ACTIVITY

Think back to when you were told difficult news, or observed difficult news being given.

* How could it have been done differently?

FURTHER READING

Journal articles

Barnett MM (2002) Effect of breaking bad news on patients' perceptions of doctors. *Journal of the Royal Society of Medicine*. **95**(7): 343–7.

Fallowfield L (1993) Giving sad and bad news. *Lancet*. **341**: 476–8.

Fallowfield LJ, Jenkins VA and Beveridge HA (2002) Truth may hurt but deceit hurts more: communication in palliative care. *Palliative Medicine*. **16**(4): 297–303.

Farrell M, Ryan S and Langrick B (2001) 'Breaking bad news' within a paediatric setting: an evaluation report of a collaborative education workshop to support health professionals. *Journal of Advanced Nursing*. **36**(6): 765–75.

Higgins D (2002) Breaking bad news in cancer care. Part 2: Practical skills. *Professional Nurse*. **17**(11): 670–1.

Pessagno RA (1998) When bad news is delivered. *Clinical Journal of Oncology Nursing*. **2**(4): 146–7.

Radziewicz R and Baile WF (2001) Communication skills: breaking bad news in the clinical setting. *Oncology Nursing Forum*. **28**(6): 951–3.

Resource books

Calman K, Doyle D and Hanks GWC (eds) (2003) *The Oxford Textbook of Palliative Medicine* (3e). Oxford University Publications, Oxford.

Faulkner A (1994) *Talking to Cancer Patients and Their Relatives*. Oxford University Press, Oxford.

Faulkner A (1998) *Effective Interaction with Patients* (2e). Churchill Livingstone, New York.

Regnard C and Hockley J (2004) *A Guide to Symptom Relief in Palliative Care* (5e). Radcliffe Medical Press, Oxford.

Twycross R (2003) *Introducing Palliative Care* (4e). Radcliffe Medical Press, Oxford.

PSYCHOLOGICAL NEEDS

4 Helping the anxious person

Claud Regnard
Margaret Kindlen
Tessa Nichol

INTERMEDIATE LEVEL

Aim of this worksheet

To understand the principles of helping the anxious person.

How to use this worksheet

- You can work through this worksheet by yourself, or with a tutor.

- Read the case study below, then work on the questions overleaf.

- The work page is on the right side, the information page is on the left.

- Work any way you want: you can try answering from your own knowledge (in which case, fold over the information page), you can use the information page (this is not cheating – you learn as you find the information) or you can use other sources of information.

- It should take you about 15 minutes. If anything is unclear, discuss it with a colleague.

- If you think any information is wrong or out of date, let us know.

- Use the activity on the back page and take this learning into your workplace.

Case study

John is a 46-year-old man, married with two children. He initially complained of increasing weakness in his legs. Always an anxious man, at first this was put down to stress. When the weakness worsened, however, investigations and examination by the neurologist suggested motor neurone disease, and subsequent progression of the signs and symptoms has confirmed the diagnosis. He wanted to know the diagnosis and was told. Today he comes to see you and is fidgety and unsettled and seems anxious.

INFORMATION PAGE

Getting started

- *Acknowledge what is happening:* This first step applies to many situations. Simply reflect back what is happening, e.g. 'You seem anxious today, how can I help?' While this may seem unnecessary, it gives John a clear message that you have noticed his anxiety and that you are taking it seriously.

- *Negotiate further discussion:* e.g. 'Can we talk about how you're feeling?'
- *Check that John can understand:* Make sure he's not deaf or distracted by a confusional state.

Mimics of anxiety

1 Some drugs can produce restlessness. This is unrelated to anxiety but can mimic the motor tension aspects of anxiety. Drugs which may cause this are cyclizine, haloperidol, hyoscine, levomepromazine (methotrimeprazine), metoclopramide and the tricyclic antidepressants (e.g. amitriptyline). The differentiating feature is that patients may deny any severe anxiety, although sometimes anxiety is part of the drug effect. A single drug alone is an unusual cause unless higher doses are being used, or the patient is very young or elderly. The risk is much greater when two or more at-risk drugs are used together and this risk can be reduced by avoiding combinations of drugs with this effect.

2 Confusional states can make a patient hyperalert and restless.

3 Pain that is not worsened by movement can make some patients restless, mainly as a distractive behaviour.

The features of anxiety

Life-threatening illness creates an uncertain future that causes anxiety which may increase as the illness progresses. Anxiety in turn makes it more difficult for the patient to cope with suffering. Features of anxiety are:

- *Thinking features* (also called 'apprehensive expectation') e.g. fear, rumination, tendency to perceive situations in a threatening way.
- *Coping features* (also called 'vigilance and scanning') e.g. irritability, poor concentration, difficulty getting to sleep, tendency to perceive bodily sensations in a threatening way.
- *Motor features* e.g. trembling, tension, restlessness.
- *Autonomic features:* hyperactivity of this system causes sweating, dry mouth, cold hands, tachycardia and diarrhoea.

In advanced disease, anxiety is often associated with depression. The Hospital Anxiety and Depression (HAD) scale is a sensitive and specific tool for generalised anxiety which can also help in identifying accompanying depression.

Supportive measures

- *Expression:* Enabling John to express his feelings and giving the information he needs can do much to ease anxiety.
- *Cognitive behavioural therapy (CBT):* Helping John to look for links between thoughts and feelings can generate more realistic interpretations. For example, feeling 'out of control with all that machinery' can be changed into 'It's good to think all that technology is there to help'. Similar approaches have been used with visualisation. CBT can result in rapid relief of anxiety.
- *Anxiety management techniques* can be helpful such as distraction or relaxation. Muscle relaxation techniques are best avoided as it can worsen the anxiety of some people who are excessively vigilant of their bodily sensations, and relaxation using visualisation or music are better alternatives.
- *Complementary therapy:* It helps to have access to massage or aromatherapy. Reflexology has a role if the therapist is willing to pass any interpretations they make to the professional and not to the patient (telling an anxious person the reflexologist 'felt something wrong' will worsen their anxiety).

Identifying and managing difficult problems

- *Anxiety state:* This is defined as a mood different from, or worse than, their usual mood and by a **persistent anxiety for > 50% of the time and for > 2 weeks**, together with four or more features of anxiety.
- *Disorganisation:* This may be mild with very poor concentration and can be eased with supportive measures, perhaps with the short-term use of mild benzodiazepines such as lorazepam. Occasionally the disorganisation is severe (tormented, **unable to care for themselves** or **unable to make a decision**) and this will usually need an antipsychotic (haloperidol or levomepromazine) and referral to a psychiatrist.

- *Somatic symptoms*, i.e. autonomic hyperactivity such as **sweating and tremor**, can be helped with drugs such as propranolol.
- *Panics and phobias:* **Feelings of impending doom** suggest a panic or phobia. Cognitive behavioural therapy seeks out triggers and explores thoughts and can be helpful with panics and phobias. Hypnosis can also help some people. Drugs such as clomipramine can help.
- *Depression* commonly accompanies anxiety and patients may be **feeling hopeless and apathetic**.

Persisting anxiety

1 Consider that depression may also be present – the two often exist together and it is common to miss depression because of the more obvious anxiety symptoms.

2 If features persist or are severe, refer for specialist advice and help.

WORK PAGE

Think   Think about what might cause restlessness *other* than anxiety.

. . . .

. . . .

. . . .

. . . .

Make a list of the features of anxiety in the following categories:

Thinking features   Motor features

. . . .

. . . .

. . . .

. . . .

Coping features   Autonomic features

. . . .

. . . .

. . . .

. . . .

Write a list of supportive measures that might help John.

. . . .

. . . .

. . . .

. . . .

Think   Consider which of these would make you concerned about John's anxiety.

Persistent anxiety for the past two weeks   Occasional forgetfulness

Unable to decide what to eat   Not bothering to shave or wash

Feelings of impending doom   Looking anxious

Sweating and tremor   Feeling hopeless and apathetic

FURTHER ACTIVITY

In a patient who seems restless or anxious:

• Is this new for that patient?

• Is it persisting for more than half the time?

Observe which features of anxiety are present.

FURTHER READING

Journal articles

Barraclough J (1997) ABC of palliative care: Depression, anxiety, and confusion. *BMJ*. **315**: 1365–8.

Bottomley A (1998) Anxiety and the adult cancer patient. *European Journal of Cancer Care (English Language Edition)*. **7**(4): 217–24.

Burns SJ, Harbuz MS, Hucklebridge F *et al.* (2001) A pilot study into the therapeutic effects of music therapy at a cancer help center. *Alternative Therapies in Health and Medicine*. **7**(1): 48–56.

Brittlebank A and Regnard C (1990) Terror or depression? A case report. *Palliative Medicine*. **4**: 317–19.

Carroll BT, Kathol RG, Noyes R Jr *et al.* (1993) Screening for depression and anxiety in cancer patients using the Hospital Anxiety and Depression Scale. *General Hospital Psychiatry*. **15**(2): 69–74.

Nordin K, Berglund G, Glimelius B *et al.* (2001) Predicting anxiety and depression among cancer patients: a clinical model. *European Journal of Cancer*. **37**(3): 376–84.

Payne DK (2000) Management of depression and anxiety in cancer patients. *Oncology (Huntington)*. **15**(4 Suppl. Pt 2): 13.

Rogers P and Gournay K (2001) Phobias: nature, assessment and treatment. *Nursing Standard*. **15**(30): 37–43.

Sheard T and Maguire P (1999) The effect of psychological interventions on anxiety and depression in cancer patients: results of two meta-analyses. *British Journal of Cancer*. **80**(11): 1770–80.

Stark D, Kiely M, Smith A *et al.* (2002) Anxiety disorders in cancer patients: their nature, associations, and relation to quality of life. *Journal of Clinical Oncology*. **20**(14): 3137–48.

Stark DP and House A (2000) Anxiety in cancer patients. *British Journal of Cancer*. **83**(10): 1261–7.

Van Fleet S (2000) Relaxation and imagery for symptom management: improving patient assessment and individualizing treatment. *Oncology Nursing Forum*. **27**(3): 501–10.

Wilkinson S, Aldridge J, Salmon I *et al.* (1999) An evaluation of aromatherapy massage in palliative care. *Palliative Medicine*. **13**(5): 409–17.

Resource books

Calman K, Doyle D and Hanks GWC (eds) (2003) *The Oxford Textbook of Palliative Medicine* (3e). Oxford University Publications, Oxford.

Faulkner A (1994) *Talking to Cancer Patients and Their Relatives*. Oxford University Press, Oxford.

Faulkner A (1998) *Effective Interaction with Patients* (2e). Churchill Livingstone, New York.

Moorey S and Greer S (2002) Cognitive techniques II: applications of cognitive techniques to common problems. In: *Cognitive Behaviour Therapy for People with Cancer*. Oxford University Press, Oxford, pp. 121–6.

Regnard C and Hockley J (2004) *A Guide to Symptom Relief in Palliative Care* (5e). Radcliffe Medical Press, Oxford.

Twycross R (2003) *Introducing Palliative Care* (4e). Radcliffe Medical Press, Oxford.

PSYCHOLOGICAL NEEDS

5 Helping the angry person

Claud Regnard
Margaret Kindlen
Tessa Nichol

INTERMEDIATE LEVEL

Aim of this worksheet

To understand the principles of helping the angry person and to avoid escalation.

How to use this worksheet

- You can work through this worksheet by yourself, or with a tutor.

- Read the case study below, then work on the questions overleaf.

- The work page is on the right side, the information page is on the left.

- Work any way you want: you can try answering from your own knowledge (in which case, fold over the information page), you can use the information page (this is not cheating – you learn as you find the information) or you can use other sources of information.

- It should take you about 15 minutes. If anything is unclear, discuss it with a colleague.

- If you think any information is wrong or out of date, let us know.

- Use the activity on the back page and take this learning into your workplace.

Case study

John is a 46-year-old man, married with two children. He initially complained of increasing weakness in his legs. Always an anxious man, at first this was put down to stress. When the weakness worsened, however, investigations and examination by the neurologist suggested motor neurone disease, and subsequent progression of the signs and symptoms has confirmed the diagnosis. He wanted to know the diagnosis and was told.

Today he comes in to see you for the first time with his brother, Peter, with whom he is very close. Peter soon starts to demand why his brother wasn't diagnosed earlier and, red-faced with anger, starts to blame you for allowing John to get into this state.

INFORMATION PAGE

Getting started

As in many situations, start by acknowledging what is going on.

- *Acknowledge Peter's anger:* e.g. 'I can see this has made you angry. How can I help?' While this may seem unnecessary, it gives the person a clear message that you have noticed their anger and that you are taking it seriously. Offering to help starts to defuse the anger. NB: Peter is expressing active anger, but a few people exhibit passive anger – a sort of controlled anger – and you may have to start by saying, 'I get the feeling that you're angry, can we talk about it?'
- *Be aware of what anger does to you:* It is normal for you to be emotionally affected when confronted by an angry person. Some professionals feel irritated in response, in which case they need to suppress this irritation to avoid escalating the anger. Other professionals become shocked at the anger being directed at them, in which case they need to be more assertive in order to be believed and help the angry person

effectively. If your reactions make it difficult for you to help an angry person (e.g. you become too angry or withdrawn to help effectively) it would be best to ask someone else to see the angry person, and for you to consider getting advice or teaching on your response to an angry person.

- *The setting:* With an angry person it is usually impossible to choose the right setting. If the setting seems particularly awkward (e.g. a busy corridor) then as the discussion progresses it is reasonable to suggest an alternative, more private venue.
- *Defusing the anger:* This should have started when you acknowledged the presence of anger – most people want to know that you are prepared to listen and help. They may want help with getting something done or help with information. Exploring the cause of the anger is part of helping to defuse it since an offer of help is not usually rejected.

The appropriateness of anger

- *Discuss the cause* e.g. 'What's happened to make you feel like this?
- *Clarify the extent of the anger* e.g. 'On a scale of 0 to 10, how angry have you been?'

Most anger is understandable in that (a) its reasons can be

understood; and (b) it is understandable that some people in distressing situations become angry.

So, Peter's anger is understandable, but it is not appropriately directed (you are seeing him for the first time), and seems out of proportion to the situation.

Apologising: when to say sorry and when it is not appropriate

When the anger is directed at you, *and that anger is appropriate* then come clean and apologise! For example: 'I'm sorry you were kept waiting for so long – it would make me angry too.'

When the anger is about the behaviour of another health professional, avoid the temptation to defend that person since

(a) it's not your place to defend others, and (b) trying to defend the other person will fail to defuse the anger and will only result in the accusation that 'You lot all stick together!' You can still show your concern without being defensive, for example, 'I can see why you're angry'. Then suggest that they speak or write to the individual to express their concerns.

Escalating anger: an important warning sign

The steps so far should by now have defused Peter's anger *within a few minutes*. At the very least, it should be no worse. Occasionally, however, the anger escalates. If this happens:
- Position yourself by the nearest exit.
- Acknowledge the escalating anger, e.g. 'I can see this has made you very angry.'
- Set limits, e.g. 'I want to help you, but your anger is

beginning to make me feel uncomfortable. If you don't feel you can control your anger I wouldn't feel comfortable continuing.' Giving them 10 minutes to calm down may allow you to start again from the beginning, e.g. 'How can I help?'
- If the person cannot accept the limits, end the interview and leave immediately to avoid being assaulted.

Persisting anger

There are several reasons for persisting anger:
- this may be a person's normal behaviour
- there may be a clinical depression
- unrealised ambitions, e.g. seeing children grow up

- loss of control because of weakness or immobility
- spiritual anger.

The last four may need additional or specialist help.

WORK PAGE

'For 2 months they couldn't make up their minds what was wrong – now look at the state John's in! I can't believe you call yourselves doctors!!'

Think How does Peter's anger make you feel?

• What can you do to start helping his anger?

. . . .

. . . .

. . . .

Which of these do you think is true about Peter's anger?

The anger is understandable	True	False
The anger is appropriately directed	True	False
The anger is proportional to the situation	True	False

How Would you react? Peter angrily blames the GP for the delay in diagnosis. What can you say?

. . . .

. . . .

. . . .

• Peter accuses you of keeping them waiting an hour (you were running 50 minutes late). What can you say?

. . . .

. . . .

. . . .

• It's clear that Peter's anger is escalating. What can you do?

. . . .

. . . .

. . . .

Think On the next visit, Peter's anger is less, but is still present. Think about what could be causing this.

. . . .

. . . .

. . . .

FURTHER ACTIVITY

Reflect on how you are affected by an angry person:

- Do you tend to react with anger?

- Do you tend to withdraw?

FURTHER READING

Journal articles

Garnham P (2001) Understanding and dealing with anger, aggression and violence. *Nursing Standard.* **16**(6): 37–42.

McCord RS, Floyd MR, Lang F *et al.* (2002) Responding effectively to patient anger directed at the physician. *Family Medicine.* **34**(5): 331–6.

Robbins PR and Tanck RH (1997) Anger and depressed affect: interindividual and intra-individual perspectives. *Journal of Psychology.* **131**(5): 489–500.

Thomas SP, Groer M and Davis M (2000) Anger and cancer: an analysis of the linkages. *Cancer Nursing.* **23**(5): 344–9.

Resource books

Calman K, Doyle D and Hanks GWC (eds) (2003) *The Oxford Textbook of Palliative Medicine* (3e). Oxford University Publications, Oxford.

Faulkner A (1994) *Talking to Cancer Patients and Their Relatives.* Oxford University Press, Oxford.

Faulkner A (1998) *Effective Interaction with Patients* (2e). Churchill Livingstone, New York.

Regnard C and Hockley J (2004) *A Guide to Symptom Relief in Palliative Care* (5e). Radcliffe Medical Press, Oxford.

Twycross R (2003) *Introducing Palliative Care* (4e). Radcliffe Medical Press, Oxford.

PSYCHOLOGICAL NEEDS

6 Answering difficult questions

Claud Regnard

INTERMEDIATE LEVEL

Aim of this worksheet

To understand some ways of answering difficult questions posed by a patient, partner or relative.

How to use this worksheet

• You can work through this worksheet by yourself, or with a tutor.

• Read the case study below, then work on the questions overleaf.

• The work page is on the right side, the information page is on the left.

• Work any way you want: you can try answering from your own knowledge (in which case, fold over the information page), you can use the information page (this is not cheating – you learn as you find the information) or you can use other sources of information.

• It should take you about 15 minutes. If anything is unclear, discuss it with a colleague.

• If you think any information is wrong or out of date, let us know.

• Use the activity on the back page and take this learning into your workplace.

Case study

John is a 46-year-old man, married with two children, who was diagnosed with motor neurone disease. He wanted to know the diagnosis and was told. He has been deteriorating rapidly this past week. During a conversation about arranging home care he suddenly asks, 'Tell me, how long have I got?'

INFORMATION PAGE

Why are some questions difficult?

People take time to adjust to the shock of advanced disease. During this time they will often seek clarification and information from health professionals. While some questions will be straightforward, other questions are more difficult to answer, e.g. 'Why has this happened to me?'

There are several reasons why such questions can seem difficult to answer:

- *Surprise:* Often the question is asked when you least expect it, adding to its difficulty.
- *The patient, partner and relative:* They require information to make rational choices, but this may conflict with the fears of advancing illness and the need to maintain hope in the face of uncertainty. These conflicts often result in difficult questions.
- *For the professional:* There are fears of admitting ignorance, being blamed, producing an emotional reaction or of dealing with a situation for which they have received little or no training.
- *Setting:* Because difficult questions are often spontaneous, the setting may be awkward, such as a busy corridor. It is reasonable to offer a quieter location if the person asking wants this.

Three first steps

1 *Acknowledge* the importance of the question. It usually takes the person much thought, anxiety and courage to ask the question. This needs to be recognised, e.g. 'That's an important question.'

2 *Find out* why the question is being asked. This avoids any misunderstanding. You could ask something like 'I wonder why you're asking me this now?' Checking gives the person an opportunity to make sure how willing they are to hear the answer. Don't assume that John is asking whether he is going to die – check it out!

3 *Are you the right person?* You need to consider if you are the most appropriate person to be answering the question. If the answer is straightforward, clear, and you are comfortable in answering, then provide the answer.

Should the person seem reluctant to hear the answer, check the following:

- You need to be satisfied that the person is not troubled with drowsiness, deafness or confusion.
- Check that the person wasn't put off because you weren't paying full attention! The most likely reason is because the question caught you unprepared. You can remedy this easily by apologising for the inattention and once more acknowledge the importance of the question.
- Finally, the person may suspect that any answer is going to be bad or difficult news. *See* the CLIP worksheet on *Breaking difficult news.*

MCQ answers: (1) A; (2) D; (3) D; (4) A; (5) A.

Is the answer still difficult?

There are good reasons why you may be unable to answer the question: inexperience; you don't have the information the person needs; or if it's an emotionally charged question (e.g. 'Am I dying?').

You cannot disclose the full facts unless the following conditions have been met:

1 The person wants to know the full facts.
2 You have all the information needed.

There are some questions that have no clear answer because full information is not available. An example would be the patient who asks when they are going to die. Again, being honest with the situation is helpful. Start by acknowledging the uncertainty: 'I can see this uncertainty is difficult for you.'

You need to be honest about how you feel: e.g. 'I don't have the experience (or knowledge) to answer that question, but I'll get someone who can' or 'I'm finding that difficult to answer' or even 'I don't know what to say'. People will respect your honesty, which demonstrates that you are taking their question seriously. It will be reassuring for the person to know that you will not abandon them so offer a future contact time: 'I'll be interested to hear how you get on with . . . If you want to talk about it with me later, please do.'

Remember: *The truth may hurt, but deceit hurts more.*

Summary points

- Difficult questions arise out of a person's uncertainty.
- Acknowledging the question is an important first step.
- Answers may be unclear or impossible.
- Being honest about not knowing improves rather than hinders relationships.
- Some answers mean more bad news.

WORK PAGE

Think **Think: how would you feel?**

. . . .
. . . .
. . . .

What makes the question difficult?

• For John:

. . . .
. . . .
. . . .

• For you:

. . . .
. . . .
. . . .

MCQ **What do you think of the following responses?**

1 Ask him why he's asking that question	Agree	Disagree
2 Answer him by saying 'Not very long'	Agree	Disagree
3 Tell him he shouldn't worry about such things	Agree	Disagree
4 Tell him that you don't have a clear answer	Agree	Disagree
5 Tell him you don't know	Agree	Disagree

Think **What can you do if there is no clear answer?**

. . . .
. . . .
. . . .

Write down the conditions that need to be met before disclosing the full facts to a patient.

. . . .
. . . .
. . . .

FURTHER ACTIVITY

Reflect on a time when someone asked you a difficult question:

- How did you feel?

- How did you answer the question?

- With hindsight, would you have answered it differently?

FURTHER READING

Journal articles

Friedrichsen MJ, Strang P and Carlsson ME (2000) Breaking bad news in the transition from curative to palliative cancer care – patient's view of the doctor giving the information. *Supportive Care in Cancer.* **8**(6): 472–8.

Jenkins V, Fallowfield L and Saul J (2001) Information needs of patients with cancer: results from a large study in UK cancer centres. *British Journal of Cancer.* **84**(1): 48–51.

Lamont EB and Christakis NA (2001) Prognostic disclosure to patients with cancer near the end of life. *Annals of Internal Medicine.* **134**(12): 1096–105.

McCague K (2001) Collusion in doctor-patient communication. Doctors should adopt patient's perspective. *BMJ.* **322**: 1063.

Noone I, Crowe M, Pillay I *et al.* (2000) Telling the truth about cancer: views of elderly patients and their relatives. *Irish Medical Journal.* **93**(4): 104–5.

Parker PA, Baile WF, de Moor C *et al.* (2001) Breaking bad news about cancer: patients' preferences for communication. *Journal of Clinical Oncology.* **19**(7): 2049–56.

Rousseau P (2000) Death denial. *Journal of Clinical Oncology.* **18**(23): 3998–9.

Ubel PA (2001) Truth in the most optimistic way. *Annals of Internal Medicine.* **134**(12): 1142–3.

Resource books

Calman K, Doyle D and Hanks GWC (eds) (2003) *The Oxford Textbook of Palliative Medicine* (3e). Oxford University Publications, Oxford.

Faulkner A (1994) *Talking to Cancer Patients and Their Relatives.* Oxford University Press, Oxford.

Faulkner A (1998) *Effective Interaction with Patients* (2e). Churchill Livingstone, New York.

Regnard C and Hockley J (2004) *A Guide to Symptom Relief in Palliative Care* (5e). Radcliffe Medical Press, Oxford.

Twycross R (2003) *Introducing Palliative Care* (4e). Radcliffe Medical Press, Oxford.

PSYCHOLOGICAL NEEDS

7 Helping the withdrawn patient

Claud Regnard
Margaret Kindlen
Tessa Nichol

ADVANCED LEVEL

Aim of this worksheet

To understand the principles of helping the withdrawn patient.

How to use this worksheet

- You can work through this worksheet by yourself, or with a tutor.

- Read the case study below, then work on the questions overleaf.

- The work page is on the right side, the information page is on the left.

- Work any way you want: you can try answering from your own knowledge (in which case, fold over the information page), you can use the information page (this is not cheating – you learn as you find the information) or you can use other sources of information.

- It should take you about 15 minutes. If anything is unclear, discuss it with a colleague.

- If you think any information is wrong or out of date, let us know.

- Use the activity on the back page and take this learning into your workplace.

Case study

John is a 46-year-old man, married with two children. He initially complained of increasing weakness in his legs. Always an anxious man, at first this was put down to stress. When the weakness worsened, however, investigations and examination suggested motor neurone disease, and subsequent progression of the signs and symptoms has confirmed the diagnosis. He wanted to know the diagnosis and was told. He is normally anxious, but ready to chat and animated. Today he seems distant and speaks to you in brief sentences or single words.

INFORMATION PAGE

Getting started

- *Acknowledge what is happening:* This first step applies to many situations. Simply reflect back your observations, e.g. 'You don't seem your usual self today.' While this may seem unnecessary, it gives John a clear message that you have noticed his withdrawal and that you are taking it seriously.

- *Negotiate further discussion:* e.g. 'Is there something I can help you with?'
- *Check that John can understand:* make sure he's not deaf or distracted by a confusional state.

Reasons for withdrawal

Although depression might be the reason, there are many other possible causes:

- Perhaps this is John's usual behaviour (this is unlikely as he was previously animated and willing to chat).
- His speech and facial expressions may be severely affected by his MND, preventing a conversation.
- His pain might be so distracting that it is preventing him from concentrating.
- A confusional state may be making him suspicious or unwilling to talk.

- Drowsiness caused by drugs, infection or a biochemical disturbance may be preventing a conversation.
- Parkinsonism caused by drugs (e.g. haloperidol, metoclopramide) may reduce facial expressions.
- Collusion may be preventing him from talking for fear of upsetting a partner or relative.
- He may be too exhausted to talk.
- He might be too frightened to talk (the 'frozen terror' syndrome).
- Guilt or shame may be present, causing him to withdraw (this may be part of a depression)

Depression

The proportion of patients with advanced disease who have a clinical depression varies between studies and depends partly on the assessment tools used. It has been suggested that 25% or more of cancer and AIDS patients suffer from depression.

The diagnosis of depression is made on the following characteristics:

- A persistent low mood (>2 weeks for >50% of the time).
- The withdrawal is a change to their usual mood.
- There is a loss of enjoyment.
- There are three or more depression-related symptoms present: diurnal variation in mood, repeated or early morning wakening, impaired concentration, loss of interest or enjoyment, feelings of hopelessness, guilt, shame or

feeling a burden to others, thoughts of self-harm, desire for hastened death.

All the features listed above *could* indicate a depression, but some are less useful than others in advanced disease. Loss of energy, appetite and sex drive are more likely to be due to the disease itself and cannot be used as diagnostic indicators. Feeling 'fed up' tells you little!

Suicidal thoughts are a less useful indicator in advanced disease, since some patients will express a realistic wish that they would rather be dead, rather than be in pain, a burden, immobile etc. In contrast, suicidal planning, thoughts of self-harm and a desire for a hastened death are more important.

Helping the withdrawn patient

In John's case, the first step is to establish the cause and treat any straightforward causes:

- Enable communication using a speech communicator.
- Treat any pain or confusional state.
- Reduce drugs that may be causing drowsiness or Parkinsonian adverse effects.
- Explore collusion if this is present (*see* CLIP worksheet on *Collusion and denial*).
- Manage anxiety (*see* CLIP worksheet *Helping the anxious person*) or anger (*see* CLIP worksheet *Helping the angry person*).

- Explore any guilt or shame: this may simply be due to incontinence, but may be a feature of depression.

If a clinical depression is present, start an antidepressant:

- Some use lofepramine 140–280 mg daily as the best balance between effectiveness and side effects, while others use the newer antidepressants such as sertraline or venlafaxine.
- The response can occur within 2 weeks (so don't delay because of a short prognosis).
- The patient is the last to notice any improvement.
- If the depression is persisting or has complicating features (e.g. agitation, paranoia), ask for advice from a psychiatric colleague.

WORK PAGE

Think   How do you start a dialogue with John?

• Think about what you need to check first.

. . . .

. . . .

List some reasons why John might be more withdrawn than usual (you don't have to put depression at the top of the list!).

. . . .

. . . .

. . . .

. . . .

. . . .

. . . .

Q: How common is depression?

10%   25%   50%   80%

Which of the following would strongly support a diagnosis of depression in John?
Ring your choices

Suicidal thoughts (e.g. 'I'd rather be dead')   Reduced sex drive

Inappropriate guilt   A change in mood

Loss of appetite   Diurnal variation (e.g. worse on waking)

Suicidal plans   Persistent, low mood for 1 week

Early morning waking   Loss of enjoyment

Feeling fed up   Feelings of hopelessness

Feeling a burden to others   Lack of energy

Think   How can you start to help John?

. . . .

. . . .

. . . .

FURTHER ACTIVITY

When you next meet a patient who is withdrawn explore:

- Is this a new problem for the patient?

- Is the patient thinking and acting clearly? (i.e. make sure the patient is not confused).

- Is the patient feeling apathetic and hopeless?

If the answer was yes to these questions, then a depression is possible. Ask an experienced colleague to review the patient with you and consider whether you should refer the patient for further assessment.

FURTHER READING

Journal articles

Breitbart W, Rosenfeld B, Pessin H *et al.* (2000) Depression, hopelessness, and desire for hastened death in terminally ill patients with cancer. *JAMA.* **284**(22): 2907–11.

Hotopf M, Chidgey J, Addington-Hall J *et al.* (2002) Depression in advanced disease: a systematic review Part 1. Prevalence and case finding. *Medicine.* **16**(2): 81–97.

Lloyd-Williams M (2001) Screening for depression in palliative care patients: a review. *European Journal of Cancer Care.* **10**(1): 31–5.

Lloyd-Williams M (2001) Screening for depression in palliative care. *American Journal of Hospice and Palliative Care.* **18**(2): 79–80.

Lloyd-Williams M (2002) Is it appropriate to screen palliative care patients for depression? *American Journal of Hospice and Palliative Care.* **19**(2): 112–14.

Lloyd-Williams M (2002) How common are thoughts of self-harm in a UK palliative care population? *Supportive Care in Cancer.* **10**(5): 422–4.

Lloyd-Williams M (2002) The stability of depression scores in patients who are receiving palliative care. *Journal of Pain and Symptom Management.* **24**(6): 593–7.

Lloyd-Williams M and Friedman T (2001) Depression in palliative care patients – a prospective study. *European Journal of Cancer Care.* **10**(4): 270–4.

Lloyd-Williams M, Friedman T and Rudd N (1999) A survey of antidepressant prescribing in the terminally ill. *Palliative Medicine.* **13**(3): 243–8.

Lloyd-Williams M, Friedman T and Rudd N (2000) Criterion validation of the Edinburgh postnatal depression scale as a screening tool for depression in patients with advanced metastatic cancer. *Journal of Pain and Symptom Management.* **20**(4): 259–65.

Lloyd-Williams M, Friedman T and Rudd N (2001) An analysis of the validity of the Hospital Anxiety and Depression scale as a screening tool in patients with advanced metastatic cancer. *Journal of Pain and Symptom Management.* **22**(6): 990–6.

Lloyd-Williams M, Spiller J and Ward J (2003) Which depression screening tools should be used in palliative care? *Palliative Medicine.* **17**(1): 40–3.

Ly KL, Chidgey J, Addington-Hall J *et al.* (2002) Depression in palliative care: a systematic review. Part 2. Treatment. *Palliative Medicine.* **16**(4): 279–84.

Nelson CJ, Rosenfeld B, Breitbart W *et al.* (2002) Spirituality, religion, and depression in the terminally ill. *Psychosomatics.* **43**(3): 213–20.

Peveler R, Carson A and Rodin G (2002) ABC of psychological medicine: Depression in medical patients. *BMJ.* **323**: 149–52.

Ripamonti C, Filiberti A, Totis A *et al.* (1999) Suicide among patients with cancer cared for at home by palliative-care teams. *Lancet.* **354**: 1877–8.

Stiefel R, Die Trill M, Berney A *et al.* (2001) Depression in palliative care: a pragmatic report from the Expert Working Group of the European Association for Palliative Care. *Supportive Care in Cancer.* **9**(7): 477–88.

Resource books

Calman K, Doyle D and Hanks GWC (eds) (2003) *The Oxford Textbook of Palliative Medicine* (3e). Oxford University Publications, Oxford.

Regnard C and Hockley J (2004) *A Guide to Symptom Relief in Palliative Care* (5e). Radcliffe Medical Press, Oxford.

Twycross R (2003) *Introducing Palliative Care* (4e). Radcliffe Medical Press, Oxford.

PSYCHOLOGICAL NEEDS

8 Collusion and denial

Paul McNamara
Claud Regnard

ADVANCED LEVEL

Aim of this worksheet

To develop some insight into collusion and denial by a patient, partner or relative.

How to use this worksheet

- You can work through this worksheet by yourself, or with a tutor.

- Read the case study below, then work on the questions overleaf.

- The work page is on the right side, the information page is on the left.

- Work any way you want: you can try answering from your own knowledge (in which case, fold over the information page), you can use the information page (this is not cheating – you learn as you find the information) or you can use other sources of information.

- It should take you about 15 minutes. If anything is unclear, discuss it with a colleague.

- If you think any information is wrong or out of date, let us know.

- Use the activity on the back page and take this learning into your workplace.

Case study

John is a 46-year-old man, married with two children, who was diagnosed with motor neurone disease. He wanted to know the diagnosis and was told. He has been deteriorating rapidly this past week. Now back at home, you have been asked to visit by his wife Dora and daughter Angela.

When you arrive they explain that John doesn't know you have been called. You decide to see John for yourself, but at the bottom of the stairs, Dora grasps your arm and tells you John doesn't know he is dying and she and Angela have decided he should not be told. Dora thinks it best if you go outside and ring the doorbell, to make it look now as if you have just called in routinely to see John.

INFORMATION PAGE

Getting started

Like much else in healthcare, it is important to keep an open mind. Don't assume that collusion and denial are bad or good – the issue is whether they are helpful or unhelpful to those involved.

Definitions

- *Collusion*: This is something you do to another person, e.g. a wife chooses not to tell her husband that he is seriously ill, or patients choose not to tell their family about their illness. It is 'denial-by proxy'.
- *Denial:* This is something you do to yourself, e.g. a patient refuses to accept the full reality of their illness. It is not the same as a gap in knowledge since you have to deny something! On the contrary, it is due to the individual struggling to cope with the knowledge they do have – it is an overload of reality.

Your reactions

When you first meet someone who is colluding in keeping information from their partner or relative, your reaction may be any of these:
- Surprise at the person's comments.
- Annoyance that someone is intervening between you and your patient.
- Confusion as to what you should say now.
- A desire to join with the person and protect the patient.
- A determination that the patient should have the opportunity to decide for themselves.
- A wish to enable the patient and person to work this out together.

The first step

1 F: Agreeing to their deception is collusion. It is not a promise you can keep without first talking to John.
2 F: This is going too far the other way – they may be right, after all!
3 F: Now you are getting cross about the collusion *and* colluding at the same time!
4 T: You need to start a dialogue with Dora and Angela to explore their feelings.
5 T: Denial is a good coping mechanism, as long as it is working for the individual.

The pros and cons of collusion and denial

The good things:

Collusion

Usually an act of love

Provides a sense of protecting the patient

Both person and patient may agree to collude!

Superficially easier for carers

Offers mutual protection

Denial

Allows information to be managed in stages

Does not prevent consent for treatment

Is a good coping mechanism

The downside:

Collusion

Occasionally it reflects control over the patient

May isolate and patronise the patient

May strain relationships because of 'secrets'

May increase anxiety or depress mood

Can create a 'conspiracy of silence' and distrust

Denial

Can prompt carers to push information

Can prompt carers to insist on sharing information

Can delay the sorting out of important business

The next step

- *What can you say that might help Dora and Angela?* It can help to reflect the loving care that is being shown to John, e.g. 'I can see that he has been hurt – you have all been hurt – by this devastating diagnosis and you do not want him to be hurt any more.' Explain that you would be guided by John in the consultation, but if he asks outright then you would take it as an indication that he is ready to start discussing the diagnosis.

- *Telling or not telling:* It is a professional's duty to find out how much the patient wants to know, not to decide whether the patient should know. *See* the CLIP worksheet *Breaking difficult news.*
- *Should you 'fudge it'?* Sometimes a delay and a further visit clarify the situation for everyone and enables greater trust.

Summary points

- Collusion is usually driven by love rather than control.
- Collusion is usually estranging and isolating for all involved (professionals too!).
- The purpose of tackling collusion is to enable closeness and honesty between those involved.
- The key to moving forward with partners and relatives is to fully acknowledge that they are behaving in the most loving way they know, but then to outline the downside. It can help to point out that although collusion may seem the most loving thing to do now, how will the 'missed opportunities' be viewed looking back in bereavement?
- There are some situations when it is not helpful to challenge collusion, e.g. if the patient is too ill to engage in the discussions needed or if the prognosis is too short to allow time for the discussions.

WORK PAGE

Think Think about:

- how you would feel

- how you would react.

. . . .

. . . .

. . . .

Dora says you know nothing about her husband and she and Angela have talked long about what they are proposing and how to do otherwise would 'destroy that dignified man up there'.

MCQ What do you think of their plan?

1	Accept their plan and step outside to ring the door bell	True	False
2	Tell them you're leaving as you feel you are here under false pretences	True	False
3	Argue that you feel this arrangement is against your ethical principles but agree not to mention his deterioration	True	False
4	Sit down with Dora and Angela to enquire why they feel this way	True	False
5	Accept that denial is an acceptable way of coping	True	False

What are the pros and cons of their approach?

Good things about collusion and denial	The downside of collusion and denial
Collusion	Collusion
Denial	Denial

You arrive at an understanding that you will not initiate discussion about his deterioration. John has been lightly dozing, but sits up and asks how much time he has left.

Think Think about how you should respond.

- What agreement would have to be agreed downstairs to enable a truthful reply?

. . . .

. . . .

- Is it your duty to tell the patient?

. . . .

. . . .

- What are the consequences if you 'fudge' it today? Do you have to sort it all out today?

. . . .

. . . .

FURTHER ACTIVITY

Reflect on a time when you colluded with someone:

- What were your reasons for colluding?

- With hindsight, was it the best way?

FURTHER READING

Journal articles

Friedrichsen MJ, Strang PM and Carlsson ME (2000) Breaking bad news in the transition from curative to palliative cancer care – patient's view of the doctor giving the information. *Supportive Care in Cancer*. 8(6): 472–8.

Jenkins V, Fallowfield L and Saul J (2001) Information needs of patients with cancer: results from a large study in UK cancer centres. *British Journal of Cancer*. 84(1): 48–51.

Lamont EB and Christakis NA (2001) Prognostic disclosure to patients with cancer near the end of life. *Annals of Internal Medicine*. 134(12): 1096–105.

McCague K (2001) Collusion in doctor-patient communication. Doctors should adopt patient's perspective. *BMJ*. 322: 1063.

Noone I, Crowe M, Pillay I *et al.* (2000) Telling the truth about cancer: views of elderly patients and their relatives. *Irish Medical Journal*. 93(4): 104–5.

Parker PA, Baile WF, de Moor C *et al.* (2001) Breaking bad news about cancer: patients' preferences for communication. *Journal of Clinical Oncology*. 19(7): 2049–56.

Rousseau P (2000) Death denial. *Journal of Clinical Oncology*. 18(23): 3998–9.

Ubel PA (2001) Truth in the most optimistic way. *Annals of Internal Medicine*. 134(12): 1142–3.

Resource books

Calman K, Doyle D and Hanks GWC (eds) (2003) *The Oxford Textbook of Palliative Medicine* (3e). Oxford University Publications, Oxford.

Faulkner A (1998) *Effective Interaction with Patients* (2e). Churchill Livingstone, New York.

Regnard C and Hockley J (2004) *A Guide to Symptom Relief in Palliative Care* (5e). Radcliffe Medical Press, Oxford.

Twycross R (2003) *Introducing Palliative Care* (4e). Radcliffe Medical Press, Oxford.

HELPING THE PATIENT WITH REDUCED
HYDRATION AND NUTRITION

1 Maintaining the environment for eating and drinking

Dorothy Matthews
Lynn Gibson
Claud Regnard
Margaret Kindlen

INTRODUCTORY LEVEL

Aim of this worksheet

To consider how to ensure the environment is best suited for eating and drinking.

How to use this worksheet

- You can work through this worksheet by yourself, or with a tutor.

- Read the case study below, then work on the questions overleaf.

- The work page is on the right side, the information page is on the left.

- Work any way you want: you can try answering from your own knowledge (in which case, fold over the information page), you can use the information page (this is not cheating – you learn as you find the information) or you can use other sources of information.

- It should take you about 15 minutes. If anything is unclear, discuss it with a colleague.

- If you think any information is wrong or out of date, let us know.

- Use the activity on the back page and take this learning into your workplace.

Case study

Ben is a 33-year-old man who has moderate learning disability together with hydrocephalus, spastic diplegia, visual impairment and epilepsy. He enjoys life, but his plans to resettle in a small group community home are halted when he is diagnosed as having a carcinoma of the kidney with lung metastases. He is normally well nourished, but he has become tense and easily startled at mealtimes and is becoming increasingly reluctant to eat.

INFORMATION PAGE

Mealtimes are social occasions

Why do we eat?: At its most basic, **hunger** makes us eat for **nutrition** and for **survival**. But we also eat for psychological reasons such as **habit, boredom, pleasure, satisfaction** or **comfort**, and because we choose to make it a **social activity**.

What influences your choice of diet?: Choices (likes/dislikes) obviously influence our choice, but this is greatly influenced by **lifestyle** (e.g. vegetarianism) **religion, external resources** (i.e. what is available locally), **budget**, and **occasion**. In illness, other factors become important such as **environment, staff numbers, medications, loss of taste**, and **physical/mental health problems**.

Environment: a matter of choice

This can have a big impact on a person's wish to eat and participate at mealtimes. When we are independent and healthy we choose when, what and where we eat, and with whom. Having this choice allows eating to be a pleasurable and social activity and not just a means of survival. For some, this means eating in the company of others. Other people, however, prefer privacy, especially if they already have difficulty eating. Illness or a loss of independence greatly reduces these choices.

Problems with the mealtime environment

- *Timing:* The living environment in the hospital, hospice or nursing home can lead to inflexible mealtimes, as daily routines can be task-oriented, with limited time allocated for serving, eating and enjoying the meal.
- *Size of area and number of people:* A crowded, small room or a large area with an open access or thoroughfare does not encourage pleasant mealtimes. Thought needs to be given to the number of people using the dining room.
- *Unintentional exclusion:* Positioning of patients, carer and furniture needs to be carefully thought out to prevent unintentional exclusion, e.g. placing a patient facing a blank wall, but hearing general activity behind them.
- *Presentation of food:* Each meal should offer variety, be attractive, be the correct temperature and an appropriate proportion size for the patient.
- *Equipment:* If necessary the patient should be assessed by an appropriate professional (i.e. physiotherapist, occupational therapist) for seating and crockery/utensils. Otherwise the usual furniture needs to be checked for table height and access.
- *Communication:* This is an important social aspect of eating and distractions or background noise such as music, stacking plates should be kept to a minimum. Relationships should be acknowledged both between patients, and between patients and staff. Wherever possible the patient's choice should be followed. Communication opportunities increase for both the patient and carer when the carer pays attention, is responsive, is at face to face level, gives eye contact, asks simple questions, creates choices, uses simple language about the meal, and allows the patient to use all sensory information such as looking, smelling and touching.

Lessons to be learnt

- *Why could Ben be tense and easily startled at mealtimes?* Ben may have a **brisk startle reflex** so that loud noises or sudden bangs would make him uncomfortable and tense. An increase in his **anxiety** because of the illness or a **new environment** (e.g. hospital) would worsen this problem.
- *What could be contributing factors in Ben's reluctance to eat?* Maybe Ben's **taste** in food could have changed, so he dislikes what is being offered. Food should be colourful and well seasoned so it stimulates the appetite using sight and smell and taste, especially given Ben's **visual impairment. Portion sizes** should be individually adjusted and consideration given to the individual needs of the patient and to the **temperature of the food** offered. Some patients can only manage small portions at one time, but may be willing to take these more frequently as snacks. **Oral problems** need to be excluded, e.g. poor dental hygiene, oral candida, apthous ulceration. **Anorexia** (loss of appetite) can also be caused by cancer, infection, anxiety, depression and many other illnesses. Finally, a number of **drugs** can reduce appetite by causing drowsiness, nausea or gastric irritation.
- *What measures could be taken to improve the mealtime experience for Ben?* If it is necessary to **help someone to feed**, the carer should **sit opposite** the person being fed, **talk calmly**, providing **verbal and non-verbal prompts** and encouragement. **Appropriate-sized mouthfuls** should be given with **sufficient time** made available to enjoy the meal. Time becomes very important in a patient who has a swallowing problem. Many people assume that anyone can assist another to eat. However, feeding a patient is not a simple procedure. Carers need to be taught how to do it, what the problems are and how they might be overcome. Most importantly, they need to know the problems of a poor environment and the risks of swallowing problems (*see* CLIP worksheet *Thinking about swallowing problems*).

Causes related to Ben's illness need to be treated (*see* CLIP worksheet *Decisions in hydration and nutrition*).

WORK PAGE

Think   Think about why we eat and what influences our choice of diet.

- Why we eat:

  . . . .

  . . . .

- What influences our choice of diet:

  . . . .

  . . . .

Write down some examples of problems with the mealtime environment that can occur for patients.

Category   Examples

Timing of meals

Company

Food

Equipment

Communication

Write your thoughts on the following questions:

- What could be making Ben tense at mealtimes?

  . . . .

  . . . .

- What could be contributing to Ben's reluctance to eat?

  . . . .

  . . . .

- What could you do to improve Ben's mealtime experience?

  . . . .

  . . . .

FURTHER ACTIVITY

Select a patient who seems to have difficulty with eating or drinking:

• Observe their environment during mealtimes and consider their individual likes, dislikes and personalities.

• Think of ways you could improve the environment for that patient.

FURTHER READING

Journal articles

Lesourd B and Mazari L (1999) Nutrition and immunity in the elderly. *Proceedings of the Nutrition Society.* **58**(3): 685–95.

Wilkes G (2000) Nutrition: the forgotten ingredient in cancer care. *American Journal of Nursing.* **100**(4): 46–51.

Williams J and Copp G (1990) Food presentation and the terminally ill. *Nursing Standard.* 4: 29–32.

Books and reports

Joint working party of the National Council for Hospice and Palliative Care Services and the ethics committee of the Association for Palliative Medicine of Great Britain and Ireland (1997) Artificial hydration (AH) for people who are terminally ill. *European Journal of Palliative Care.* 4: 124.

BMA (1993) *Withholding and Withdrawing Life-prolonging Medical Treatment – Guidance for Decision-making.* BMJ Publishing Group, London.

DoH (2001) *The Essence of Care: Patient Focused Bench Marking for Health Care Practitioners.* DoH, London.

Klein MD, Morris S and Dunn M (1999) *Mealtime Participation Guide.* Therapy Skill Builders, San Antonio.

Herber H, Blackburn GL and Go VLG (1999) *Nutritional Oncology.* Academic Press, San Diego.

HELPING THE PATIENT WITH REDUCED
HYDRATION AND NUTRITION

2 Balancing the diet

Dorothy Matthews
Lynn Gibson
Claud Regnard

INTERMEDIATE LEVEL

Aim of this worksheet

To understand the principles of maintaining a balanced diet.

How to use this worksheet

- You can work through this worksheet by yourself, or with a tutor.

- Read the case study below, then work on the questions overleaf.

- The work page is on the right side, the information page is on the left.

- Work any way you want: you can try answering from your own knowledge (in which case, fold over the information page), you can use the information page (this is not cheating – you learn as you find the information) or you can use other sources of information.

- It should take you about 15 minutes. If anything is unclear, discuss it with a colleague.

- If you think any information is wrong or out of date, let us know.

- Use the activity on the back page and take this learning into your workplace.

Case study

Ben is a 33-year-old man, who has moderate learning disability together with hydrocephalus, spastic diplegia, and visual impairment and epilepsy. He enjoys life but his plan to settle in a small group community home was halted when he is diagnosed as having a carcinoma of the kidney with lung metastases. He is normally well nourished but staff are now concerned about maintaining Ben's adequate nutritional status. He weighs 68 kg and is 2 m tall.

INFORMATION PAGE

Importance of a balanced diet

Nutrition is a priority in an individual's treatment and provides the foundation for all other care. The only exception to this is the end stages of a life-threatening illness when it becomes more important to give hydration and feeding for pleasure rather than survival.

Having a correct diet means eating a variety of foods in the correct proportions. The six basic food groups – and the amounts to be eaten from each group for a healthy, balanced diet – are:

Milk and dairy foods: 17% total intake

Vitamins, minerals, essential fats: Less than 1%

Meat, fish and alternatives: 12% total intake

Fruit and vegetables: 32% total intake

Fats and sugars: 5% total intake

Bread, other cereals and potatoes: 33% total intake

Despite these figures, the concept of a 'healthy' diet is based on averages for a population and current knowledge. Some people can remain healthy on different proportions – this particularly applies to 'micronutrients' (vitamins, minerals and essential fats), whose requirements are probably genetically determined and will vary with individuals.

Planning nutritional support

Nutritional support should be considered for anybody unable to maintain their nutritional status by their usual diet. There are many factors which may influence food intake and need to be considered when planning nutritional support. Examples are surgery, radiotherapy, chemotherapy, physical or mental illness, advanced disease, and Ben's behaviour and his environment.

If Ben has difficulty accepting a balanced diet, he will start to lose weight. This can be checked by calculating his Body Mass Index (BMI). This should normally be more than 20.

Modifying the diet

- *Timing and frequency of food and drink:* Patients may be unable to eat their usual portions. Ben may prefer to 'graze' all day with snacks 'little and often' rather than main meals.
- *Altering food consistency:* Ben may benefit from very soft foods or even liquids if he finds it difficult to chew or has a sore mouth.

How much food do people need? People differ in the amount of energy (calories) they require and that is what affects the amount of food, in total, that individuals need. However much people need, the proportions of food from the different groups should remain the same. So, for example, someone with a low daily energy requirement of say 1200 calories, would need the same proportions of food from the five food groups, as someone with a high daily requirement of 3000 calories. Things that affect people's overall energy needs are:

- *Gender:* Women tend to need less energy than men.
- *Age:* Older adults need less energy than adolescents and young adults.
- *Being overweight:* Being heavier than the healthy weight range for an individual's height means less energy is required to achieve a healthy weight.
- *Being very inactive:* The less active a person is, the lower their energy needs.

Recommended daily calorie needs: Women = 2000 calories. Men = 2500 calories. A man with a physically demanding job would need 3000 calories, while a frail, elderly woman may only need 1500 calories. Ben is a young man who would need 2000 calories normally, but if he becomes less active because of his illness he may manage with smaller amounts.

It is calculated by dividing the weight in kilograms by the square of the height: for Ben this is 68 kg divided by $2\,m \times 2\,m$, so $68 \div 4 = 17$. A BMI of 17 is low, showing that Ben is undernourished.

The effects of a poor diet include muscle weakness, fatigue, skin problems (dryness, thinning, oedema, pressure ulcers), vitamin and mineral deficiencies, anaemia, infections, heart failure, hypoglycaemia and a reduced ability to withstand infection, physical injury and emotional stress.

- *Altering food choice:* Taste changes may mean foods that Ben previously liked are now disliked and those previously disliked now enjoyed.
- *Fortifying food:* Food may be fortified with protein and energy if Ben is unable to eat and drink sufficient amounts. This can be done using commercial products or store cupboard ingredients (*see* CLIP worksheet *Enriching and fortifying the diet*).

WORK PAGE

 This pie chart shows the proportions of the six basic food groups in a healthy diet. Join each food type with the correct section of the chart.

| Milk and dairy products | Meat and fish | Fats and sugars | Vitamins, minerals, etc. | Fruit and vegetables | Bread, cereals, potatoes |

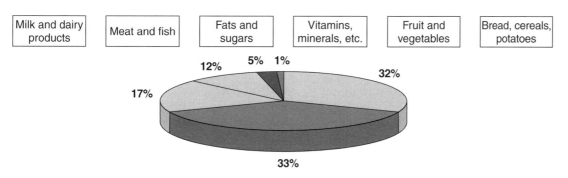

Think ⟨Ring⟩ the number of calories you think the following people should be eating each day:

A man with a physically demanding job	500	1000	1500	2000	3000	5000
A frail, 95-year-old, inactive woman	500	1000	1500	2000	3000	5000
Ben (33-year-old man with cancer)	500	1000	1500	2000	3000	5000

The Body Mass Index (BMI) is (weight in kilograms/height squared). Work out Ben's BMI – what does this tell you about Ben?

. . . .

. . . .

. . . .

. . . .

. . . .

Think Think how you could increase Ben's nutrition *without* increasing the amount of food given at one sitting.

. . . .

. . . .

. . . .

. . . .

. . . .

FURTHER ACTIVITY

For one of your patients: work out what proportion of the five basic food groups make up their daily intake.

Work out your own BMI (if you dare!).

FURTHER READING

Journal articles

Lesourd B and Mazari L (1999) Nutrition and immunity in the elderly. *Proceedings of the Nutrition Society.* **58**(3): 685–95.

Stratton RJ and Elia M (2000) Are oral nutritional supplements of benefit to patients in the community? Findings from a systematic review. *Current Opinion in Clinical Nutrition and Metabolic Care.* **3**(4): 311–15.

Wilkes G (2000) Nutrition: the forgotten ingredient in cancer care. *American Journal of Nursing.* 100(4): 46–51.

Williams J and Copp G (1990) Food presentation and the terminally ill. *Nursing Standard.* 4: 29–32.

Books and reports

BMA (1993) *Withholding and Withdrawing Life-prolonging Medical Treatment – Guidance for Decision-making.* BMJ Publishing Group, London.

DoH (2001) *The Essence of Care: Patient Focused Bench Marking for Health Care Practitioners.* DoH, London.

Herber H, Blackburn GL and Go VLG (1999) *Nutritional Oncology.* Academic Press, San Diego.

Joint working party of the National Council for Hospice and Palliative Care Services and the ethics committee of the Association for Palliative Medicine of Great Britain and Ireland (1997) Artificial hydration (AH) for people who are terminally ill. *European Journal of Palliative Care.* 4: 124.

Klein MD, Morris S and Dunn M (1999) *Mealtime Participation Guide.* Therapy Skill Builders, San Antonio.

HELPING THE PATIENT WITH REDUCED
HYDRATION AND NUTRITION

3 Enriching and fortifying the diet

Dorothy Matthews
Lynn Gibson
Claud Regnard
Margaret Kindlen

INTERMEDIATE LEVEL

Aim of this worksheet

To understand how the diet can be enriched and supplemented.

How to use this worksheet

- You can work through this worksheet by yourself, or with a tutor.

- Read the case study below, then work on the questions overleaf.

- The work page is on the right side, the information page is on the left.

- Work any way you want: you can try answering from your own knowledge (in which case, fold over the information page), you can use the information page (this is not cheating – you learn as you find the information) or you can use other sources of information.

- It should take you about 15 minutes. If anything is unclear, discuss it with a colleague.

- If you think any information is wrong or out of date, let us know.

- Use the activity on the back page and take this learning into your workplace.

Case study

Ben is a 33-year-old man, who has moderate learning disability together with hydrocephalus, spastic diplegia, and visual impairment and epilepsy. He enjoys life but his plan to settle in a small group community home was halted when he is diagnosed as having a carcinoma of the kidney with lung metastases. He is normally well nourished but staff are now concerned about maintaining Ben's adequate nutritional status. His Body Mass Index (BMI) is low at 17.

INFORMATION PAGE

Fortifying the diet

- *Milk:* To fortify milk, whisk or liquidise 3–4 heaped table-spoons of dried milk powder into whole (silver top) milk. Try to use at least 1 pint of this 'fortified milk' each day. This seems a lot to take but it can be kept chilled and sipped through the day, and can be used in drinks, e.g. hot chocolate, Horlicks, Bournvita and Ovaltine, sauces, custard, soups, puddings, on cereals and for milk shakes with flavouring.
- *Cream:* Add cream to cereals, porridge, sauces, soups, mashed potato and puddings.
- *Condensed milk:* Add to hot and cold puddings.
- *Evaporated milk:* Add to sauces, custards, jelly, puddings and coffee.

- *Cheese:* Grated cheese can be added to sauces, potatoes, scrambled egg and vegetables or as a topping to soup and lots of savoury dishes.
- *Eggs:* These can be used to make baked custard, beaten into hot puddings, mixed into potatoes for savoury pies or using chopped hard boiled eggs to sprinkle over vegetables or salad.
- *Butter and margarine:* Add to potatoes, melt on top of vegetables and pasta, spread thickly on bread.
- *Mayonnaise:* Use in sandwiches, with fish and on savoury biscuits.
- *Sugar:* Add to drinks, cereals and puddings.
- *Preserves:* Use on bread and add to puddings.

Dietary supplements

- These may be used to improve an inadequate diet or may be used as a sole source of nutrition if taken in sufficient quantity. They can be used on their own (chilled and sipped through the day) or added to a meal. Savoury supplements can be used as a starter, and sweet supplements can be used as a sweet, while neutral taste supplements can be added to existing foods in the diet.
- Most are called 'complete feeds' since they all provide proteins, vitamins, minerals and trace elements to meet requirements. There is no evidence that one type is any better than another, but they seem to be more effective in those with a BMI less than 20 or in those who are rapidly losing weight (Stratton and Elia, 2000).

- The dietician can give appropriate advice on the most suitable supplements available.
- Sip feeds contain whole proteins, hydrolysed fat and carbohydrate. They come in a range of flavours both sweet and savoury and are preserved:
  - as powder in a packet – e.g. Complan, Build-Up (can be bought over the counter)
  - in a can or carton – Entera-high energy drink supplement, Enlive-high energy fruit juice supplements, Ensure supplement.
- Many of these supplements are prescription-only from the GP or consultant.

Energy supplements

Carbohydrates (in the form of glucose polymers in powder or liquid form) are virtually tasteless and may be added to many foods. These supplements would be used to increase the energy content of the food, e.g. Maxijul.

Making clinical decisions with Ben

The overriding need is for Ben to maintain adequate nutrition and comfort whilst ensuring a good quality of life.
- *Exclude the following as causes:* anxiety or depression, breath-lessness, swallowing problems, weakness or disability preventing intake, constipation, nausea and vomiting, infection or odour, drugs (causing nausea, mucosal irritation or gastric stasis), poor food presentation.

- *Is Ben's nutritional status poor or deteriorating?* Consider fortifying and supplementing Ben's diet with the supplements above.
- *Can the anorexia be helped by corticosteroids?* Useful if a brief (1–4 week) effect is wanted. Dexamethasone 2–4 mg once in the morning may help (*see* CLIP worksheet *The cachexia syndrome*).

WORK PAGE

 What easily available foods could you use to add extra calories and nutrients to Ben's food? How could you use them in Ben's diet?

Easily available food	How would you use the food?
e.g. cream	e.g. add to cereals, porridge, sauces, soups, mashed potato and puddings.

. . . .

. . . .

. . . .

. . . .

. . . .

There are many commercial dietary supplements on the market. List as many as you can and how they could add to Ben's diet.

. . . .

. . . .

. . . .

. . . .

Think Think about how these supplements could be included in Ben's diet.

. . . .

. . . .

. . . .

. . . .

Think Think about how you could help Ben's lack of appetite and poor nutritional intake.

. . . .

. . . .

. . . .

. . . .

FURTHER ACTIVITY

Select a patient who has a BMI below 15:

- Plan a daily menu, fortifying their diet with easily available 'store-cupboard' ingredients to boost the nutritional intake.

FURTHER READING

Journal articles

Lesourd B and Mazari L (1999) Nutrition and immunity in the elderly. *Proceedings of the Nutrition Society.* **58**(3): 685–95.

Stratton RJ and Elia M (2000) Are oral nutritional supplements of benefit to patients in the community? Findings from a systematic review. *Current Opinion in Clinical Nutrition and Metabolic Care.* **3**(4): 311–15.

Wilkes G (2000) Nutrition: the forgotten ingredient in cancer care. *American Journal of Nursing.* **100**(4): 46–51.

Williams J and Copp G (1990) Food presentation and the terminally ill. *Nursing Standard.* **4**: 29–32.

Books and reports

BMA (1993) *Withholding and Withdrawing Life-prolonging Medical Treatment – Guidance for Decision-making.* BMJ Publishing Group, London.

DoH (2001) *The Essence of Care: Patient Focused Bench Marking for Health Care Practitioners.* DoH, London.

Herber H, Blackburn GL and Go VLG (1999) *Nutritional Oncology.* Academic Press, San Diego.

Joint working party of the National Council for Hospice and Palliative Care Services and the ethics committee of the Association for Palliative Medicine of Great Britain and Ireland (1997) Artificial hydration (AH) for people who are terminally ill. *European Journal of Palliative Care.* **4**: 124.

Klein MD, Morris S and Dunn M (1999) *Mealtime Participation Guide.* Therapy Skill Builders, San Antonio.

HELPING THE PATIENT WITH REDUCED
HYDRATION AND NUTRITION

4 Decisions in hydration and nutrition

Claud Regnard
Dorothy Matthews
Lynn Gibson

INTERMEDIATE LEVEL

Aim of this worksheet

To consider the causes and approaches to reduced hydration and nutrition in advanced disease.

How to use this worksheet

- You can work through this worksheet by yourself, or with a tutor.

- Read the case study below, then work on the questions overleaf.

- The work page is on the right side, the information page is on the left.

- Work any way you want: you can try answering from your own knowledge (in which case, fold over the information page), you can use the information page (this is not cheating – you learn as you find the information) or you can use other sources of information.

- It should take you about 15 minutes. If anything is unclear, discuss it with a colleague.

- If you think any information is wrong or out of date, let us know.

- Use the activity on the back page and take this learning into your workplace.

Case study

Ben is a 33-year-old man who has a moderate learning disability together with hydrocephalus, spastic diplegia, visual impairment and epilepsy. He enjoys life, but his plans to resettle in a small group community hospital are halted when he is diagnosed as having a carcinoma of the kidney with lung metastases. He is normally well nourished, but in the three months since being told he has lost 11 kg in weight. Today he is listless and thirsty.

INFORMATION PAGE

Causes of reduced hydration and nutrition

- *Physical disability:* Paralysis, weakness or any difficulty with co-ordination will make it difficult or impossible for Ben to feed or drink. Breathlessness can make it difficult to eat or drink if it is severe enough. Swallowing problems have many causes (*see* CLIP worksheet *Thinking about swallowing problems*).
- *Physical illness:* Constipation, infection, nausea or vomiting are common causes. Cancer can reduce appetite as well as increasing the loss of fat and muscle, a syndrome known as cachexia (*see* CLIP worksheet *The cachexia syndrome*). Many illnesses can result in loss of fluid, e.g. raised temperature, diarrhoea, vomiting, high levels of glucose or calcium.
- *Psychological:* Anxiety, low mood or depression can reduce the interest in food. Remember also that a competent person may choose to leave their intake unchanged.
- *Behavioural:* Food-related behaviours can occur for many reasons, and may be worsened by the stress of physical illness.
- *Current treatment:* Recent radiotherapy, chemotherapy or surgery will all reduce appetite. Some drugs can have the same effect directly (e.g. phenytoin) or indirectly by causing constipation or nausea.
- *Environmental:* Some odours can reduce appetite (e.g. smells from frying food, bowels or wounds). Poorly presented food is a common cause in hospital, while a lack of privacy can be a problem for someone who has difficulty eating.

Reasons for and against hydration and nutrition

- *For hydration:* This is **simple** to administer by mouth if Ben is given help. If swallowing is difficult, a **subcutaneous (SC) infusion** can be used in the short term, or a tube into the stomach can be inserted easily under light sedation with an endoscope to form a percutaneous endoscopic gastrostomy (**PEG**). Hydration ensures **good oral health**, helps to **prevent pressure sores**, and **prevents thirst**.
- *For feeding:* Adequate nutrition prevents pressure sores, prevents hunger, and prevents the symptoms of nutritional deficiency. If swallowing problems are present a PEG can be used.
- *Against hydration:* **Refusal** by an individual to have a SC line or PEG placed must be accepted if the person is competent for that decision. In very ill patients, hydration can cause problems with **bronchial secretions**, **vomiting** or **incontinence**. Experience also demonstrates that **many patients in their last days are comfortable** without hydration.
- *Against feeding:* This **can be more difficult**, especially if swallowing problems are present. **Refusal** by an individual to have a intravenous line or PEG placed must be accepted if the person is competent for that decision. In an ill patient the **prognosis may be too short for feeding to be of help**. Many ill patients **are not hungry** and have no desire for food. **Feeding does not prevent the death of a terminal patient. It does not prolong survival in a patient with advanced disease.**

Clinical decisions for Ben

- *Is the prognosis short (i.e. day by day deterioration)?* Hydration and nutrition are often unnecessary in a terminal patient who is comfortable and settled.
- *Does Ben want to leave the intake unchanged?* As long as depression has been excluded, and he is able to make a reasoned choice about his intake, then his choice must be accepted.
- *Are swallowing problems present?* Ask a speech therapist for advice (*see* CLIP worksheet *Thinking about swallowing problems*).
- *Are treatable problems present?* Examples are nausea, vomiting, constipation, anxiety, depression, drugs.
- *Can you help with feeding or change food presentation?* Ben may need help with feeding and drinking. Check the food is appetising, varied and in small portions. Ensure a pleasant atmosphere.

Advising and treating Ben

The overriding need is for comfort. Hydrating and feeding Ben will not prevent him dying from his cancer, but it will help him to feel as well as possible so that he can cope with his problems.

- *Hydration:* He is having symptoms from a lack of fluid and replacing fluid will help him to feel better. He may be able to drink enough, otherwise the subcutaneous route can be used easily in any setting.
- *Nutrition:* The value of nutrition depends on his choice and prognosis. If he wants food, he should have this regardless of the prognosis. If his deterioration is slow (week by week, or month by month deterioration), extra nutrition in the form of supplements may help prevent symptoms due to nutritional deficiencies. His appetite can be stimulated using low dose steroids, e.g. dexamethasone 4 mg once in the morning (*see* CLIP worksheet *The cachexia syndrome*).

WORK PAGE

Think   Think of possible causes for Ben's weight and fluid loss in each of the following categories:

Physical disability:

. . . .

Physical illness:

. . . .

Psychological:

. . . .

Behavioural:

. . . .

Current treatment:

. . . .

Environmental:

. . . .

Write down reasons for and against giving Ben fluid and food.

	For	Against
Giving fluids (hydration)		
Giving food (nutrition)		

Think   His listlessness and dry mouth suggest he is short of fluids. Think about what you would advise Ben to do.

. . . .

. . . .

FURTHER ACTIVITY

Taste a selection of commercially available supplements:

- Reflect on whether you would prefer these preparations or high energy, natural, foods.

FURTHER READING

Journal articles

Burge FI (1996) Dehydration and provision of fluids in palliative care. What is the evidence? *Canadian Family Physician*. **42**: 2383–8.

Burnham P (1996) Nourishing knowledge. *Nursing Times*. **92**: 78–9.

Dunphy K, Finlay I, Rathbone G *et al.* (1995) Rehydration in palliative and terminal care: if not – why not? *Palliative Medicine*. **9**(3): 221–8.

Fainsinger RL and Bruera E (1997) When to treat dehydration in a terminally patient? *Supportive Care in Cancer*. **5**: 205–11.

Fainsinger RL, MacEachern T, Miller MJ *et al.* (1994) The use of hypodermoclysis for rehydration in terminally ill cancer patients. *Journal of Pain and Symptom Management*. **9**: 298–302.

Grindel CG, Whitner K and Barsevick A (1996) Quality of life and nutritional support in patients with cancer. *Cancer Practitioner*. **4**: 81–7.

Holmes S (1998) The challenge of providing nutritional support for the dying. *International Journal of Palliative Nursing*. **4**: 26–31.

Lesourd B and Mazari L (1999) Nutrition and immunity in the elderly. *Proceedings of the Nutrition Society*. **58**(3): 685–95.

Morita T, Tei Y, Tsunoda J *et al.* (2001) Determinants of the sensation of thirst in terminally ill cancer patients. *Supportive Care in Cancer*. **9**(3): 177–86.

Stratton RJ and Elia M (2000) Are oral nutritional supplements of benefit to patients in the community? Findings from a systematic review. *Current Opinion in Clinical Nutrition and Metabolic Care*. **3**(4): 311–15.

Wilkes G (2000) Nutrition: the forgotten ingredient in cancer care. *American Journal of Nursing*. **100**(4): 46–51.

Williams J and Copp G (1990) Food presentation and the terminally ill. *Nursing Standard*. **4**: 29–32.

Winter SM (2000) Terminal nutrition: framing the debate for the withdrawal of nutritional support in terminally ill patients. *American Journal of Medicine*. **109**(9): 723–6.

Books and reports

BMA (1993) *Withholding and Withdrawing Life-prolonging Medical Treatment – Guidance for Decision-making*. BMJ Publishing Group, London.

DoH (2001) *The Essence of Care: Patient Focused Bench Marking for Health Care Practitioners*. DoH, London.

Herber H, Blackburn GL and Go VLG (1999) *Nutritional Oncology*. Academic Press, San Diego.

Joint working party of the National Council for Hospice and Palliative Care Services and the ethics committee of the Association for Palliative Medicine of Great Britain and Ireland (1997) Artificial hydration (AH) for people who are terminally ill. *European Journal of Palliative Care*. **4**: 124.

Klein MD, Morris S and Dunn M (1999) *Mealtime Participation Guide*. Therapy Skill Builders, San Antonio.

HELPING THE PATIENT WITH REDUCED
HYDRATION AND NUTRITION

5 Thinking about swallowing problems

Claud Regnard
Dorothy Matthews
Lynn Gibson
Sue Clark

INTERMEDIATE LEVEL

Aim of this worksheet

To consider the causes and approaches to swallowing problems in advanced disease.

How to use this worksheet

- You can work through this worksheet by yourself, or with a tutor.

- Read the case study below, then work on the questions overleaf.

- The work page is on the right side, the information page is on the left.

- Work any way you want: you can try answering from your own knowledge (in which case, fold over the information page), you can use the information page (this is not cheating – you learn as you find the information) or you can use other sources of information.

- It should take you about 15 minutes. If anything is unclear, discuss it with a colleague.

- If you think any information is wrong or out of date, let us know.

- Use the activity on the back page and take this learning into your workplace.

Case study

Ben is a 33-year-old man who has a moderate learning disability together with hydrocephalus, spastic diplegia, visual impairment and epilepsy. He is diagnosed as having a carcinoma of the kidney with lung metastases. Ben is usually well nourished, but in three months he has lost 11 kg in weight. He has always found eating and drinking difficult but now coughs and splutters when drinking. He has had three chest infections in as many weeks.

INFORMATION PAGE

Causes of difficulty swallowing (dysphagia)

- *Mucosal problems:* **Dryness** from any cause can make swallowing very difficult. If the mucosa is damaged, **pain** will make it difficult to swallow. Causes of mucosal damage are **infection** (e.g. candida, herpes, apthous ulcers), **local cancer** causing pain, **cancer treatment** (chemotherapy or radiotherapy involving the mouth, pharynx or oesophagus). **Drugs** can affect swallowing by causing dryness (e.g. amitriptyline, morphine, cyclizine), or causing ulceration (e.g. NSAIDs).
- *Neurological problems:* Both sensation and muscular control are essential for effective swallowing. Any cause of **nerve damage** (e.g. cancer, surgery) will cause problems with sensation or muscle control. Damage to the cortex of the brain (e.g. **dementia**, **stroke**) or to the cerebellum (e.g. cancer) can cause problems with co-ordination of the swallowing muscles. Some conditions cause degeneration of the connecting nerve cells that control muscles (motor neurones) e.g. **motor neurone disease**.
- *Muscular problems:* Nearly 40 muscles are involved in swallowing and each must co-ordinate correctly with its neighbour for swallowing to occur correctly. Any of the **neurological problems** above may cause problems. In addition, **surgical removal** of muscle, or **scarring of muscle** (due to surgery or radiotherapy) can cause difficulties.
- *Blockages:* These mainly affect the oesophagus and can be caused by **cancer**, **scarring**, or inflammation due to **infection**.

Signs and symptoms of dysphagia

General features:
- *Signs:* Dehydration and weight loss are the most likely signs. The total time taken from the first movement of the tongue to the last movement of the larynx (the oropharyngeal transit time) is usually less than 1 second with liquids – times longer than this are abnormal. Patients will usually refuse all food if the transit time is longer than 10 seconds.
- *Symptoms:* Food refusal and pain on eating may indicate a problem with swallowing. Repeated chest infections can occur if food or fluid is getting into the lungs (aspiration). Patients can sense accurately the position of an obstruction and this information is important in separating out swallowing causes in the mouth and pharynx from those in the oesophagus.

Preparation phase problems:
- *Signs:* Leakage of food or liquid from the mouth, food collecting between the gums and the cheek, reduced or poorly co-ordinated tongue movements preventing food from forming a bolus and moving food from the front to the back of the mouth, prolonged chewing due to pain in the mouth, reduced sensation or muscular weakness.
- *Symptoms:* Difficulty moving food or liquids to the back of the tongue or pain in the mouth on chewing.

Swallowing and pharyngeal phase problems:
- *Signs:* Delayed swallowing phase, choking and coughing before, during or after the swallow, 'gurgly' quality to the voice after drinking due to material entering the larynx, nasal regurgitation or copious sputum.
- *Symptoms:* A sensation of food 'sticking' at the mouth or throat, feeling of choking or pain in the throat on swallowing.

Oesophageal phase problems:
- *Signs:* Usually none unless aspiration is causing repeated chest infections.
- *Symptoms:* Sensation of food sticking in the chest or abdomen that is worse with solid food (the level of the sensation invariably matches the site of the blockage), pain on swallowing or heartburn due to reflux of stomach contents into the oesophagus.

Helping Ben

- *Gather information:* Check for all the signs and symptoms above. Monitor food and drink intake.
- *Think about Ben's need for hydration and feeding:* See CLIP worksheet *Decisions in hydration and nutrition.*
- *Ensure that any infection or pain is treated:* e.g. candida. See CLIP worksheet *Oral problems.*
- *Ask for help:* If you suspect a swallowing problem then which person is needed depends on where the problem lies:
  - *Mouth or pharynx:* These patients should be seen by a swallowing therapist. They are speech therapists with a special interest in swallowing. After an initial assessment they may arrange for investigations of swallowing which help to formulate solutions to make swallowing easier, as well as give advice on whether it is safe to continue with oral feeding and drinking.
  - *Oesophagus:* These patients need referral to a gastroenterologist who may organise a barium or gastrograffin swallow as well as a look with a flexible viewing tube (an endoscope). If there is an obstruction they may be able to treat this by dilatation, laser or inserting a stent to keep the oesophageal passage open.

If the assessments show that Ben needs extra hydration and food then it may be necessary to consider a non-oral route – see CLIP worksheet *Using non-oral routes.*

- *Simple help:* Thickened liquids and foods (mousse, creamed soup) can often be swallowed more easily. Swallowing with the head tilted forward can reduce aspiration.

WORK PAGE

There are four stages of swallowing:

- *Preparation phase:* chewing and moving the food and liquid backwards.
- *Swallowing:* moving the contents over the back of the tongue into the pharynx.
- *Pharyngeal:* moving the contents towards the opening of the gullet (oesophagus).
- *Oesophageal:* moving contents down through the oesophagus to the stomach.

Think What could affect Ben's swallowing? Think about causes in the following categories:

Problems with the lining (mucosa):

. . . .

Neurological (nerve and brain) problems:

. . . .

Muscle problems:

. . . .

Blockages:

. . . .

Write down the signs (changes you can feel or see) and symptoms (problems the patient complains of) when swallowing is affected.

	Signs you can feel or see	Symptoms patient complains of
General features		
Preparation phase		
Swallowing and pharyngeal phase		
Oesophageal phase		

Think Think about what you can do to help Ben.

. . . .

. . . .

FURTHER ACTIVITY

If one of your clients was experiencing problems with swallowing:

- what would you do?

- who would you contact?

FURTHER READING

Journal articles

Dwolatzky T, Berezovski S, Friedmann R *et al.* (2001) A prospective comparison of the use of nasogastric and percutaneous endoscopic gastrostomy tubes for long-term enteral feeding in older people. *Clinical Nutrition.* **20**(6): 535–40.

Fuh JL, Lee RC, Lin CH *et al.* (1997) Swallowing difficulty in Parkinson's disease. *Clinical Neurology and Neurosurgery.* **99**: 106–12.

Groher ME (1994) Determination of the risks and benefits of oral feeding. *Dysphagia.* **9**: 233–4.

Lazarus CL (2000) Management of swallowing disorders in head and neck cancer patients: optimal patterns of care. *Seminars in Speech and Language.* **21**(4): 293–309.

Leslie P, Carding PN and Wilson JA (2003) Investigation and management of chronic dysphagia. *BMJ.* **326**: 433–6.

Magnus V (2001) Dysphagia training for nurses in an acute hospital setting – a pragmatic approach. *International Journal of Language and Communication Disorders.* **36**(Suppl.): 375–8.

McHorney CA, Bricker DE, Kramer AE *et al.* (2000) The SWAL-QOL outcomes tool for oropharyngeal dysphagia in adults: I. Conceptual foundation and item development. *Dysphagia.* **15**: 115–21.

McHorney CA, Bricker DE, Robbins J *et al.* (2000) The SWAL-QOL outcomes tool for oropharyngeal dysphagia in adults: II. Item reduction and preliminary scaling. *Dysphagia.* **15**: 134–5.

Park RHR, Allison MC, Lang J *et al.* (1992) Randomised comparison of percutaneous gastrostomy and nasogastric tube feeding in patients with persisting neurological dysphagia. *BMJ.* **304**: 1406–9.

Regnard CFB (2003) Dysphagia, dyspepsia and hiccups. In: K Calman, GW Hanks and D Doyle (eds) *The Oxford Textbook of Palliative Medicine* (3e). Oxford University Publications, Oxford.

Scott AG and Austin HE (1994) Nasogastric feeding in the management of severe dysphagia in motor neurone disease. *Palliative Medicine.* **8**: 45–9.

Thomas FJ and Wiles CM (1999) Dysphagia and nutritional status in multiple sclerosis. *Journal of Neurology.* **246**: 677–82.

Wasson K, Tate H and Hayes C (2001) Food refusal and dysphagia in older people with dementia: ethical and practical issues. *International Journal of Palliative Nursing.* **7**(10): 465–71.

Resource books

Langley J (1994) *Working with Swallowing Disorders.* Winslow Publications, Bicester.

Logemann JA (1983) *Evaluation and Treatment of Swallowing Disorders.* College Hill Press, San Diego.

North G *et al.* (1996) *Dysphagia. A guide for people who are having difficulties eating and drinking.* North Derbyshire Community Health Trust, Chesterfield.

HELPING THE PATIENT WITH REDUCED
HYDRATION AND NUTRITION

6 Using non-oral routes

Dorothy Matthews
Lynn Gibson
Claud Regnard
Margaret Kindlen

ADVANCED LEVEL

Aim of this worksheet

To consider the non-oral routes of hydration and nutrition in advanced disease.

How to use this worksheet

- You can work through this worksheet by yourself, or with a tutor.

- Read the case study below, then work on the questions overleaf.

- The work page is on the right side, the information page is on the left.

- Work any way you want: you can try answering from your own knowledge (in which case, fold over the information page), you can use the information page (this is not cheating – you learn as you find the information) or you can use other sources of information.

- It should take you about 15 minutes. If anything is unclear, discuss it with a colleague.

- If you think any information is wrong or out of date, let us know.

- Use the activity on the back page and take this learning into your workplace.

Case study

Ben is a 33-year-old man who has a moderate learning disability together with hydro-cephalus, spastic diplegia, visual impairment and epilepsy. He is diagnosed as having a carcinoma of the kidney with lung metastases. Ben is usually well nourished, but in three months he has lost 11 kg in weight. He can no longer swallow without aspirating fluids.

INFORMATION PAGE

Indications for a non-oral route

For mouth and pharynx problems, the advice of a swallowing therapist (usually a speech therapist with a special interest in swallowing) is essential. For oesophageal problems the advice of a gastroenterologist is necessary.

Non-oral feeding should be considered if:
- If the mouth to pharynx swallow takes longer than usual. The oropharyngeal transit (OT) time is the time a swallow takes from the first tongue movement to the last movement of the larynx. This can be assessed at the bedside. It is usually less than one second. Long meal times are inevitable when the OT is long.
- The swallowing problems are causing the person to become **reluctant to eat**.
- Mealtimes are taking so long that the person is losing interest in food and they are **losing weight**.
- They are not managing to take enough fluids to keep well hydrated, e.g. **persistent vomiting**.

- They need extra feeding in preparation for treatment such as an **operation** or **chemotherapy**.

Non-oral feeding is needed if:
- Investigations show an oesophageal obstruction that cannot be treated.
- The **OT time is 10 seconds** or more – patients will usually stop eating because the effort is too great.
- More than 10% of swallowed material is aspirated – this can only be assessed with an X-ray test where the swallow is filmed using special dye (videofluoroscopy).
- In someone with swallowing difficulties, **repeated chest infections** are an indication that aspiration is becoming a problem.

Insufficient reasons for a non-oral route: convenience; staff shortages; refusing food (reasons for refusal must be assessed first); long mealtimes in the absence of swallowing problems; drooling or messy eating.

Types of non-oral routes

Nasogastric tube:
- *Advantages:* alternative when the patient does not want a gastrostomy, easily inserted (fine tube inserted into nasal cavity and down into stomach), safe (inserted under medical supervision), no anaesthetic required for insertion, easily reversed, rapid commencement of enteral feeds, few contraindications to placement.
- *Disadvantages:* does not prevent aspiration, discomfort on insertion, easily displaced (increased risk of pulmonary aspiration and likelihood of sub-optimal feed delivery), reflux (due to lower oesophageal sphincter being held open), frequent placement is uncomfortable and distressing, altered body image (aesthetically unacceptable), long term problems (nose bleeds, nasopharyngeal erosions, sinus pain, laryngeal injury), does not greatly reduce the sensation of hunger (Stratton, 2002, 1999)

Gastrostomy tube:
- *Indications:* long-term feeding (usually >2 weeks), prolonged need for increased nutrient intake (e.g. cystic fibrosis), inability to tolerate nasogastric tube on two occasions, conditions causing severe swallowing problems (e.g. advanced dementia, stroke, MND, MS, paralysis, head and neck cancer, oesophageal cancer).
- *Methods of gastrostomy insertion:*
  - Percutaneous endoscopic gastrostomy (PEG): an endoscope is passed into the stomach under light sedation. A gastrostomy tube is then inserted through the skin (the 'percutaneous' bit).
  - Percutaneous fluoroscopic gastrostomy (PFG): a nasogastric tube is inserted into the stomach and used to inflate the stomach with gas. The gastrostomy tube is then inserted under X-ray control (the 'fluoroscopic' bit). This is used when an endoscope cannot be inserted, e.g. tumours of the head and neck.
  - Surgical gastrostomy: the stomach is entered during a

small operation under general anaesthetic. The tube is replaced after 6 weeks with a low profile button gastrostomy.
- *Advantages:* less often displaced, less aspiration, often preferred for convenience and cosmetic reasons, more secure long term option, more efficient at delivering feed (because of larger bore), easily removed and replaced.
- *Disadvantages:* can be accidentally or deliberately removed, complications of endoscopy (sedation and aspiration), may need endoscopic removal, tube blockage, exit site infection. Does not greatly reduce hunger.
- *Gastrostomy compared with nasogastric tube:* PEGs have been shown to be a better way of ensuring caloric intake – this is because gastrostomy tubes are of larger diameter and nasogastric tubes are frequently displaced.
- *Replacement:* this is easily done through the existing tract.

Parenteral route:
- *Subcutaneous:* this uses a tiny plastic tube inserted under the skin. It is used in palliative care to give people extra fluids. It is more comfortable and easier to monitor in any setting. It cannot be used for nutrition.
- *Intravenous (peripheral):* uses plastic tube inserted into an arm vein. It is useful for giving fluids short-term or rapidly.
- *Intravenous (central):* this uses a long tube inserted under local anaesthetic into the large veins near the heart. It is used for giving nutrition, but is almost never needed in palliative care.

Jejunal feeding:
- *Indications:* early post-operative feeding since small bowel less affected by postoperative ileus), delayed gastric emptying, increased risk of aspiration, pharynx or oesophagus inaccessible (e.g. head and neck tumours).
- *Access:* this can be done through a gastrostomy.

What to choose for Ben: a gastrostomy may offer the best balance of risks and benefits.

WORK PAGE

Non-oral routes mean giving fluids or food through any route other than through the mouth, e.g. nasogastric tube, intravenous drip, gastrostomy.

 Ring those situations you think might need a non-oral route of feeding or hydration.

Swallowing difficulty without weight loss   Swallowing difficulty with weight loss

Taking 10 seconds to swallow   Insufficient staff to help with feeding

Persistent vomiting   Refusing food

Repeated chest infections   Preparing for surgery

Long meal times in absence of swallowing problems

Write down the advantages and disadvantages of the following three non-oral routes:

Route	Advantages	Disadvantages
Nasogastric tube		
Gastrostomy, e.g. PEG		
Parenteral (SC or IV)		

 Think about what route you would choose for Ben.

FURTHER ACTIVITY

When you next have a patient who is having difficulties with their food or drinks:

* Look up the weight charts and consider the implications of introducing non-oral feeding.

FURTHER READING

Journal articles

Ashby M, Game P, Devitt P *et al.* (1991) Percutaneous gastrostomy as a venting procedure in palliative care. *Palliative Medicine.* **5**: 147–50.

Boyd KJ and Beeken L (1994) Tube feeding in palliative care: benefits and problems. *Palliative Medicine.* **8**: 156–8.

Finucane TE and Bynum JPW (1996) Use of tube feeding to prevent aspiration pneumonia. *Lancet.* **348**: 1421–4.

Goodhall L (1997) Tube feeding dilemmas: can artificial nutrition and hydration be legally or ethically withheld or withdrawn? *Journal of Advanced Nursing.* **25**: 217–22.

Laing B, Smithers M and Harper J (1994) Percutaneous fluoroscopic gastrostomy: a safe option? *Medical Journal of Australia.* **161**: 308–10.

Loeb M, McGeer A, McArthur M *et al.* (1999) Risk factors for pneumonia and other lower respiratory tract infections in elderly residents of long-term care facilities. *Archives of Internal Medicine.* **159**: 2058–64.

Meehan SE, Wood RAB and Cuschieri A (1984) Percutaneous cervical pharyngostomy: a comfortable and convenient alternative to protracted nasogastric intubation. *American Journal of Surgery.* **148**: 325–30.

Mitchell SL, Kiely DK and Lipsitz LA (1997) The risk factors and impact on survival of feeding tube placement in nursing home residents with severe cognitive impairment. *Archives of Internal Medicine.* **157**: 327–32.

Myssiorek D, Siegel D and Vambutas A (1998) Fluoroscopically placed gastrostomies in the head and neck patient. *Laryngoscope.* **108**: 1557–60.

Park RHR, Allison MC, Lang J *et al.* (1992) Randomised comparison of percutaneous gastrostomy and nasogastric tube feeding in patients with persisting neurological dysphagia. *BMJ.* **304**: 1406–9.

Regnard CFB (2003) Dysphagia, dyspepsia and hiccups. In: K Calman, GW Hanks and D Doyle (eds) *The Oxford Textbook of Palliative Medicine* (3e). Oxford University Publications, Oxford.

Rudberg MA, Egleston BL, Grant MD *et al.* (2000) Effectiveness of feeding tubes in nursing home residents with swallowing disorders. *Journal of Parenteral and Enteral Nutrition.* **24**: 97–102.

Scott AG and Austin HE (1994) Nasogastric feeding in the management of severe dysphagia in motor neurone disease. *Palliative Medicine.* **8**: 45–9.

Stratton R (2002) Use and benefits of enteral nutrition. *Primary Health Care.* **12**(2): 25–30.

Stratton RJ and Elia M (1999) The effects of enteral tube feeding and parenteral nutrition on appetite sensations and food intake in health and disease. *Clinical Nutrition.* **18**(2): 63–70.

Stratton RJ, Stubbs RJ and Elia M (1998) Interrelationship between circulating leptin concentrations, hunger, and energy intake in healthy subjects receiving tube feeding. *Journal of Parenteral and Enteral Nutrition.* **22**(6): 335–9.

HELPING THE PATIENT WITH REDUCED
HYDRATION AND NUTRITION

7 Managing a gastrostomy

Dorothy Matthews
Lynn Gibson
Claud Regnard
Margaret Kindlen

ADVANCED LEVEL

Aim of this worksheet

To understand the principles of managing a gastrostomy.

How to use this worksheet

- You can work through this worksheet by yourself, or with a tutor.
- Read the case study below, then work on the questions overleaf.
- The work page is on the right side, the information page is on the left.
- Work any way you want: you can try answering from your own knowledge (in which case, fold over the information page), you can use the information page (this is not cheating – you learn as you find the information) or you can use other sources of information.
- It should take you about 15 minutes. If anything is unclear, discuss it with a colleague.
- If you think any information is wrong or out of date, let us know.
- Use the activity on the back page and take this learning into your workplace.

Case study

Ben is a 33-year-old man who has a moderate learning disability together with hydro-cephalus, spastic diplegia, visual impairment and epilepsy. He has been diagnosed as having a carcinoma of the kidney with lung metastases. A decline in Ben's nutritional status meant decisions relating to maintaining his weight and general overall condition had to be made. As Ben has a relatively good quality of life it was decided by Ben's family and the palliative care team to arrange for Ben to have a percutaneous endoscopic gastrostomy (PEG). The staff caring for Ben would like further advice on after-care and problems relating to the PEG.

INFORMATION PAGE

Gastrostomy

1 T: It is an opening through the abdominal wall into the stomach through which a feeding tube can be passed.
2 F: PEG = percutaneous endoscopic gastrostomy since an endoscope is used to insert the tube.
3 F: X-ray control or surgery can be used (only surgery needs a general anaesthetic).
4 T: With good after care, gastrostomies can last for years (*see also* CLIP worksheet on *Using non-oral routes*).

5 T: In a patient with a swallowing disorder, the risk is higher with a nasogastric tube.

Initially Ben was given a PEG with a small tube exiting from the stoma site. This was changed after six weeks to a low-profile PEG tube 'button' which is discreet and comfortable to use and is favoured especially by young people.

Initial care of the PEG site (if you have a local PEG team, follow their protocols)

For a new gastrostomy:
1 The external fixation plate should be left intact for 72 hours to minimise gastric leakage and allow adherence of the stoma to abdominal wall.
2 Several days after the procedure, the external fixation plate should be moved slightly to prevent adherence.
3 Each day:
   • always wash hands before caring for PEG sites.
   • clean the newly formed stoma site using sterile saline solution.
   • rotate the tube to avoid adherence to the tract.

When the stoma site has healed:
• Cleaning should be done daily using water or mild soap solution.
• A dressing is not necessary unless there is a heavy discharge.
• Bathing and showering are allowed at this stage.
• The tube should be flushed with 25–50 ml of water between feeds and after drug administration to prevent blockages. The frequency of flushes and the amount of water used will depend on frequency of feeds and whether medication is being given through the PEG.

Possible problems

• *Redness around the stoma:*
   – *Skin excoriation:* Is the fixation too tight or not being cleaned regularly? Is it too loose, causing leakage? This inflammation and reddened skin can be prevented by use of barrier creams. If the stoma site is leaking gastric contents, ensure that the fixation plate is in the correct position.
   – *Local infection:* Are you using good hygiene techniques? Infection occurs in 3–15% of cases, so a good hygiene technique is essential. Dressings may lead to moisture accumulation. Turning the tube daily prevents crusts forming and the development of scar tissue. If a local cellulitis is suspected (redness spreading well beyond the stoma), antibiotics should be given through the gastrostomy (usually flucloxacillin) and a wound swab should be taken for culture and sensitivity.
• *Tube blockage:* Why has it happened? Can it be reduced by regular flushing? Try flushing with a small diameter syringe to exert more pressure. If water does not clear the blockage, soda water or carbonised liquid may clear the tube. Pineapple juice contains a proteolytic enzyme which

can be used to digest a blockage caused by feeds. Regular use of cranberry juice can reduce blockages. Some drugs coagulate with feeds and cause blockage (e.g. antacids, carbamazepine, phenytoin) and they need to be well diluted (at least an equal volume of water) or given at least one hour separate from a feed.
• *Dislodged tube:* Has this been pulled too hard? If this is a new gastrostomy of 10 days or less, contact the team who inserted the tube. If the gastrostomy is well established then a urinary Foley catheter should be inserted in the first instance to keep the stoma patent until a replacement can be obtained.
• *Nausea and vomiting:* This may due to the infusion running too fast or volumes being too large. Some patients need a prokinetic (metoclopramide or domperidone) to encourage gastric emptying.
• *Chest infections:* These can be due to aspiration of feeds. There is no evidence that non-oral feeding reduces the risk of aspiration. Maintaining the head of the bed at a minimum of 30 degrees may help; and consider using metoclopramide to increase gastric emptying.

After-care

• Oral hygiene should not be overlooked. This can be avoided with good regular oral hygiene as a part of routine care.
• Ben should be weighed regularly, his weight recorded, intake recorded and a check made that the prescribed amount is given. All of these are less important once his cancer progresses.
• Ben's tube size and date of insertion and removal method should be recorded.

• Details for delivery of supplies and feed for Ben should be made available.
• Balloon-inflated tubes should be regularly checked (size varies 5–30 ml).
• Be innovative with volumes and schedules. NB: A flexible feeding regime constitutes a good quality of life.
• Stratton (2002) found that 83% of patients on home artificial nutrition still had a desire to eat.

WORK PAGE

MCQ Write down your answers to these questions:

1 A gastrostomy passes food directly to the stomach	True	False
2 PEG stands for percutaneous exterior gastrostomy	True	False
3 Insertion needs a general anaesthetic	True	False
4 A gastrostomy can be used long term	True	False
5 The risk of aspiration is lower with a gastrostomy	True	False

What can you do for the following problems?

Problem   **Your solution**

Redness around the stoma

. . . .

. . . .

Blocked tube

. . . .

. . . .

Dislodged tube

. . . .

. . . .

Vomiting after feeds

. . . .

. . . .

Increase in chest infections

. . . .

. . . .

Think Think about what after-care Ben will need.

. . . .

. . . .

FURTHER ACTIVITY

The next time you have a patient with a gastrostomy:

- list the advantages for that patient

- observe any problems the patient is having and consider ways of helping.

FURTHER READING

Journal articles

Arrowsmith H (1996) Nursing management of patients receiving gastrostomy feeding. *British Journal of Nursing.* **5**: 268–73.

Boyd KJ and Beeken L (1994) Tube feeding in palliative care: benefits and problems. *Palliative Medicine.* **8**: 156–8.

Campos ACL, Butters M and Meguid MM (1990) Home enteral nutrition via gastrostomy in advanced head and neck cancer patients. *Head and Neck.* **12**: 137–42.

Dwolatzky T, Berezovski S, Friedmann R *et al.* (2001) A prospective comparison of the use of nasogastric and percutaneous endoscopic gastrostomy tubes for long-term enteral feeding in older people. *Clinical Nutrition.* **20**(6): 535–40.

Gauderer MW (2002) Percutaneous endoscopic gastrostomy and the evolution of contemporary long-term enteral access. *Clinical Nutrition.* **21**(2): 103–10.

Goodhall L (1997) Tube feeding dilemmas: can artificial nutrition and hydration be legally or ethically withheld or withdrawn? *Journal of Advanced Nursing.* **25**: 217–22.

Howell M (2002) Do nurses know enough about percutaneous endoscopic gastrostomy? *Nursing Times.* **98**(17): 40–2.

Kimber CP and Beasley SW (1999) Limitations of percutaneous endoscopic gastrostomy in facilitating enteral nutrition in children: review of the shortcomings of a new technique. *Journal of Paediatric and Child Health.* **35**: 427–31.

Laing B, Smithers M and Harper J (1994) Percutaneous fluoroscopic gastrostomy: a safe option? *Medical Journal of Australia.* **161**: 308–10.

Larson D, Burton DD, Schroeder KW *et al.* (1987) Percutaneous endoscopic gastrostomy. Indicates success, complications and mortality in 314 consecutive patients. *Gastoenterology.* **93**: 48–52.

Mandal A, Steel A, Davidson AR *et al.* (2000) Day-case percutaneous endoscopic gastrostomy: a viable proposition? *Postgraduate Medical Journal.* **76**: 157–9.

Myssiorek D, Siegel D and Vambutas A (1998) Fluoroscopically placed gastrostomies in the head and neck patient. *Laryngoscope.* **108**: 1557–60.

Norton B, Homer-Ward M, Donelly MT *et al.* (1996) A randomised prospective comparison of percutaneous endoscopic gastrostomy and nasogastric tube feeding after dysphagic stroke. *BMJ.* **312**: 13–16.

Pennington C (2002) To PEG or not to PEG. *Clinical Medicine.* **2**(3): 250–5.

Raha S and Woodhouse K (1993) Who should have a PEG? *Age and Ageing.* **22**: 313–15.

Stratton R (2002) Use and benefits of enteral nutrition. *Primary Health Care.* **12**(2): 25–30.

White S (1998) Percutaneous endoscopic gastrostomy PEG. *Nursing Standard.* **12**: April 1–7.

HELPING THE PATIENT WITH REDUCED
HYDRATION AND NUTRITION

8 The cachexia syndrome

Claud Regnard
Margaret Kindlen

ADVANCED LEVEL

Aim of this worksheet

To consider the features and causes of the cachexia syndrome in advanced disease.

How to use this worksheet

- You can work through this worksheet by yourself, or with a tutor.

- Read the case study below, then work on the questions overleaf.

- The work page is on the right side, the information page is on the left.

- Work any way you want: you can try answering from your own knowledge (in which case, fold over the information page), you can use the information page (this is not cheating – you learn as you find the information) or you can use other sources of information.

- It should take you about 15 minutes. If anything is unclear, discuss it with a colleague.

- If you think any information is wrong or out of date, let us know.

- Use the activity on the back page and take this learning into your workplace.

Case study

Ben is a 33-year-old man who has a moderate learning disability together with hydro-cephalus, spastic diplegia, visual impairment and epilepsy. He is diagnosed as having a carcinoma of the kidney with lung metastases. Ben is usually well nourished, but in three months he has lost 11 kg in weight. He is refusing food and becoming less active.

INFORMATION PAGE

Description

1 T: Cachexia is a syndrome, i.e. a collection of signs and symptoms.
2 F: The weight loss is both fat and skeletal muscle – up to three-quarters of both can be lost.
3 T: Cachexia is seen in cancer patients (especially cancers of the stomach, pancreas and lung), but is also seen in AIDS, end-stage cardiac disease and chronic infection (e.g. tuberculosis), but not in neurological diseases.
4 F: Cachexia is not the same as starvation since apart from loss of fat, other processes are very different:

- up to 75% skeletal muscle breaks down (in starvation there is a reduction in protein breakdown)
- the liver increases in size (in starvation it reduces)
- lactate production produces non-productive energy cycles (in starvation glucose turnover reduces)
- resting energy use can be increased (it is reduced in starvation).

5 F: This process is not the result of the cancer competing for energy (cancers do not usually use up more than 1% of the body's energy needs).

Mechanism

- Cachexia is mediated by the body's own cytokines produced as part of a systemic inflammatory response (SIR) to the presence of cancer. Cytokines are low molecular weight proteins that integrate cell activity and over 100 are known.
- Some cytokines, such as tumour necrosis factor and interleukin 6, cause loss of appetite (anorexia), reduce the ability of the bowel to absorb nutrients, reduce the action of insulin and activate useless energy cycles.
- Additional chemicals such as proteolytic initiation factor and insulin growth factor encourage muscle loss.

The effects of cachexia on Ben

- *Loss of weight:* This is the most obvious outward sign and will be one cause of Ben's 11 kg loss in 3 months.
- *Weakness:* This is causing Ben's reduced mobility and is partly due to the dramatic loss of skeletal muscle.
- *Fatigue:* This means a loss of energy and adds to the problems of Ben's reduced mobility.
- *Pressure area damage:* The reduced mobility and less efficient healing mean that Ben is at increased risk.
- *Body image:* The sudden change in appearance is often distressing and Ben will be aware of the change.
- *Reduced survival:* Cancer patients with cachexia do not survive as long as cancer patients who do not have cachexia.

- *Breathlessness:* This is common in advanced cancer, even in the absence of any direct involvement of the lungs by cancer. The cause may be a combination of skeletal muscle loss and anaemia.
- *Reduced mobility:* This has many causes including muscle loss, inefficient use of energy, anaemia and breathlessness.
- *Anaemia:* This is probably a direct effect on the bone marrow causing fewer red cells to be produced.
- *Fever:* Effects on the hypothalamus can result in pyrexia with sweats.
- *Oedema:* This will further reduce Ben's mobility and make it difficult for him to wear shoes. Low pressure stockings can often help.

Treatment

Therapy for cachexia is in three areas:
1 *Support for the distress of cachexia:* This includes exploring body and sexual image, catering advice, coping strategies for fatigue and support for psychological adjustment disorders.
2 *Nutrition:* Although extra nutrition replaces deficiencies and may partly restore body image through fat deposition, it does not usually reverse cachexia. In particular, loss of skeletal muscle is not reversed. Even total parenteral nutrition results in more weight by putting on fat, but no increase in muscle strength, which can make the situation worse.
3 *Appetite stimulants:* Corticosteroids (e.g. dexamethasone, prednisolone) are commonly used but have a limited action of 4 weeks and can have troublesome long-term adverse effects (proximal muscle weakness, increase in blood glucose, reduced healing, suppressed immunity to infection). However, corticosteroids have the advantage of inducing a sense of well-being and do improve the quality of life for many patients. Megestrol acetate is effective in doses of 800 mg/day but is expensive and can cause troublesome fluid retention. Cyproheptidine and hydrazine sulphate have been shown to be no better than placebo – hydrazine may actually reduce survival.
4 *See also* CLIP worksheets *Enriching and fortifying the diet* and *Maintaining the environment for eating and drinking.*
5 *Blocking/inhibiting cytokines and SIR:* NSAIDs such as ibuprofen have been shown to have a modest ability to inhibit cachexia. A possible alternative is the use of eicosapentaenoic acid (EPA), a fatty acid derived from fish oil. Given in doses of 2–6 g/day together with 600 calories it is capable of reversing weight loss in cachectic pancreatic cancer patients, and can increase their survival. Concentrated omega-3 fish oils are available from chemists and contain up to 30% EPA.

In the future, it is possible that the cachexia process may prove to be as important a target as tumour growth.

WORK PAGE

MCQ Which of the following statements about cachexia are true and which are false?

Features are loss of appetite, weight loss, fatigue, anaemia and oedema	True	False
Loss of fat is the main cause of weight loss	True	False
Cachexia can occur in patients with severe heart disease	True	False
Most of its effects are due to starvation	True	False
The cancer competes with the body for energy	True	False

Think Think about how cachexia could affect Ben.

. . . .

. . . .

. . . .

Think Think about what you can do to help Ben.

- Psychological support

. . . .

. . . .

. . . .

- Nutrition

. . . .

. . . .

. . . .

- Stimulating the appetite

. . . .

. . . .

. . . .

FURTHER ACTIVITY

For a patient with weight loss due to cancer, AIDS or end-stage cardiac disease:

- What features of the cachexia syndrome are present?

- What effect is reduced mobility and loss of body image having on the patient?

FURTHER READING

Journal articles

Anker S and Sharma R (2002) The syndrome of cardiac cachexia. *International Journal of Cardiology*. 85(1): 51.

Barber MD, Ross JA and Fearon KC (1999) Cancer cachexia. *Surgical Oncology*. 8(3): 133–41.

Barber MD, Fearon KC, Tisdale MJ *et al.* (2001) Effect of a fish oil-enriched nutritional supplement on metabolic mediators in patients with pancreatic cancer cachexia. *Nutrition and Cancer*. 40(2): 118–24.

Berry C and Clark AL (2000) Catabolism in chronic heart failure. *European Heart Journal*. 21(7): 521–32.

Brown JK (2002) A systematic review of the evidence on symptom management of cancer-related anorexia and cachexia. *Oncology Nursing Forum*. 29(3): 517–32.

Fearon K and Moses A (2002) Cancer cachexia. *International Journal of Cardiology*. 85(1): 73.

Fearon KC, Barber MD and Moses AG (2001) The cancer cachexia syndrome. *Surgical Oncology Clinics of North America*. 10(1): 109–26.

Lundholm K, Gelin J, Hytlander A *et al.* (1994) Anti-inflammatory treatment may prolong survival in undernourished patients with metastatic solid tumours. *Cancer Research*. 54: 5602–6.

Macmillan DC, Wigmore SJ, Fearon KCH *et al.* (1999) A prospective randomised study of megestrol acetate and ibuprofen in gastrointestinal cancer patients with weight loss. *British Journal of Cancer*. 79: 495–500.

Mantovani G (2000) Cachexia and anorexia. *Supportive Care in Cancer*. 8(6): 506–9.

Nelson KA (2000) Modern management of the cancer anorexia-cachexia syndrome. *Current Oncology Reports*. 2(4): 362–8.

O'Gorman P, McMillan DC and McArdle CS (1998) Impact of weight loss, appetite and the inflammatory response on quality of life in gastrointestinal cancer patients. *Nutrition and Cancer*. 32: 76–80.

Plauth M and Schutz E (2002) Cachexia in liver cirrhosis. *International Journal of Cardiology*. 85(1): 83.

Schols A (2002) Pulmonary cachexia. *International Journal of Cardiology*. 85(1): 101.

Strasser F and Bruera ED (2002) Update on anorexia and cachexia. *Hematology – Oncology Clinics of North America*. 16(3): 589–617.

Tisdale MJ (2000) Metabolic abnormalities in cachexia and anorexia. *Nutrition*. 16(10): 1013–14.

Walsmith J and Roubenoff R (2002) Cachexia in rheumatoid arthritis. *International Journal of Cardiology*. 85(1): 89.

PROCEDURES IN PALLIATIVE CARE

1 Setting up a Graseby syringe driver

Claud Regnard
Margaret Kindlen
Sarah Alport

INTERMEDIATE LEVEL

Aim of this worksheet

To understand how to set up a Graseby syringe driver.

How to use this worksheet

- You can work through this worksheet by yourself, or with a tutor.

- Read the case study below, then work on the questions overleaf.

- The work page is on the right side, the information page is on the left.

- Work any way you want: you can try answering from your own knowledge (in which case, fold over the information page), you can use the information page (this is not cheating – you learn as you find the information) or you can use other sources of information.

- It should take you about 15 minutes. If anything is unclear, discuss it with a colleague.

- If you think any information is wrong or out of date, let us know.

- Use the activity on the back page and take this learning into your workplace.

Case study

Mary is a 28-year-old woman, married, with two small children. Six months ago, she was found to have an advanced cancer of the cervix and was treated with pelvic radiotherapy and started chemotherapy. Her pain responded to morphine, but she has now been admitted with nausea and vomiting. It is decided to give her drugs as a 24-hour subcutaneous infusion through a Graseby syringe driver.

INFORMATION PAGE

The Graseby syringe driver

1 F: There are two syringe drivers:
   * the MS26, which is calibrated in mm per day and used most commonly in palliative care
   * the MS16, calibrated in mm per hour and used when rapid infusions are needed.
2 F: The boost button on the MS26 moves the plunger forward by 0.23 mm after a single activation. With a 10 ml syringe it would take more than 30 boosts to come close to a four-hourly dose. Therefore the boost button is totally unsuitable for 'top up' medication in palliative care.
3 F: Both syringe drivers can take a range of syringe sizes: 5 ml, 10 ml, 20 ml, 30 ml. The most commonly used size is 10 ml. Some 30 ml syringes will fit but are best avoided because of their bulk.
4 T: The reason you can use different sized syringes of any make is that the drivers are calibrated using the distance that the syringe plunger travels, not volume. If the measured distance was 48 mm and 24 was dialled up this would make *half* the syringe run through in 24 hours on a MS26 (i.e. the *whole* syringe will run through in 2 days). On an MS16 *half* the contents would run through in 1 hour (i.e. the *whole* syringe will run through in 2 hours). Whatever you dial up is the distance the plunger will travel in one day for the MS26 and 1 hour for the MS16.
5 T: Plastic IV cannulae are better tolerated and last longer than metal butterfly needles. Plastic cannula also significantly reduce the risk of needle-stick injuries to staff. Ideally use plastic IV cannulae without a side port, e.g. Insyte. The cannula and infusion site are often covered with OpSite or similar.
6 F: The syringe drivers are not even drip-proof and are vulnerable to any water dropped on them – they certainly won't survive long in a shower!

Syringe driver medication

Diamorphine is the opioid of choice in this situation. Since it is three times more potent than oral morphine, the correct dose would be one third of her present daily oral morphine dose, i.e. 20 mg diamorphine in 24 hours.

Her cyclizine can be continued at the same dose, i.e. 75 mg in 24 hours.

The laxative can be stopped until the vomiting stops.

Of the drugs that could be used in palliative care, three cause too much local irritation to be used: chlorpromazine, diazepam and prochlorperazine. Cyclizine and levomepromazine (methotrimeprazine) cause some irritation in some patients.

Many other drugs have been shown that they can be safely and effectively given by the subcutaneous infusion route: cyclizine, dexamethasone, haloperidol, hyoscine butylbromide, hyoscine hydrobromide, ketamine, midazolam, metoclopramide and octreotide.

Setting up the syringe driver

There are several issues to think about:

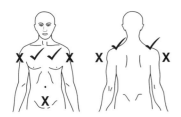

* *Infusion site:* ideally the site needs to be one that does not move too much and that patients can avoid lying on. This excludes the abdomen and the upper arms ✗. The best sites are the upper chest for drugs and upper back for hydration ✓ (for the upper back, use a site above the spine of the scapula).
* *What connector?* Ideally this should have a small filling volume, but this is not essential.
* *Should I use a filter?* There is no evidence that filters reduce infection or prevent site irritation.

Setting the rate

This causes people the most worry. In reality it is easy:

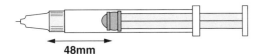

48mm

1 Measure the distance the syringe plunger has to travel (in mm).
2 Dial this amount on the syringe driver (if it's 48 mm, dial 48).
3 Fill the connecting tubing (i.e. do this *after* measuring the syringe).*
4 The first syringe will run through 1–2 hours early, but subsequent syringes will run on time.
5 Switch on the pump by inserting the battery (an alarm will sound) and pressing the boost button once.

*Some teams advocate filling the tubing before measuring, but this means the rate has to be reset the next day with the risk of an additional error being made.

WORK PAGE

MCQ

1 The Graseby MS26 is calibrated in mm per hour   T   F

2 The boost button on the MS26 is a useful way for patients to 'top up' their   T   F
medication

3 The syringe volume must not be more than 10 ml   T   F

4 You measure the plunger travel as 48 mm; dialling up 24 on an MS26 ensures the   T   F
contents will take 2 days to run through

5 The use of IV plastic cannulae inserted subcutaneously reduces local reactions   T   F

6 The syringe drivers are shower proof   T   F

Before she started vomiting Mary was taking:

- morphine as MXL 60 mg once daily

- co-danthrusate twice daily

- cyclizine 25 mg 8-hourly.

What changes would you make to Mary's medication when you change to a syringe driver?

. . . .

. . . .

. . . .

Think   Think about the following:

- What helps to decide a good site for the needle?

- Does the length and diameter of the connecting tube matter?

- What about a filter?

Ring the correct answers to the following:

- When I measure the syringe I have to measure:

     The whole syringe   The plunger   The distance the plunger has to travel

- I should fill up the connecting tubing:

         Before I measure the syringe   After I measure the syringe

FURTHER ACTIVITY

Look at a chart for a Graseby syringe driver and work out how the rate was calculated.

FURTHER READING

Journal articles

Bruera E, Neumann CM, Pituskin E *et al.* (1999) A randomized controlled trial of local injections of hyaluronidase versus placebo in cancer patients receiving subcutaneous hydration. *Annals of Oncology.* 10(10): 1255–8.

Donnelly M (1999) The benefits of hypodermoclysis. *Nursing Standard.* 13(52): 44–5.

Frisoli A Jr, de Paula AP, Feldman D *et al.* (2000) Subcutaneous hydration by hypodermoclysis. A practical and low cost treatment for elderly patients. *Drugs and Aging.* 16(4): 313–19.

Fudin J, Smith HS, Toledo-Binette CS *et al.* (2000) Use of continuous ambulatory infusions of concentrated subcutaneous (s.q.) hydromorphone versus intravenous (i.v.) morphine: cost implications for palliative care. *American Journal of Hospice and Palliative Care.* 17(5): 347–53.

Hunt R, Fazekas B, Thorne D *et al.* (1999) A comparison of subcutaneous morphine and fentanyl in hospice cancer patients. *Journal of Pain and Symptom Management.* 18(2): 111–19.

Jain S, Mansfield B and Wilcox MH (1999) Subcutaneous fluid administration – better than the intravenous approach? *Journal of Hospital Infection.* 41(4): 269–72.

Negro S, Azuara ML, Sanchez Y *et al.* (2002) Physical compatibility and in vivo evaluation of drug mixtures for subcutaneous infusion to cancer patients in palliative care. *Supportive Care in Cancer.* 10(1): 65–70.

Nelson KA, Glare PA, Walsh D *et al.* (1997) A prospective, within-patient, crossover study of continuous intravenous and subcutaneous morphine for chronic cancer pain. *Journal of Pain and Symptom Management.* 13(5): 262–7.

O'Doherty CA, Hall EJ, Schofield L *et al.* (2001) Drugs and syringe drivers: a survey of adult specialist palliative care practice in the United Kingdom and Eire. *Palliative Medicine.* 15(2): 149–54.

Ross JR, Saunders Y, Cochrane M *et al.* (2002) A prospective, within-patient comparison between metal butterfly needles and Teflon cannulae in subcutaneous infusion of drugs to terminally ill hospice patients. *Palliative Medicine.* 16(1): 13–16.

Torre MC (2002) Subcutaneous infusion: non-metal cannulae vs metal butterfly needles. *British Journal of Community Nursing.* 7(7): 365–9.

Resource books and website

Calman K, Doyle D and Hanks GWC (eds) (2003) *The Oxford Textbook of Palliative Medicine* (3e). Oxford University Publications, Oxford.

Regnard C and Hockley J (2004) *A Guide to Symptom Relief in Palliative Care* (5e). Radcliffe Medical Press, Oxford.

Twycross RG and Wilcock A (2001) *Symptom Management in Advanced Cancer* (3e). Radcliffe Medical Press, Oxford.

www.palliativedrugs.com – Updated website for the *Palliative Care Formulary.*

PROCEDURES IN PALLIATIVE CARE

2 Problems with a subcutaneous infusion

Claud Regnard
Margaret Kindlen
Sarah Alport

INTERMEDIATE LEVEL

Aim of this worksheet

To understand how to sort out problems with a subcutaneous infusion.

How to use this worksheet

- You can work through this worksheet by yourself, or with a tutor.

- Read the case study below, then work on the questions overleaf.

- The work page is on the right side, the information page is on the left.

- Work any way you want: you can try answering from your own knowledge (in which case, fold over the information page), you can use the information page (this is not cheating – you learn as you find the information) or you can use other sources of information.

- It should take you about 15 minutes. If anything is unclear, discuss it with a colleague.

- If you think any information is wrong or out of date, let us know.

- Use the activity on the back page and take this learning into your workplace.

Case study

Mary is a 28-year-old woman, married, with two small children. Six months ago, she was found to have an advanced cancer of the cervix and was treated with pelvic radiotherapy and started chemotherapy. Her pain responded to oral morphine, but because she was troubled with nausea and vomiting it was decided to give her drugs as a 24-hour subcutaneous infusion through a Graseby syringe driver. The infusion has been running well for the past three days, but today her pain and nausea have returned.

INFORMATION PAGE

Types of subcutaneous (SC) infusion

- *Drug infusions:* These use Graseby syringe drivers to deliver drugs. The infusions usually last 24 hours (using Graseby MS26 pumps), but occasionally are done over 1–4 hours (using Graseby MS16 pumps). *See* CLIP worksheet on *Setting up a Graseby syringe driver.*

- *SC hydration (hypodermoclysis):* This infuses up to 2 litres/24 hours of rehydration fluids. No pumps are used, only gravity. *See* CLIP worksheet *Using non-oral routes.*

Problems with syringe drivers

The best way is to start at the pump and think through the possible problems:

- *Pump:* Rundown batteries (action: replace); pump switched off due to back pressure caused by blockage (action: clear the blockage by checking connecting tubing and cannula as below); pump failure – a rare cause (action: replace pump).

- *Syringe:* This may have become dislodged (action: put back in position).
- *Connecting tubing:* This may leak (a break or disconnection) or may have become blocked (due a kink or drug precipitation) (action: reconnect or replace tubing).
- *Cannula:* This can become blocked through blood, or because of drug precipitation (action: replace the cannula).

Problems with subcutaneous sites

Several problems can occur:

- *Inflammation:* This is usually due to drug irritation (chlorpromazine, diazepam and prochlorperazine should never be used subcutaneously because of severe irritation). Metal butterfly needles are more likely to cause local irritation than plastic cannula (action: change to a new site, consider changing to a plastic cannula).
- *Infection:* This is unusual but is likely if there is a clear area of spreading cellulitis around the infusion (action: change to a new site; the infection may need systemic flucloxacillin).
- *Leakage of drug from the infusion site:* This can happen with older sites (7 days or more) even in the absence of inflammation (action: change to a new site).

- *Bleeding from the infusion site*: This can occur on insertion but stops within minutes. If it persists this may be due to a coagulation disorder (action: if bleeding stops within minutes of insertion, flush cannula with 1 ml 0.9% saline, then start infusion; if bleeding persists or starts in an established site, exclude a coagulation disorder and consider alternative routes of drug administration).
- *Swelling:* This is common in subcutaneous infusions and a mild swelling only needs observation. Infusions for hydration can cause uncomfortable swelling if the wrong sites are used such as the thigh or upper chest. The upper back is the best site for large volumes (action: observe if mild, otherwise change site).

Problems with drugs

- *Licensed and unlicensed use:* Diamorphine, hyoscine hydrobromide and levomepromazine (methotrimeprazine) are the only drugs licensed for subcutaneous administration. However 'licensed' means a licence for marketing. It is now accepted in the UK that it is acceptable to use unlicensed routes or purposes *if* there is documented evidence that this is an acceptable and safe practice.

  There is now extensive experience of using the following drugs safely by the SC route: cyclizine, dexamethasone, insulin, erythropoietin, haloperidol, heparin, hydromorphone, hyoscine butylbromide, hyoscine hydrobromide, levomepromazine, midazolam, metoclopramide and octreotide.

  Experience is growing in the use of other drugs by the SC route such as fentanyl, ketamine and oxycodone.

- *Drug incompatibility:* If this results in precipitation, then this can cause blockage. This may be seen as a cloudiness in the syringe, or small crystals on the walls of the syringe. Most of the drugs used in syringe drivers are compatible with each other. The main exception is cyclizine which is incompatible with many drugs.

  However, the absence of precipitation does not mean that drugs are compatible and if possible it is best to limit the number of drugs in a syringe to two. Other drugs can be given by other routes (e.g. PR) or those that are long-acting can be give once daily (e.g. haloperidol or levomepromazine).

  See www.palliativedrugs.com for current compatibility data.

WORK PAGE

Think What should you check and what would you do about it? (Hint: start at the skin.)

Area to check	Possible problem(s)	Action
Pump		
Syringe		
Connecting tubing		
Cannula		
Skin		

Think What drugs are suitable for subcutaneous administration? (Ring) those drugs that *should not* be used subcutaneously

chlorpromazine	diamorphine	haloperidol
hyoscine butylbromide	hyoscine hydrobromide	metoclopramide
cyclizine	prochlorperazine	midazolam
levomepromazine	dexamethasone	diazepam

Only *three* of these drugs are licensed for subcutaneous infusion. Underline these three drugs.

Mary becomes much more settled on her syringe driver. You are called one evening, however, because her pain and nausea have returned once more and the nurse has noticed a cloudiness to the syringe contents.

Q: What do you think has happened?

. . . .

. . . .

. . . .

FURTHER ACTIVITY

Look at each part of a subcutaneous infusion on a patient.

• What problems could occur?

FURTHER READING

Journal articles

Bruera E, Neumann CM, Pituskin E *et al.* (1999) A randomized controlled trial of local injections of hyaluronidase versus placebo in cancer patients receiving subcutaneous hydration. *Annals of Oncology.* 10(10): 1255–8.

Donnelly M (1999) The benefits of hypodermoclysis. *Nursing Standard.* 13(52): 44–5.

Frisoli A Jr, de Paula AP, Feldman D *et al.* (2000) Subcutaneous hydration by hypodermoclysis. A practical and low cost treatment for elderly patients. *Drugs and Aging.* 16(4): 313–19.

Fudin J, Smith HS, Toledo-Binette CS *et al.* (2000) Use of continuous ambulatory infusions of concentrated subcutaneous (s.q.) hydromorphone versus intravenous (i.v.) morphine: cost implications for palliative care. *American Journal of Hospice and Palliative Care.* 17(5): 347–53.

Hunt R, Fazekas B, Thorne D *et al.* (1999) A comparison of subcutaneous morphine and fentanyl in hospice cancer patients. *Journal of Pain and Symptom Management.* 18(2): 111–19.

Jain S, Mansfield B and Wilcox MH (1999) Subcutaneous fluid administration – better than the intravenous approach? *Journal of Hospital Infection.* 41(4): 269–72.

Negro S, Azuara ML, Sanchez Y *et al.* (2002) Physical compatibility and in vivo evaluation of drug mixtures for subcutaneous infusion to cancer patients in palliative care. *Supportive Care in Cancer.* 10(1): 65–70.

Nelson KA, Glare PA, Walsh D *et al.* (1997) A prospective, within-patient, crossover study of continuous intravenous and subcutaneous morphine for chronic cancer pain. *Journal of Pain and Symptom Management.* 13(5): 262–7.

O'Doherty CA, Hall EJ, Schofield L *et al.* (2001) Drugs and syringe drivers: a survey of adult specialist palliative care practice in the United Kingdom and Eire. *Palliative Medicine.* 15(2): 149–54.

Ross JR, Saunders Y, Cochrane M *et al.* (2002) A prospective, within-patient comparison between metal butterfly needles and Teflon cannulae in subcutaneous infusion of drugs to terminally ill hospice patients. *Palliative Medicine.* 16(1): 13–16.

Torre MC (2002) Subcutaneous infusion: non-metal cannulae vs metal butterfly needles. *British Journal of Community Nursing.* 7(7): 365–9.

Resource books and website

Calman K, Doyle D and Hanks GWC (eds) (2003) *The Oxford Textbook of Palliative Medicine* (3e). Oxford University Publications, Oxford.

Regnard C and Hockley J (2004) *A Guide to Symptom Relief in Palliative Care* (5e). Radcliffe Medical Press, Oxford.

Twycross RG and Wilcock A (2001) *Symptom Management in Advanced Cancer* (3e). Radcliffe Medical Press, Oxford.

www.palliativedrugs.com – Updated website for the *Palliative Care Formulary.*

PROCEDURES IN PALLIATIVE CARE

3 Spinal analgesia: problems with two drugs

Claud Regnard
Margaret Kindlen

ADVANCED LEVEL

Aim of this worksheet

To recognise and manage the adverse effects of spinal diamorphine and bupivacaine.

How to use this worksheet

- You can work through this worksheet by yourself, or with a tutor.

- Read the case study below, then work on the questions overleaf.

- The work page is on the right side, the information page is on the left.

- Work any way you want: you can try answering from your own knowledge (in which case, fold over the information page), you can use the information page (this is not cheating – you learn as you find the information) or you can use other sources of information.

- It should take you about 15 minutes. If anything is unclear, discuss it with a colleague.

- If you think any information is wrong or out of date, let us know.

- Use the activity on the back page and take this learning into your workplace.

Case study

Mary is a 28-year-old woman, married, with two small children. Six months ago, she was found to have an advanced cancer of the cervix and was treated with pelvic radiotherapy and started chemotherapy. Despite this, the tumour has persisted and she is now troubled with a bearing down pain in her perineum, and a burning pain in both legs. Her pains have been diagnosed as being a tenesmus pain and a neuropathic pain. The pain has been severe for the past few weeks and has not responded to increasing doses of morphine, anticonvulsants, antidepressants or ketamine. She has had an intrathecal line inserted.

INFORMATION PAGE

The effects of diamorphine and bupivacaine

- *Sensory block:* This is not meant to be a catch but you could have ticked both boxes:
  - You would expect a local anaesthetic to have this effect (remember trying to have a cup of tea after going to the dentist!). It will also block pain and temperature sensation.
  - Diamorphine will block the sensation of some types of pain, but not the other sensations.
- *Muscle paralysis:* Only bupivacaine will do this.
- *Low blood pressure:* Bupivacaine does this by blocking the sympathetic nerves, causing blood vessels to dilate which drops the blood pressure. Diamorphine does not have this effect.
- *Respiratory depression:* Both drugs can cause this but by different mechanisms:
  - diamorphine depresses respiration by an effect on the respiratory centre (= central effect)
  - bupivacaine will do this *if* the drug reaches high enough to the block nerve supply to the respiratory muscles (= peripheral effect). This is an emergency since the patient will require ventilation
  - unopposed action of systemic opioid. This can occur if pain relief is sudden. Therefore the usual practice is to reduce the systemic opioid dose by 30–50% before starting spinal analgesia.
- *Urinary retention:* Both can cause this, although the mechanism for diamorphine is unclear.

- *Constipation:* Only diamorphine can do this, and it seems to be a systemic effect, although it is unusual with intrathecal diamorphine because of the very low doses used, e.g. 5 mg/24 hours.
- *Itching:* This is an unusual effect of diamorphine caused by histamine release.
- *Nausea:* This seems to be a central effect of diamorphine.
- *Small pupils:* Both drugs can produce this:
  - it is a direct effect of diamorphine
  - bupivacaine does it by blocking the sympathetic nerves (which normally widen the pupils).
- *Red face:* This is another sympathetic blocking action of bupivacaine.
- *Increased heart rate:* This can occur with lowered blood pressure due to bupivacaine.
- *Slow heart rate:* This is seen in epidural administrations if the bupivacaine has been injected into a blood vessel in the epidural space – the effect is due to a direct effect on the heart. This is very unusual with intrathecal spinals.
- *Convulsions:* Caused by blood injection of bupivacaine, or due to the accumulation of epidural doses of bupivacaine. It is not seen in continuous intrathecal infusions.
- *Antibacterial:* Surprisingly, some work in Sweden has shown that bupivacaine is itself antibacterial, thereby reducing the risk of infection if it is used. Diamorphine does not have this effect.

Side effects of diamorphine and bupivacaine

- *My arms have gone weak:* Emergency. Suggests the bupivacaine has reached C6 – breathing will stop very quickly and immediate resuscitation will be needed (Ambu bag, intubation, O$_2$ and IV line).
- *I feel faint:* Urgent. Suggests the BP is dropping. Will need an IV line of 0.9% saline. Ephedrine 30 mg may be needed IV if BP is very low (systolic < 80 mmHg).
- *I'm desperate for a wee:* Soon. Suggests urinary retention and Mary may need a catheter.
- *I feel awful:* Urgent. There may be many reasons for this complaint. Low BP is one. An unusual cause is bupivacaine toxicity (much more common with epidurals) with the risk of convulsions. Close monitoring is required.
- *Nurse – I can't wake Mary:* Emergency. The cause may be

either respiratory depression or severe hypotension. If respiratory depression is caused by the morphine, IV naloxone will be required (400 microg diluted to 10 ml, given slowly IV, then by infusion).

- *I hate this numbness in my legs:* Soon. Numbness due to bupivacaine is uncommon if there is no previous nerve damage. If previous treatment or tumour has damaged nerves, numbness and weakness can occur at quite low doses of bupivacaine (e.g. 6 ml 0.25% per 24 hours intrathecal). The bupivacaine can be reduced and the diamorphine increased, or other drugs added such as clonidine. Sometimes pain relief can only be achieved at the expense of some numbness or weakness – not every patient is able to accept this.

WORK PAGE

Diamorphine is used rather than morphine because, in the UK, it is widely available in a form that is free of preservatives or additives (morphine is available in this form, but is not commonly stocked in the UK). The commonest drugs to use are diamorphine and bupivacaine, often together. They are compatible.

 Below are a number of effects of diamorphine or bupivacaine. If you think a particular effect is due to diamorphine, put a ✓ in the diamorphine box, if not put a ✗. Do the same for bupivacaine.

Effects	Diamorphine	Bupivacaine	Effects	Diamorphine	Bupivacaine
Sensory block	☐	☐	Nausea	☐	☐
Muscle paralysis	☐	☐	Small pupils	☐	☐
Low blood pressure	☐	☐	Red face	☐	☐
Respiratory depression	☐	☐	Raised heart rate	☐	☐
Urinary retention	☐	☐	Slow heart rate	☐	☐
Constipation	☐	☐	Convulsions	☐	☐
Itching	☐	☐	Antibacterial	☐	☐

Discuss With a colleague, discuss the treatment of the following problems Mary might complain of:

Mary's problem	Is urgent action needed? Emergency, Urgent or Soon?	What should you do?
'My arms have gone weak'		
'I feel faint'		
'I'm desperate for a wee'		
'I feel awful'		
'Nurse – I can't wake Mary'		
'I hate this numbness in my legs'		

FURTHER ACTIVITY

What observations would you make before starting a spinal line?

FURTHER READING

Journal articles

Anderson P (1991) Intrathecal narcotics for the relief of pain from head and neck cancer. *Archives of Otolaryngological Head Neck Surgeons.* **117**: 1277–80.

Burton M (1990) Long-term pain relief produced by intrathecal morphine infusion in 53 patients. *Journal of Neurosurgery.* **72**: 200–9.

Crul B and Delhaas E (1991) Technical complications during long term subarachnoid or epidural administration of morphine in terminally ill cancer patients: a review of 140 cases. *Regional Anaesthesia.* **16**: 209–13.

Dahm P, Nitescu P, Appelgren L *et al.* (1998) Efficacy and technical complications of long-term continuous intraspinal infusions of opioid and/or bupivacaine in refractory nonmalignant pain: a comparison between the epidural and the intrathecal approach with externalized or implanted catheters and infusion pumps. *Clinical Journal of Pain.* **14**(1): 4–16.

Day R (2001) The use of epidural and intrathecal analgesia in palliative care. *International Journal of Palliative Nursing.* **7**(8): 369–74.

Gesten Y and Vainio A (1997) Long term intrathecal infusion of morphine in home care of patients with advanced cancer. *Acta Anaethesiology Scandanavica.* **47**: 12–17.

Gustaffson L (1988) Clinical experience of long term treatment with epidural and intrathecal opioids – a nationwide survey. *Acta Analgesia Scandanavica.* **32**: 253–9.

Krames ES (1993) Intrathecal infusional therapies for intractable pain patient management guidelines. *Journal of Pain and Symptom Management.* **8**: 36–46.

Krames E and Gershow J (1985) Continuous infusion of spinally administered narcotics for the relief of pain due to malignant disorders. *Cancer.* **56**: 696–702.

Lema MJ (2001) Invasive analgesia techniques for advanced cancer pain. *Surgical Oncology Clinics of North America.* **10**(1): 127–36.

Mercadante S (1998) Controversies over spinal treatment in advanced cancer patients. *Supportive Care in Cancer.* **6**(6): 495–502.

Mercadante S (1999) Problems of long-term spinal opioid treatment in advanced cancer patients. *Pain.* **79**(1): 1–13.

Nitescu P, Appelgren L, Linder LE *et al.* (1990) Epidural versus intrathecal morphine-bupivacaine: assessment of consecutive treatments in advanced cancer pain. *Journal of Pain and Symptom Management.* **5**(1): 18–26.

Nitescu P, Appelgren L, Hultman E *et al.* (1991) Long-term, open catheterization of the spinal subarachnoid space for continuous infusion of narcotic and bupivacaine in patients with 'refractory' cancer pain. A technique of catheterization and its problems and complications. *Clinical Journal of Pain.* **7**(2): 143–61.

Nitescu P, Sjoberg M, Appelgren L *et al.* (1995) Complications of intrathecal opioids and bupivacaine in the treatment of 'refractory' cancer pain. *Clinical Journal of Pain.* **11**(1): 45–62.

Sjoberg M, Appelgren L, Einarsson S *et al.* (1991) Long-term intrathecal morphine and bupivacaine in 'refractory' cancer pain. I. Results from the first series of 52 patients. *Acta Anaesthesiologica Scandinavica.* **35**(1): 30–43.

Sjoberg M, Karlsson PA, Nordborg C *et al.* (1992) Neuropathologic findings after long-term intrathecal infusion of morphine and bupivacaine for pain treatment in cancer patients. *Anesthesiology.* **76**(2): 173–86.

Sjoberg M, Nitescu P, Appelgren L *et al.* (1994) Long-term intrathecal morphine and bupivacaine in patients with refractory cancer pain. Results from a morphine:bupivacaine dose regimen of 0.5:4.75 mg/ml. *Anesthesiology.* **80**(2): 284–97.

Tumber PS and Fitzgibbon DR (1998) The control of severe cancer pain by continuous intrathecal infusion and patient controlled intrathecal analgesia with morphine, bupivacaine and clonidine. *Pain.* **78**(3): 217–20.

van Dongen RT, Crul BJ and van Egmond J (1999) Intrathecal coadministration of bupivacaine diminishes morphine dose progression during long-term intrathecal infusion in cancer patients. *Clinical Journal of Pain.* **15**(3): 166–72.

Resource book

Calman K, Doyle D and Hanks GWC (eds) (2003) *The Oxford Textbook of Palliative Medicine* (3e). Oxford University Publications, Oxford.

PROCEDURES IN PALLIATIVE CARE

4 Spinal analgesia: problems with the line

Claud Regnard
Margaret Kindlen
Sarah Alport

ADVANCED LEVEL

Aim of this worksheet

To recognise and manage the problems of spinal lines.

How to use this worksheet

- You can work through this worksheet by yourself, or with a tutor.

- Read the case study below, then work on the questions overleaf.

- The work page is on the right side, the information page is on the left.

- Work any way you want: you can try answering from your own knowledge (in which case, fold over the information page), you can use the information page (this is not cheating – you learn as you find the information) or you can use other sources of information.

- It should take you about 15 minutes. If anything is unclear, discuss it with a colleague.

- If you think any information is wrong or out of date, let us know.

- Use the activity on the back page and take this learning into your workplace.

Case study

Mary is a 28-year-old woman, married, with two small children. Six months ago, she was found to have an advanced cancer of the cervix and was treated with pelvic radiotherapy and started chemotherapy. Despite this, the tumour has persisted and she is now troubled with a bearing down pain in her perineum, and a burning pain in both legs. Her pains have been diagnosed as being a tenesmus pain and a neuropathic pain. The pain has been severe for the past few weeks and has not responded to increasing doses of morphine, anticonvulsants, antidepressants or ketamine. She has had an intrathecal line inserted which worked initially, but now the pain has returned.

INFORMATION PAGE

The pain worsens whilst on the intrathecal spinal line

Such a situation seems difficult at first because spinal analgesia is more complex than most analgesia and sorting out this problem seems daunting. In fact there are only a few possibilities. Start at the end of the line furthest away from the patient:

- *Pump:*
  - *If this is working* then has the syringe become dislodged?
  - *If the pump has stopped* then check the battery. Occasionally the pump stops because the line is blocked – remember this for later.
- *Filters:*
  - *Is there air in the filters?* This can slow the flow – remove the filter and fill with the spinal drug.
  - *Is the screw fitting cracked?* Filter connections crack very easily and then leak: replace.
- *Connecting line:*
  - *Is the line kinked?* Straighten.
  - *Is a connector leaking?* Replace the leaking joint.
- *Spinal hub:*
  - This joins the very narrow spinal line to the much bigger connecting line. The connection is made by a screw fitting which tightens onto, and grips, the spinal line. Occasionally this loosens and results in leakage. Overtightening will block the line.

- *Spinal line:*
  - *Is the line displaced?* Occasionally the line comes out of the intrathecal space and the efficacy of the analgesics drops either because they are now entering the epidural space or, more likely, they are going into subcutaneous tissues. This can be checked by trying to withdraw CSF. Disconnect the connecting line, leaving one bacterial filter and draw on the syringe – with modest suction you can withdraw 1 ml (discard this), then withdraw a further 1.5 ml. To check this is CSF, check it for sugar content with a urine test stick (CSF has a little sugar, whilst spinal line contents do not).
  - *Is the line blocked?* This is unusual, but the commonest cause is that the line has become kinked in the subcutaneous tissues. This sometimes happens in more mobile or active patients. Ask the person who inserted the line to review the patient.
- *Other possibilities:* There may be a new pain which is outside the area being affected by the spinal line. Alternatively, tolerance may have occurred to bupivacaine, but this usually is seen when bupivacaine is used on its own. In epidural lines, other possibilities are that the line tip is in a vein or is blocked by local fibrosis.

Infection and spinal lines

MCQ answers:

1 T: It has activity against a range of bacteria and fungi.
2 F: Since you are using bacterial filters and bupivacaine is antimicrobial, the injected solution is the least likely route of entry for infection. Because spinal analgesia involves infusing drugs close to, or into, the intrathecal space, there is an understandable fear of meningitis with intrathecals, and epidural abscess with epidural lines. With intrathecal lines the infection rate is less than 5% and deaths from meningitis are rare.
3 F: The exit site is much more of a risk as the bacteria can travel along the spinal line tract. Since the line is inert it should produce no skin reaction – therefore *any* redness is an indication of local infection and would be an indication for antibiotics in the presence of pyrexia. The exit site should be checked regularly (at least weekly) and sprayed with povidone iodine powder.

4 F: Serious intraspinal infection is unusual, even when the patient has an existing source of infection. There is a higher risk in severely immunocompromised patients such as AIDS patients in whom a spinal line would pose a higher risk.
5 T: The filters are guaranteed by the manufacturers for only a few days, but research has shown they are still active after a month. Since the bupivacaine is antimicrobial and regular line disconnections increase the risk of infection, the distal filters are changed weekly and the filter nearest to the exit site is changed monthly.
6 T: Pyrexia in a patient with a spinal line is usually caused by sources such as chest or urine (so a urine test would be useful). With intrathecal lines, a CSF sample would be withdrawn (without a filter) for culture.

WORK PAGE

Mary has been doing well at home for several weeks with her intrathecal spinal line. Her husband telephones you one evening to tell you that the pain has been getting worse since tea time and now is nearly as bad as before her spinal line was put in.

 What could have happened and how can you check?

	What could have happened?	How can you check that this is the cause?

The pump

. . . .

. . . .

Connection line and filters

. . . .

. . . .

Spinal line

. . . .

. . . .

Other

. . . .

. . . .

Her line is running well again, but next time you visit she seems unwell and sleepy. As you touch her hand she seems pyrexial and a quick axillary temperature check shows a temperature of 38.5°C.

MCQ **What should you check? Could the line be the cause? Not sure? Well, try this multiple choice instead!**

1	Bupivacaine is an antimicrobial (i.e. it kills bacteria and fungi)	False	True
2	The likeliest source of infection is from the injected analgesic mixture	False	True
3	The exit site of the spinal line should be uncovered only on rare occasions	False	True
4	You should never use a spinal line in the presence of existing infection	False	True
5	Bacterial filters can be left in use for up to one month	False	True
6	A urine test would be helpful in this situation	False	True

FURTHER ACTIVITY

What observations would you make to ensure that the spinal line was working properly?

FURTHER READING

Journal articles

Anderson P (1991) Intrathecal narcotics for the relief of pain from head and neck cancer. *Archives of Otolaryngological Head Neck Surgeons.* 117: 1277–80.

Burton M (1990) Long-term pain relief produced by intrathecal morphine infusion in 53 patients. *Journal of Neurosurgery.* 72: 200–9.

Crul B and Delhaas E (1991) Technical complications during long term subarachnoid or epidural administration of morphine in terminally ill cancer patients: a review of 140 cases. *Regional Anaesthesia.* 16: 209–13.

Dahm P, Nitescu P, Appelgren L et al. (1998) Efficacy and technical complications of long-term continuous intraspinal infusions of opioid and/or bupivacaine in refractory nonmalignant pain: a comparison between the epidural and the intrathecal approach with externalized or implanted catheters and infusion pumps. *Clinical Journal of Pain.* 14(1): 4–16.

Day R (2001) The use of epidural and intrathecal analgesia in palliative care. *International Journal of Palliative Nursing.* 7(8): 369–74.

Gesten Y and Vainio A (1997) Long term intrathecal infusion of morphine in home care of patients with advanced cancer. *Acta Anaethesiology Scandanavica.* 47: 12–17.

Gustaffson L (1988) Clinical experience of long term treatment with epidural and intrathecal opioids – a nationwide survey. *Acta Analgesia Scandanavica.* 32: 253–9.

Krames ES (1993) Intrathecal infusional therapies for intractable pain patient management guidelines. *Journal of Pain and Symptom Management.* 8: 36–46.

Krames E and Gershow J (1985) Continuous infusion of spinally administered narcotics for the relief of pain due to malignant disorders. *Cancer.* 56: 696–702.

Lema MJ (2001) Invasive analgesia techniques for advanced cancer pain. *Surgical Oncology Clinics of North America.* 10(1): 127–36.

Mercadante S (1998) Controversies over spinal treatment in advanced cancer patients. *Supportive Care in Cancer.* 6(6): 495–502.

Mercadante S (1999) Problems of long-term spinal opioid treatment in advanced cancer patients. *Pain.* 79(1): 1–13.

Nitescu P, Appelgren L, Linder LE et al. (1990) Epidural versus intrathecal morphine-bupivacaine: assessment of consecutive treatments in advanced cancer pain. *Journal of Pain and Symptom Management.* 5(1): 18–26.

Nitescu P, Appelgren L, Hultman E et al. (1991) Long-term, open catheterization of the spinal subarachnoid space for continuous infusion of narcotic and bupivacaine in patients with 'refractory' cancer pain. A technique of catheterization and its problems and complications. *Clinical Journal of Pain.* 7(2): 143–61.

Nitescu P, Sjoberg M, Appelgren L et al. (1995) Complications of intrathecal opioids and bupivacaine in the treatment of 'refractory' cancer pain. *Clinical Journal of Pain.* 11(1): 45–62.

Sjoberg M, Appelgren L, Einarsson S et al. (1991) Long-term intrathecal morphine and bupivacaine in 'refractory' cancer pain. I. Results from the first series of 52 patients. *Acta Anaesthesiologica Scandinavica.* 35(1): 30–43.

Sjoberg M, Karlsson PA, Nordborg C et al. (1992) Neuropathologic findings after long-term intrathecal infusion of morphine and bupivacaine for pain treatment in cancer patients. *Anesthesiology.* 76(2): 173–86.

Sjoberg M, Nitescu P, Appelgren L et al. (1994) Long-term intrathecal morphine and bupivacaine in patients with refractory cancer pain. Results from a morphine: bupivacaine dose regimen of 0.5:4.75 mg/ml. *Anesthesiology.* 80(2): 284–97.

Tumber PS and Fitzgibbon DR (1998) The control of severe cancer pain by continuous intrathecal infusion and patient controlled intrathecal analgesia with morphine, bupivacaine and clonidine. *Pain.* 78(3): 217–20.

van Dongen RT, Crul BJ and van Egmond J (1999) Intrathecal coadministration of bupivacaine diminishes morphine dose progression during long-term intrathecal infusion in cancer patients. *Clinical Journal of Pain.* 15(3): 166–72.

Resource book

Calman K, Doyle D and Hanks GWC (eds) (2003) *The Oxford Textbook of Palliative Medicine* (3e). Oxford University Publications, Oxford.

HELPING THE PERSON WITH COMMUNICATION
DIFFICULTIES

1 Conditions causing communication difficulties

Claud Regnard
Christine K Armstrong
Dorothy Matthews
Lynn Gibson

INTRODUCTORY LEVEL

Aim of this worksheet

To review the conditions that cause communication difficulties.

How to use this worksheet

- You can work through this worksheet by yourself, or with a tutor.

- The work page is on the right side, the information page is on the left.

- Work any way you want: you can try answering from your own knowledge (in which case, fold over the information page), you can use the information page (this is not cheating – you learn as you find the information) or you can use other sources of information.

- It should take you about 15 minutes. If anything is unclear, discuss it with a colleague.

- If you think any information is wrong or out of date, let us know.

- Use the activity on the back page and take this learning into your workplace.

INFORMATION PAGE

Conditions that result in people developing alternative communication

The potential list of causes is longer than you may have thought and you should have put a ring around ALL of the conditions. In children with IQs < 70, **Down's syndrome** and **perinatal encephalopathies** are the commonest causes. Between 3–4 per 1000 school children will have an IQ < 30, and they will have to use alternative means of communication. In adults, the **dementias** are the commonest cause.

- *Development:* e.g. microcephaly, hydrocephalus
- *Bulbar palsy:* motor neurone disease
- *Degeneration:* e.g. senile dementia, Alzheimer's, Parkinson's disease
- *Genetics:* e.g. trisomy 21 (Down's syndrome), Klinefelter's syndrome (XXY), cri du chat syndrome, fragile-X syndrome, Prader-Willi syndrome
- *Hypoxia:* e.g. cerebral palsy (some types affect expression only, others affect expression and comprehension)
- *Infection:* e.g. congenital rubella, toxoplasmosis, herpes simplex, cytomegalovirus, AIDS-related
- *Malignancy:* primary or secondary tumours of the brain, paraneoplastic dementia
- *Metabolism:* e.g. galactosaemia, adrenoleucodystrophy

- *Psychiatric:* conditions such as severe depression or psychosis will hinder or prevent communication, any acute confusional state will hinder communication
- *Trauma:* to the brain
- *Toxins:* e.g. organophosphates, carbon monoxide, drugs, bacterial infections, antenatal toxins (alcohol, warfarin, opioids, organic solvents)
- *Vascular system:* e.g. cerebral infarction or haemorrhage, haemolytic uraemia syndrome

Many of these causes damage comprehension such as the dementias and encephalopathies (remember that *any* cause of severe drowsiness or coma will make communication difficult).

In some causes comprehension is normal, but the body is affected such that speech and writing become impossible. Examples are motor neurone disease and cerebral palsy (dyskinetic and spastic diplegia types).

A number of the causes affect comprehension and the body together, causing major communication difficulties. Examples are other types of cerebral palsy (spastic hemiplegia, bilateral hemiplegia, ataxic and tetraplegia types) and the leucodystrophies.

Some thoughts about people with communication difficulties

1 F: *Communication difficulty* implies that it is only the patient who is having difficulty communicating. In reality, patients have to *communicate in alternative ways* because of their condition, while carers often have difficulty in understanding what is being communicated. The problem lies with both the patient and the carer.

2 F: In many people with alternative communication, expression (giving information) is affected differently from comprehension (receiving information). Some conditions severely affect expression, but leave comprehension intact (e.g. dyskinetic and spastic types of cerebral palsy, motor neurone disease).

3 T: Staff often have the skills to pick up distress but lack confidence in their ability. Much of the communication is picked up intuitively rather than by observation.

4 F: It is very important we learn to pick up signs of pain or distress in a comatose patient.

5 F: There is usually nothing wrong with pain receptors. However, it is true that people with alternative communication can be *indifferent* to pain. This is partly due to loss of understanding of the implications of pain and reduced anticipation of the distress it causes. In practice, lack of information can lead to increased fear, and there is evidence of 11% of patients with developmental disabilities having low thresholds to pain.

6 T: Close and documented observation is the key to understanding.

An alternative language

Whenever we communicate face-to-face we don't just use words or writing. *Our face* tells a great deal about us. The whole face reveals emotions such as joy, contentment, fear, anger and sadness. Parts of our face also give clues such as dilated pupils (fear or attraction), pallor (fear or pain), frown (puzzlement or distress) or biting our lower lip (anxiety, fear). *Our voice* can provide clues through its tone and quality. Moaning, grunting, crying and screaming all have different meanings. *Hands* are used extensively to emphasise, illustrate or hide our feelings. *Posture* shows our feelings and can indicate whether we are being defensive, trusting or frightened.

Principles

- Many conditions can force children and adults to use alternative communication.
- Expression and comprehension of information can be affected differently.
- These patients are not insensitive to pain.

WORK PAGE

 Think (Ring) any of these that you think *could* cause people communication difficulties. Underline the commonest causes.

organophosphates	trisomy 21	acute hypercalcaemia	motor neurone disease
AIDS	dementia	cerebral infarction	rubella encephalitis
Parkinson's disease	psychosis	tetraplegic cerebral palsy	head injury
adrenoleucodystrophy	coma	cerebral tumour	stroke (CVA)

 MCQ

1 The problem in communication difficulties is with the patient	True	False
2 A severe communication difficulty is usually accompanied by poor comprehension	True	False
3 Carers have the skills to understand people with communication difficulties	True	False
4 Communication is not relevant in a dying, comatose patient	True	False
5 Pain insensitivity is common in people with communication difficulties	True	False
6 The most important part of communication is recognising usual behaviour	True	False

 Imagine that you have lost the ability to speak or write. How could others realise that you are in pain?

Could you use any of these to show you have pain?   Yes ✓ No ✗   How?

face?

. . . .

voice?

. . . .

hands?

. . . .

posture?

. . . .

 Think Think about the principles you have learnt from this worksheet.

FURTHER ACTIVITY

Find a colleague with whom there is mutual trust and identify a patient with any communication difficulty.

• Feedback to one another your observations on the patient.

• Discuss your individual feelings.

• Identify what you learnt from the experience and plan how you will learn more.

FURTHER READING

Books and journal articles

Astor R (2001) Detecting pain in people with profound learning disabilities. *Nursing Times.* **97**: 38–9.

Fray MT (2000) *Caring for Kathleen: A Sister's Story About Down's Syndrome and Dementia.* BILD Publications, Kidderminster.

Fullerton A (2002) Examining the comfort of the unconscious patient. *European Journal of Palliative Care.* **9**: 232–3.

Hatton C (1998) Intellectual disabilities: epidemiology and causes. In: E Emerson *et al.* (eds) *Clinical Psychology and People with Intellectual Disabilities.* John Wiley and Sons, Chichester.

Hunt A (2001) *Towards an understanding of pain in the child with severe neurological impairment. Development of a behaviour rating scale for assessing pain.* PhD thesis. University of Manchester, Manchester.

Kovach CR, Weissman DE, Griffe J *et al.* (1999) Assessment and treatment of discomfort for people with late-stage dementia. *Journal of Pain and Symptom Management.* **18**: 412–19.

Lloyd-Williams M (1996) An audit of palliative care in dementia. *European Journal of Cancer Care.* **5**: 53–5.

Manfredi PL, Breurer B, Meier D *et al.* (2003) Pain assessment in elderly patients with severe dementia. *Journal of Pain and Symptom Management.* **25**: 48–52.

Marler R and Cunningham C (1995) *Down's Syndrome and Alzheimer's Disease: A Guide for Carers.* Down's Syndrome Association, London.

Porter J, Ouvry C, Morgan M *et al.* (2001) Interpreting the communication of people with profound multiple learning difficulties. *British Journal of Learning Disabilities.* **29**: 12–16.

Regnard C, Matthews D, Gibson L *et al.* (2003) Difficulties in identifying distress and its causes in people with severe communication problems. *International Journal of Palliative Nursing.* **9**(3): 173–6.

Ware J (1996) *Creating a Responsive Environment for People with Profound Multiple Learning Difficulties.* Fulton, London.

Other resources

www.downs-syndrome.org.uk – Down's Syndrome Association.

www.downset.org/DownsEd – Down's Syndrome Educational Trust.

HELPING THE PERSON WITH COMMUNICATION
DIFFICULTIES

2 Identifying distress

Claud Regnard
Dorothy Matthews
Lynn Gibson
Christine Jensen
Christine Armstrong

INTRODUCTORY LEVEL

Aim of this worksheet

To consider ways and means of identifying distress in a person using alternative methods of communication.

How to use this worksheet

- You can work through this worksheet by yourself, or with a tutor.

- Read the case study below, then work on the questions overleaf.

- The work page is on the right side, the information page is on the left.

- Work any way you want: you can try answering from your own knowledge (in which case, fold over the information page), you can use the information page (this is not cheating – you learn as you find the information) or you can use other sources of information.

- It should take you about 15 minutes. If anything is unclear, discuss it with a colleague.

- If you think any information is wrong or out of date, let us know.

- Use the activity on the back page and take this learning into your workplace.

Case study

Margaret is a 50-year-old lady with Down's syndrome. She attended a 'special school' when she was young. She was always friendly and happy except for a short time when she was with foster parents. After that she moved in with her sister and manages to look after herself at home while her sister works. Margaret is usually responsive to others, but over the past few days she has been reluctant to communicate, ignores carers and grimaces during interventions.

INFORMATION PAGE

Behaviours and signs of distress (the 'language' of distress)

There are many ways that Margaret could express her distress:

- *Expressive:* These may be of two types:
  - *verbal:* these may be using language (simple descriptions, e.g. 'I'm not right', associated words, e.g. always using the words 'My knee hurts' for any distress), or using sounds (crying, screaming, sighing, moaning, grunting)
  - *facial:* these may be simple expressions (grimacing, clenched teeth, shut eyes, wide open eyes, frowning, biting lower lip) or more complex (where patients look sad or angry).
- *Adaptive:* Rubbing or holding a painful area, keeping an area still, approaching staff, avoiding stimulation, reduced or absent function (reduced movement, lying or sitting).
- *Distractive:* Rocking (or other rhythmic movements), pacing, biting hand or lip, gesturing, clenched fists.
- *Postural:* Increased muscle tension (extension or flexion), altered posture, flinching, head in hands, limping, pulling cover or clothes over head, knees drawn up.
- *Autonomic:* This may be either sympathetic (the flight or fight response with ↑pulse rate, ↑BP, wide pupils, pallor, and sweating) or parasympathetic (in response to nausea or visceral pain with ↓BP and ↓pulse rate)

The language of observable communication (LOC)*

Like any language, you have to:

1 know what the words mean
2 learn a basic vocabulary
3 know how the words are put together and
4 make sense of what the person is saying.

In people using alternative communication, the language is made up mainly of behaviours, signs and verbal expressions (which may be sounds only, or words that indicate distress but do not describe it). Compared to spoken language, the vocabulary in LOC is small, the grammar is basic and the pattern of expressions is unique to each individual. The difficulty is knowing what these behaviours, signs and expressions mean (i.e. it's *us* who have difficulty understanding the person expressing LOC). They can only be understood with close observation.

Some of the LOC 'words' can suggest a meaning when taken together or when seen in their context:

- *Nausea:* This tends to cause an autonomic response with pallor, cold sweating, a slow pulse and vomiting.
- *Fear:* Increased pulse, dilated pupils, tremor, and increased respirations, perhaps associated with a particular situation.
- *Frustration:* Crying or screaming, rapid and purposeless movements, looking angry, perhaps associated with a particular situation.
- *Leg pain:* Holding leg still, rubbing leg, limping, refusing to move.
- *Margaret's grimacing and ignoring of carers:* This tells us very little – we need more information.

*LOC: The abbreviation 'Loq' was formerly used as a stage direction and comes from the Latin, *loquitur*, meaning 'he/she speaks'.

Understanding LOC

A real difficulty is that any cause of distress can be accompanied by any behaviour, sign or expression. Although some LOC 'words' are the same or similar in most patients (e.g. the reactions to fear), each individual uses their own 'dialect' of LOC. Although staff are often skilled in picking up distress they often have little confidence in their observation and perceive their observations intuitively as a 'hunch'. We therefore need more information:

- *Is this behaviour or sign new?* For this we need to know their usual behaviour by recording baseline behaviour and asking the main or previous carers what they know. We know it is new in Margaret.

- *Is this behaviour or sign associated with known distress?* For this we need to identify LOC 'words' with known cause of distress (e.g. during an episode of constipation, or in a frightening situation). This can only be done if behaviour, signs and expressions are regularly documented.
- *Is this individual's behaviour unique?* For this we need to document the behaviours in a large number of individuals, estimate the cause of distress and the response to treatment (in order to confirm the cause). This is best done as a research project.

Principles

- The language of distress consists of behaviours, signs and expressions.
- The language of observable communication (LOC) may be unique to each individual.

- Documentation of LOC is essential if each individual is to be understood.
- The problem is *our* understanding. Distress may be hidden but it is never silent.

WORK PAGE

Write down different ways in which Margaret could respond to distress.

Words or sounds	
Facial expression	
Actions by Margaret that try to ease any pain she has	
Actions by Margaret that distract her from distress	
Changes in body posture	
Reflex nervous system responses	

Using your list above (or the one at the top of the opposite page), which behaviours and signs might suggest the following causes of distress:

• Nausea: . . . .

• Fear: . . . .

• Frustration: . . . .

• Leg pain: . . . .

• Margaret's grimacing and ignoring of carers: . . . .

Like us, you may have found this exercise difficult, especially when it came to interpreting Margaret's behaviour.

Write below the extra information you would need to understand Margaret and how you would get that information.

Problem	Information needed	How to obtain information
Is this behaviour or sign new?		
Is this behaviour or sign associated with known distress?		
Is this individual's behaviour unique?		

FURTHER ACTIVITY

Think of a typical day in your life:

- Write down all the times you use non-verbal language.

FURTHER READING

Books and journal articles

Astor R (2001) Detecting pain in people with profound learning disabilities. *Nursing Times*. **97**: 38–9.

Banat D, Summers S and Pring T (2002) An investigation into carers' perceptions of the verbal comprehension ability of adults with severe learning disabilities. *British Journal of Developmental Disabilities*. **30**: 78–81.

Craig KD and Prkachin KM (1993) Non-verbal measures of pain. In: R Melzack (ed.) *Pain Measurement and Assessment*. Raven Press, New York.

Davies D and Evans L (2001) Assessing pain in people with profound learning disabilities. *British Journal of Nursing*. **10**: 513–16.

Fisher-Morris M and Gellatly A (1997) The experience and expression of pain in Alzheimer patients. *Age and Ageing*. **26**: 497–500.

Fray MT (2000) *Caring for Kathleen: A Sister's Story About Down's Syndrome and Dementia*. BILD Publications, Kidderminster.

Fullerton A (2002) Examining the comfort of the unconscious patient. *European Journal of Palliative Care*. **9**: 232–3.

Hadjistavropoulos T, LaChapelle DL, MacLeod FK *et al.* (2000) Measuring movement-exacerbated pain in cognitively impaired frail elders. *Clinical Journal of Pain*. **16**: 54–63.

Hunt A (2001) *Towards an understanding of pain in the child with severe neurological impairment. Development of a behaviour rating scale for assessing pain*. PhD thesis. University of Manchester, Manchester.

Hurley AC, Volicer BJ, Hanrahan PA *et al.* (1992) Assessment of discomfort in advanced Alzheimer patients. *Research in Nursing and Health*. **15**: 369–77.

Ingram R (1991) Learning difficulties and communication. *Nursing Standard*. **5**: 36–9.

Kovach CR, Weissman DE, Griffe J *et al.* (1999) Assessment and treatment of discomfort for people with late-stage dementia. *Journal of Pain and Symptom Management*. **18**: 412–19.

Manfredi PL, Breurer B, Meier D *et al.* (2003) Pain assessment in elderly patients with severe dementia. *Journal of Pain and Symptom Management*. **25**: 48–52.

Porter J, Ouvry C, Morgan M *et al.* (2001) Interpreting the communication of people with profound multiple learning difficulties. *British Journal of Learning Disabilities*. **29**: 12–16.

Regnard C, Matthews D, Gibson L *et al.* (2003) Difficulties in identifying distress and its causes in people with severe communication problems. *International Journal of Palliative Nursing*. **9**(3): 173–6.

Simons W and Malabar R (1995) Assessing pain in elderly patients who cannot respond verbally. *Journal of Advanced Nursing*. **22**: 663–9.

Whitehouse R, Chamberlain P and Tunna K (2000) Dementia in people with learning disability: a preliminary study into care staff knowledge and attributions. *British Journal of Learning Disabilities*. **28**: 148–53.

HELPING THE PERSON WITH COMMUNICATION DIFFICULTIES

3 Down's syndrome

Claud Regnard
Margaret Kindlen
Christine K Armstrong
Dorothy Matthews
Lynn Gibson

INTERMEDIATE LEVEL

Aim of this worksheet

To introduce the health professional to the person with Down's syndrome.

How to use this worksheet

- You can work through this worksheet by yourself, or with a tutor.

- Read the case study below, then work on the questions overleaf.

- The work page is on the right side, the information page is on the left.

- Work any way you want: you can try answering from your own knowledge (in which case, fold over the information page), you can use the information page (this is not cheating – you learn as you find the information) or you can use other sources of information.

- It should take you about 15 minutes. If anything is unclear, discuss it with a colleague.

- If you think any information is wrong or out of date, let us know.

- Use the activity on the back page and take this learning into your workplace.

Case study

Margaret is a 50-year-old lady with Down's syndrome. She attended a 'special school' when she was young. She was always friendly and happy except for a short time when she was with foster parents. After that she moved in with her sister and manages to look after herself at home while her sister works.

INFORMATION PAGE

The nature of Down's syndrome

Documented in 1866, it was only explained in 1959. It is a genetic abnormality caused by an extra chromosome. There are three 21st chromosomes instead of the usual two, hence the other name for Down's syndrome, Trisomy 21. There are other rare forms of chromosomal disorder.

The mother's age is a key risk. Although 70% of Down's people are born to women under 35, the risk of a baby with Down's syndrome is 15 times higher if the mother is aged 40, compared with a mother aged 21 (1 in 100 births for mothers age 40 compared with 1 in 1500 births aged 21).

One-third of Down's syndrome babies are identified before birth, but recent advances in testing before birth may increase that number. Improved care has resulted in 80% being aged over 50.

How the person with Down's syndrome is affected

People with Down's syndrome have an affectionate, happy personality with an inherent sense of fun, but they also have a number of difficulties which make it more harder for them to interact and join with their peers:

- *Communication problems:*
  - *Eye problems:* Cataracts, squints and nystagmus can cause difficulties with vision.
  - *Speech problems:* There can be two reasons for this: (1) poor tongue control causing difficulty in forming words (dysarthria) and (2) hearing loss which can delay or prevent language development.
  - *Hearing problems:* Frequent middle ear disease can result in up to 70% hearing loss.
  - *Learning disability:* This can be very mild, allowing a high level of involvement in society. For others, their learning disability can be severe, with very delayed development.
- *Mobility problems:*
  - *Reduced muscle tone:* This delays walking. As babies they are often 'floppy'. *Poor co-ordination.*
  - *Lax ligaments* produce hypermobile joints. *Low foot arches* produce flat feet and make walking more difficult.
- *Reduced life expectancy:*
  - Current research shows that 80% of Down's syndrome people alive today are over 50 years old.
  - *Chest infections:* Nasal problems, middle ear infections and reduced muscle tone can all result in repeated respiratory infections and progressive lung damage over the years.
  - *Congenital heart disease:* A range of defects can occur in 40% of individuals which if severe, or not treated, can result in death in the first year of life.
  - *Malignancies:* Down's syndrome is associated with an increased likelihood of acute lymphoblastic leukaemia. If it appears in childhood, 60–70% can be cured, but survival is much less likely in older people with Down's syndrome. Other cancers are no more common in Down's syndrome, but they now live long enough to develop the same cancers as the rest of the population.
  - *Alzheimer's dementia:* By the age of 50–60, a rapidly progressive type of dementia develops with deteriorating intellect and mobility, mood and personality changes, hallucinations, swallowing problems, a tendency to seizures (fits) and sudden muscle jerks. Most people with this form of dementia die within two years.
  - *Thyroid problems:* The thyroid can become under-active which will need treatment.
- *Appearance:* This makes most people with Down's syndrome recognisable. They are short, have sloping eyes, a flat face (with a short bridged nose, low set small ears, and in some a protruding tongue), broad and flat hands (with a single crease and incurling fifth finger), and a smaller head.

Margaret's vulnerability

- *Prejudice:* Her appearance makes her easily recognisable. People make assumptions about her ability to comprehend, when in reality she can often understand very well what is happening. Consequently contact is avoided (through embarrassment), screening or contraception are withheld, or treatments are not given (on the assumption she cannot give consent).
- *Vulnerability:* Her trusting and friendly nature makes her vulnerable to physical, psychological and sexual abuse. Although male Down's people are infertile, females like Margaret are fertile and can have children. Margaret has the same rights to protection (security and contraception) as all of us.
- *Identifying distress:* Although behaviour changes can become repetitive, this can be due to aggression, fear or physical problems. The number of possible physical problems Down's syndrome people can suffer demands that physical causes are checked whenever behaviour changes. (*See* CLIP worksheet on *Identifying distress*.)

WORK PAGE

Think   What is the risk of having a baby with Down's syndrome? (Ring) your answer.

Mother age 21	1 in 100	1 in 200	1 in 1500
Mother age 40	1 in 100	1 in 200	1 in 1500

Think   What is the life expectancy of a person with Down's syndrome? (Ring) your answer.

20 years   40 years   80% die before 50 years   80% are over 50 years age

What problems could have affected Margaret?

* Communication: . . . .

. . . .

. . . .

* Mobility: . . . .

. . . .

. . . .

* Illness: . . . .

. . . .

. . . .

* Appearance: . . . .

. . . .

. . . .

What are the consequences for Margaret in the following areas?

1 Prejudice by others: . . . .

. . . .

. . . .

2 Vulnerability: . . . .

. . . .

. . . .

3 Identifying distress: . . . .

. . . .

. . . .

FURTHER ACTIVITY

In Down's syndrome:

- In what ways are clients vulnerable both within and outside their usual setting?

- Observe (or ask colleagues) what the clients do to indicate they are distressed.

- What physical healthcare needs do they need?

FURTHER READING

Journal articles

Alderson P (2001) Down's syndrome: cost, quality and value of life. *Social Science and Medicine*. **53**(5): 627–38.

Barr O, Gilgunn J, Kane T *et al.* (1999) Health screening for people with learning disabilities by community learning disability nursing in Northern Ireland. *Journal of Advanced Nursing*. **29**(6): 1482–91.

Cosgrave MP, McCarron M, Anderson M *et al.* (1998) Cognitive decline in Down syndrome: a validity/reliability study of the test for severe impairment. *American Journal of Mental Retardation*. **103**(2): 193–7.

Cosgrave MP, Tyrrell J, McCarron M *et al.* (1999) Age at onset of dementia and age of menopause in women with Down's syndrome. *Journal of Intellectual Disability Research*. **43**: 461–5.

McCarron M (1999) Some issues in caring for people with dual disability of Down's Syndrome and Alzheimer dementia. *Journal of Learning Disabilities for Nursing and Health Care*. **3B**: 123–9.

Miller B (1998) Palliative care for people with non-malignant disease. *Nursing Times*. **94**: 52–3.

Prasher VP (1995) End stage dementia in adults with Down syndrome. *International Journal of Geriatric Psychiatry*. **10**: 1067–9.

Prasher VP and Filer A (1995) Behavioural disturbance in people with Down's syndrome and dementia. *Journal of Intellectual Disability Research*. **39**(5): 432–6.

Tuffrey-Wynne I (2002) The palliative care needs of people with intellectual disabilities: a case study. *International Journal of Palliative Nursing*. **8**(5): 222–32.

Resource books and websites

Fray MT (2000) *Caring for Kathleen: A Sister's Story About Down's Syndrome and Dementia*. BILD Publications, Kidderminster.

Kerr D (1997) *Down's Syndrome and Dementia*. The Venture Press, Birmingham.

Marler R and Cunningham C (1995) *Down's Syndrome and Alzheimer's Disease: A Guide for Carers*. Down's Syndrome Association, London.

www.downs-syndrome.org.uk – Down's Syndrome Association.

www.downset.org/DownsEd – Down's Syndrome Educational Trust.

HELPING THE PERSON WITH COMMUNICATION
DIFFICULTIES

4 Epilepsy

Claud Regnard
Christine K Armstrong
Dorothy Matthews
Lynn Gibson

INTERMEDIATE LEVEL

Aim of this worksheet

To introduce the health professional to the person with epilepsy.

How to use this worksheet

- You can work through this worksheet by yourself, or with a tutor.

- Read the case study below, then work on the questions overleaf.

- The work page is on the right side, the information page is on the left.

- Work any way you want: you can try answering from your own knowledge (in which case, fold over the information page), you can use the information page (this is not cheating – you learn as you find the information) or you can use other sources of information.

- It should take you about 15 minutes. If anything is unclear, discuss it with a colleague.

- If you think any information is wrong or out of date, let us know.

- Use the activity on the back page and take this learning into your workplace.

Case study

Margaret is a 57-year-old lady with Down's syndrome who has always lived at home with her sister. About 2 years ago it was noticed that Margaret was becoming quieter, less lively, with less sparkle to her personality. At times she would be unsure where she was or what day it was. Her sister thought these changes were related to Margaret getting older, then she suffered a 'shaking, funny turn'.

INFORMATION PAGE

Nature and prevalence of epilepsy

- *What it is:* The brain is a highly complex structure composed of billions of nerve cells called neurones. The neurones are responsible for a wide range of functions including awareness, consciousness, movement and posture. A sudden, temporary overactivity of the neurones in one area of the brain may cause a seizure.
- *Prevalence:* Epilepsy is the most common neurological condition in the general population, with a prevalence rate of about 5–10 per 1000 (about 1 in 200). Anyone can develop epilepsy, it occurs in all races and social classes.

- *Epilepsy in learning disabilities:* About one in five people with a learning disability have epilepsy, which is 40 times higher than the average population and increases in proportion with the severity of the disability. However, of those with a profound or severe learning disability, at least 40–50% of those people will have epilepsy. Both epilepsy and learning disability are outward symptoms of underlying brain dysfunction or damage, but there is no evidence to suggest that there is a direct link between epilepsy and intelligence.

The causes, diagnosis and types of epilepsy

- *Causes:* The possible causes of epilepsy include – **inherited causes** (20%), congenital malformation, **infection**, **brain tumours**, vascular disease (e.g. **stroke**), **head injury** and **Alzheimer's dementia**. Learning disabilities are not a cause, but some conditions cause both. A direct cause cannot be identified in approximately 60% of cases. Some situations can trigger a seizure (e.g. **flashing lights**, **antidepressants**, **drug withdrawal**, **pyrexia**), but there is no evidence that emotion (e.g. fear, stress or anger) or tiredness can trigger a seizure. **Alcohol** is not a cause of epilepsy, but it can worsen existing seizures.
- *Diagnosis:* Epilepsy can be difficult to diagnose and is dependent on clinical observations and investigations such as an EEG (electroencephalogram). An ambulatory EEG allows the brain activity to be recorded over a 24-hour period.

- *Types of epilepsy:*
  - *Generalised epilepsy:* This involves abnormal electrical activity affecting the whole brain, during which there will be a loss of consciousness. In a major seizure (a 'Tonic-Clonic' seizure) the person stiffens (the tonic phase) and then convulses or jerks (the clonic phase). They may make strange noises, salivate excessively and be incontinent. Other types of generalised seizure can be much less dramatic – an 'absence' seizure can look like a very brief daydream.
  - *Partial (focal) epilepsy:* This disturbance is confined to a local area of the brain, causing either simple partial or complex partial seizures. This may show as shaking of an arm with the patient fully conscious. Partial epilepsy usually indicates a damaged area in the brain.

The effects of epilepsy

Epilepsy and seizures affect people in different ways. Some people might have to make several changes in their lives to live more safely, while others will only have to make a few changes.

It is important to recognise that a diagnosis of epilepsy can bring with it a social prejudice, which can result in as many difficulties as are caused by the seizures themselves. People with learning disabilities may feel that their epilepsy restricts their quality of life far more than does their learning disability. Epilepsy care for people with learning disabilities should achieve a standard that allows these patients to live to their full potential.

Treating epilepsy

- *Ensure safety and make the person comfortable:* Loosen clothing, remove spectacles, support and protect the head. Move objects that could be harmful. *Do not* put anything in the mouth; do not attempt to restrain convulsive movements; do not give anything to drink until the patient is fully awake and do not move the person unless they are in danger.
- *In a partial seizure:* Gently protect the person from danger, speak gently and calmly to aid reorientation to the surroundings. Stay with the person until they can resume normal activities. Seizure patients are individual and recovery patterns will differ from one person to another.
- *If the seizure is persisting:* Most seizures are self-limiting, but if a seizure is prolonged or a person experiences status epilepticus, emergency treatment is necessary. Diazepam

may be administered rectally or midazolam can be administered either nasally or buccally (between the cheek and teeth).
- *Ensure recovery is safe:* Once movements have stopped put the person into the recovery position and check the airway is clear. Allow recovery in his/her own time, talk quietly and offer reassurance.
- *Start or adjust anticonvulsant medication:* This is highly effective for some types of seizures, e.g. sodium valproate. Individual titration is the key to successful treatment. The most common problem is not taking the medication correctly. It is important for patients and their carers to co-operate in the treatment regime to control seizures. This is more likely to be successful if they understand the condition and the reasons for the prescribed treatment.

WORK PAGE

Think   How common do you think epilepsy is? (Ring) the figures you think are correct.

In the general population:	1 in 5	1 in 50	1 in 200	1 in 2000
In learning disabilities:	1 in 5	1 in 50	1 in 200	1 in 2000

Think   (Ring) the conditions you think cause epilepsy and those you think might trigger a seizure.

Possible causes of epilepsy		Possible triggers of a seizure	
Head injury	Infection	Pyrexia	Fear
Inherited disorders	Learning disability	Flashing lights	Antidepressants
Alzheimer's dementia	Tumour	Tiredness	Anger
Stroke	Alcohol	Stress	Diazepam withdrawal

What should you do if a patient has a major (tonic-clonic) seizure?

• Immediately:

. . . .

. . . .

. . . .

. . . .

• To ensure safety:

. . . .

. . . .

. . . .

. . . .

• If the seizure is persisting:

. . . .

. . . .

. . . .

. . . .

FURTHER ACTIVITY

For a client with epilepsy:

- Find out what warning signs or behaviour the client shows before a seizure (observe, ask a colleague or check through clinical records).

- Note any medication they are taking to prevent seizures and check the adverse effects in the current *British National Formulary*.

FURTHER READING

Journal articles

Bourdet SV, Gidal BE and Alldredge BK (2001) Pharmacologic management of epilepsy in the elderly. *Journal of the American Pharmaceutical Association*. **41**(3): 421–36.

Chadwick D and Smith D (2002) The misdiagnosis of epilepsy: the rate of misdiagnosis and wide treatment choices are arguments for specialist care of epilepsy. *BMJ*. **324**: 495–6.

Cunninham O and Zaagman P (2000) Modern management of epilepsy (keeping the person in focus). *Learning Disability Practice*. **3:** 16–19.

Dodrill CB (2002) Progressive cognitive decline in adolescents and adults with epilepsy. *Progress in Brain Research*. **135**: 399–407.

Ellis N, Upton D and Thompson P (2000) Epilepsy and the family: a review of current literature. *Seizure*. **9**(1): 22–30.

Loughran S and O'Brien D (2002) Epilepsy liaison nursing. *Nursing Times*. **98**(10): 32–4.

MacDonald D, Torrance N, Wood S *et al.* (2000) General practice based nurse specialists: taking a lead in improving the care of people with epilepsy. *Seizure*. **9**: 31–5.

Management of epilepsy in adolescents and adults (2000) *Lancet*. **356**: 323–9.

Welsh M (2001) The practice nurse's role in the management of epilepsy. *British Journal of Community Nursing*. **6**(3): 112–17.

HELPING THE PERSON WITH COMMUNICATION
DIFFICULTIES

5 Dementia

Claud Regnard
Margaret Kindlen
Christine K Armstrong
Dorothy Matthews
Lynn Gibson

INTERMEDIATE LEVEL

Aim of this worksheet

To introduce the health professional to the person with dementia.

How to use this worksheet

- You can work through this worksheet by yourself, or with a tutor.

- Read the case study below, then work on the questions overleaf.

- The work page is on the right side, the information page is on the left.

- Work any way you want: you can try answering from your own knowledge (in which case, fold over the information page), you can use the information page (this is not cheating – you learn as you find the information) or you can use other sources of information.

- It should take you about 15 minutes. If anything is unclear, discuss it with a colleague.

- If you think any information is wrong or out of date, let us know.

- Use the activity on the back page and take this learning into your workplace.

Case study

Margaret is a 57-year-old lady with Down's syndrome who has always lived at home with her sister. About two years ago it was noticed that Margaret was becoming quieter, less lively, with less sparkle to her personality. At times she would be unsure where she was or what day it was. Her sister thought these changes were related to Margaret getting older. She now has difficulty remembering the way back to her bedroom and occasionally does not recognise her sister and her carers.

INFORMATION PAGE

Margaret's difficulties

Old age does not cause these problems by itself, but any of the others could:

- *Bacterial infections* can cause confusion and rigors due to a high temperature.
- *Cancer* can cause confusion by a number of mechanisms.
- *Brain tumours* are an uncommon cause of confusion but can cause epileptic fits (seizures).
- *Epilepsy* can develop due to a number of reasons. In older people this can be due to brain damage caused by strokes or previous head injury.

- *Depression* could explain her more withdrawn behaviour.
- *Recent fall* can cause a clot to form slowly between the brain and skull (a subdural haematoma) which can cause the problems that Margaret has.
- *Viral infections* can cause confusion and a high temperature. Some viruses can infect the brain directly.
- *Dementia* is associated with Down's syndrome and can present with fits, visual hallucinations, swallowing problems and a rapidly progressing dementia.

The nature of dementia

Dementia is a progressive reduction in cognitive abilities (the ability to think, remember, learn and reason), leading to reduced capacity for self care and self direction. Five per cent of people over 65 years have dementia, rising to 20% of people over the age of 80 years.

There are several types:
- *Alzheimer's disease* accounts for 50% of cases.
- *Vascular dementia* is due to problems in the brain's blood supply and accounts for 15%.
- *Lewy body dementia* accounts for 15% overall.
- *Mixed and other rare types* account for the remainder.

The effects of dementia

- *Cognitive difficulties:*
  - *Memory:* Recent memory is most affected so that people remember the name of a teacher, but not what happened yesterday.
  - *Speech:* The wrong words can be used (dysphasia) or no speech at all (aphasia).
  - *Loss of self-help skills:* There is increasing difficulty in carrying out a sequence of tasks (apraxia).
  - Difficulty in recognition of people and objects.
- *Behavioural difficulties:*
  - These include agitation, aggression, wandering, delusions, hallucinations, disturbed sleeping patterns, sexual dysinhibition and mood disturbance (including anxiety and depression).
  - 70–80% of people with dementia can suffer these problems which are distressing to both the patient and carers, and may be the cause of admission to hospital or nursing home.

  - Behavioural problems can be worsened by drugs (depression due to H2-blockers and NSAIDs; increased sensitivity to neuroleptics), stresses such as changes in carer or environment, or the loss of a carer.
- *Dementia associated with Down's syndrome:* This can have a more rapid course and some features are more common such as epileptic seizures and visual hallucinations. Some patients are also troubled with sudden muscle jerks (myoclonic jerks). The commonest presentation is a change in behaviour.
- *The effects on carers:* The multiple changes in abilities, behaviour and personality put heavy pressure onto the carers and partners. The unpredictability of knowing how much time is left can make it difficult for carers to plan how they are going to respond and cope. For these reasons dementia has been defined as 'The Long Bereavement.'

Caring for Margaret

- *Safety:* She will be more vulnerable to accidents and may need more monitoring. However, this needs to be balanced against the need to maintain as much of her independence as possible. Reminders (calendars, pictures indicating her bedroom, verbal clues about time, people and place) can help her cope with some of her memory loss. Sudden changes in behaviour may be due to an unrelated physical cause which needs treatment.
- *Relationships:* Good quality care is provided through the preservation of relationships.

- *Interest:* Stimulation is important, although she may find more complex activities (e.g. going to a concert) more difficult to cope with. When caring for people with Alzheimer's, the concept that everyone has an identity, a history, a life before dementia must also be acknowledged.
- *Environment:* this may need some changes to provide reminders, improve safety and provide stimulation. However, the care and environment need to balance stimulation with safety and preventing sensory overload.

WORK PAGE

Think   What could be happening to Margaret? Ring possible causes of Margaret's problems.

Chest infection	Old age	Cancer
Brain tumour	Epilepsy	Depression
Recent fall	Alzheimer's	Viral infection

What effects might dementia have on Margaret?

• Effects on her thinking skills:

. . . .

. . . .

• Effects on behaviour:

. . . .

. . . .

• Effects on her carers:

. . . .

. . . .

What could help Margaret and her sister cope?

• Maintaining safety

. . . .

. . . .

• Maintaining relationships

. . . .

. . . .

• Maintaining interest

. . . .

. . . .

• Maintaining her environment

. . . .

. . . .

FURTHER ACTIVITY

For clients with dementia:

• How do their problems make communication difficult with carers?

• Note how the client communicates when they are content.

• Note how the client communicates distress.

FURTHER READING

Journal articles

Bonner LT and Peskind ER (2002) Pharmacologic treatments of dementia. *Medical Clinics of North America*. **86**(3): 657–74.

Clifford DB (2002) AIDS dementia. *Medical Clinics of North America*. **86**(3): 537–50.

Cosgrave MP, McCarron M, Anderson M *et al.* (1998) Cognitive decline in Down syndrome: a validity/reliability study of the test for severe impairment. *American Journal of Mental Retardation*. **103**(2): 193–7.

Kertesz A and Munoz DG (2002) Frontotemporal dementia. *Medical Clinics of North America*. **86**(3): 501–18.

Kukull WA and Bowen JD (2002) Dementia epidemiology. *Medical Clinics of North America*. **86**(3): 573–90.

Leverenz JB and McKeith IG (2002) Dementia with Lewy bodies. *Medical Clinics of North America*. **86**(3): 519–35.

McCarron M (1999) Some issues in caring for people with dual disability of Down's Syndrome and Alzheimer dementia. *Journal of Learning Disabilities for Nursing and Health Care*. **3B**: 123–9.

Prasher VP (1995) End stage dementia in adults with Down syndrome. *International Journal of Geriatric Psychiatry*. **10**: 1067–9.

Prasher VP and Filer A (1995) Behavioural disturbance in people with Down's syndrome and dementia. *Journal of Intellectual Disability Research*. **39**(5): 432–6.

Roman GC (2002) Vascular dementia revisited: diagnosis, pathogenesis, treatment, and prevention. *Medical Clinics of North America*. **86**(3): 477–99.

Ross GW and Bowen JD (2002) The diagnosis and differential diagnosis of dementia. *Medical Clinics of North America*. **86**(3): 455–76.

Teri L, Logsdon RG and McCurry SM (2002) Nonpharmacologic treatment of behavioral disturbance in dementia. *Medical Clinics of North America*. **86**(3): 641–56.

Tsuang DW and Bird TD (2002) Genetics of dementia. *Medical Clinics of North America*. **86**(3): 591–614.

Resource books and websites

Fray MT (2000) *Caring for Kathleen: A Sister's Story About Down's Syndrome and Dementia*. BILD Publications, Kidderminster.

Kerr D (1997) *Down's Syndrome and Dementia*. The Venture Press, Birmingham.

Marler R and Cunningham C (1995) *Down's Syndrome and Alzheimer's Disease: A Guide for Carers*. Down's Syndrome Association, London.

www.downs-syndrome.org.uk – Down's Syndrome Association.

www.downset.org/DownsEd – Down's Syndrome Educational Trust.

THE LAST HOURS AND DAYS

1 Adjustments

Claud Regnard
Janet Jackson
Sarah Alport
Margaret Younger

INTERMEDIATE LEVEL

Aim of this worksheet

To explore the adjustments for the patient and partner, and how to adjust medication in the last hours and days.

How to use this worksheet

- You can work through this worksheet by yourself, or with a tutor.

- Read the case study below, then work on the questions overleaf.

- The work page is on the right side, the information page is on the left.

- Work any way you want: you can try answering from your own knowledge (in which case, fold over the information page), you can use the information page (this is not cheating – you learn as you find the information) or you can use other sources of information.

- It should take you about 15 minutes. If anything is unclear, discuss it with a colleague.

- If you think any information is wrong or out of date, let us know.

- Use the activity on the back page and take this learning into your workplace.

Case study

Michael is a 57-year-old man with severe learning disability who lives in a community home with three other men with learning disability. Michael was diagnosed with gastric carcinoma some months ago, but presented too late for treatment. He has begun to deteriorate rapidly, is smoking fewer cigarettes and now has difficulty swallowing his tablets. He is extremely weak and unable to move in bed without assistance.

INFORMATION PAGE

Aims in last 48 hours of life

- *Controlling physical symptoms:* Adjustments (psychological or social) are impossible as long as troublesome pain, nausea or breathlessness are present.
- *Give explanations:* Lack of information is the commonest cause of problems. Like drugs, information must titrated to the individual. *See* CLIP worksheets *Breaking difficult news* and *Collusion and denial.*
- *Anticipate changes:* Although it is not possible to anticipate every crisis, planning ahead is essential. For example, many patients suffer from bronchial secretions at the end of life and having hyoscine hydrobromide available is sensible.
- *Individualise care:* Drugs, like information, need to be titrated to the individual.
- *Stop unnecessary drugs:* It is often possible to simplify drug regimes as a patient deteriorates (see below).
- *Continue other drugs by the appropriate route:* The subcutaneous and buccal routes are useful and kind alternatives.
- *Give and take adequate support:* Duty demands we provide support, but clinical governance insists we also accept help, advice and support when we are unsure of the situation.
- *Set realistic goals:* Goals change as a patient deteriorates, but can still foster hope even if that is now about comfort. Resuscitation issues may need to be discussed – *see* CLIP worksheet *Issues around resuscitation.* Working to a clear plan can be very helpful – a good example is the Liverpool Care of the Dying Pathway (Ellershaw and Ward, 2003).
- *Explain changes to the partner and family:* They also need as much (or as little) information as they need.
- *Help partner and family understand the changes:* Changes are frightening, but it is often comforting to explain the natural course of a death and how gentle it is for most people.
- *Ensure the environment is appropriate:* Comfortable and as quiet (or noisy) as they want.
- *Ensure that religious care is offered if wanted:* Ask the patient, partner or family if they would like to talk to a chaplain or other spiritual advisor about death and dying.
- *Hydration and feeding* in the last hours have few advantages. Very few dying patients want to eat, while most only want sips of water. Encouraging feeding may cause vomiting. Dehydration causing thirst can be helped by hydration, but too much hydration risks increasing bronchial secretions.

Helping the partner or relative to adjust

- Adjusting to loss is never easy.
- It is common to cope by shuttling back and forth between denial and realism, but this is unsettling for many people.
- The road of life has its potholes and its distant views – looking only at the potholes avoids tripping but lacks interest, whilst looking only at the views means we miss the potholes. Most people need to do both!
- Denial can seem inappropriate at the end of life, but careful listening reveals that most are people being intermittently realistic (e.g. 'I do hope he can get well enough for that holiday, but he does look an awful lot worse').
- People need to adjust at their own pace and forcing the pace is unhelpful.
- If you, as the professional, feel at a loss, contact your local palliative care team for help and advice. Nobody has a library of the right things to say. Don't punish yourself for not making things 'better'. Being there, listening and giving explanations when asked will be the most help. Making a difference is what counts.

Adjusting medication

First think of Michael's drugs you know you can stop. For example, laxatives can often be stopped. If you have been ensuring a comfortable stool before the deterioration, most people can manage for up to 2 weeks without a laxative.

Next think of those drugs you know Michael needs to continue:

- Morphine needs to continue, but by a different route. The subcutaneous route is the commonest, but for convenience diamorphine is used since it is very soluble and can be used in low volumes. Divide the total daily morphine dose by 3 to find out the 24-hour diamorphine dose. Some dying patients need a lower dose – reduce if they become more unsettled on switching to diamorphine. *See* CLIP worksheet on *Changing opioids.*
- Cyclizine would be helpful to control any continuing nausea or vomiting. It can be given in suppository form, or mixed with diamorphine and given subcutaneously (concentrations of cyclizine above 10 mg/ml will precipitate).

This leaves the drugs you might not be sure about:

- Amitriptyline can be stopped if he is deteriorating rapidly since its effects will last at least a further 24–36 hours.
- Dexamethasone is usually stopped in a rapidly deteriorating patient, regardless of the length of previous treatment. In patients deteriorating more slowly, steroids can be safely stopped if the treatment has been for less than 3 weeks, but if they have been taking steroids for 1 month or more it may be necessary to continue the dexamethasone by SC infusion to avoid the 'washed out' feeling of adrenocortical insufficiency.
- Temazepam can be stopped if the treatment has been less than 3 weeks. In many patients, however, treatment has been much longer and a benzodiazepine will need to be continued to avoid agitation due to withdrawal.
- Cigarettes are rarely continued by very ill patients. Beware, however, of agitation due to nicotine withdrawal. This is simply treated by using a nicotine patch.

WORK PAGE

Think   What are the aims of a professional in the last hours and days?

. . . .

. . . .

. . . .

Michael's family are very worried that Michael is not eating and only taking sips of water.

Before thinking of what to say to his family, write down the advantages and disadvantages of hydration and feeding in the last stages of life.

Advantages	Disadvantages

Q: What do you say to Michael's family?

. . . .

. . . .

What changes would you make to Michael's treatment sheet?

Drug	Stop? Continue? Change to what drug and dose?
Morphine CR 60 mg twice daily	
Cyclizine 50 mg three times daily	
Amitriptyline 100 mg at night	
Temazepam 40 mg at night	
Dexamethasone 8 mg daily	
Co-danthrusate 4 capsules daily	
15 cigarettes daily	

FURTHER ACTIVITY

Think back to the last dying patient you cared for:

• What adjustments did the patient and partner/relative have to make?

FURTHER READING

Journal articles

Bolund C (1993) Loss, mourning and growth in the process of dying. *Palliative Medicine.* **7**(2): 17–25.

Chapman CR and Gavrin J (1995) Suffering and the dying patient. *Journal of Pharmaceutical Care in Pain and Symptom Control.* **3**: 67–90.

Edmonds P, Karlsen S, Khan S *et al.* (2001) A comparison of the palliative care needs of patients dying from chronic respiratory diseases and lung cancer. *Palliative Medicine.* **15**(4): 287–95.

Ellershaw J and Ward C (2003) Care of the dying patient: the last hours and days of life. *BMJ.* **326**: 30–4.

Frager G (2001) Improving end-of-life care: Listening to voices from the trenches. *Journal of Pain and Symptom Management.* **21**(3): 249–50.

Higginson IJ, Astin P and Dolan S (1998) Where do cancer patients die? Ten-year trends in the place of death of cancer patients in England. *Palliative Medicine.* **12**(5): 353–63.

Jaccaud M (1990) The dreams of dying cancer patients at the end of life. *Psychotherapies.* **10**(2): 77–84.

Luddington L, Cox S, Higginson I *et al.* (2001) The need for palliative care for patients with non-cancer diseases: a review of the evidence. *International Journal of Palliative Nursing.* **7**(5): 221–6.

Owen C, Tennant C, Levi J *et al.* (1994) Cancer patients' attitudes to final events in life: Wish for death, attitudes to cessation of treatment, suicide and euthanasia. *Psycho-Oncology.* **3**(1): 1–9.

Seamark DA, Williams S, Hall M *et al.* (1998) Dying from cancer in community hospitals or a hospice: Closest lay carers' perceptions. *British Journal of General Practice.* **48**(431): 1317–21.

Steinhauser KE, Clipp EC and Tulsky JA (2002) Evolution in measuring the quality of dying. *Journal of Palliative Medicine.* **5**(3): 407–14.

Wennman-Larsen A and Tishelman C (2002) Advanced home care for cancer patients at the end of life: a qualitative study of hopes and expectations of family caregivers. *Scandinavian Journal of Caring Sciences.* **16**(3): 240–7.

Resource book

Stedeford A (1984) *Facing Death: patients, families and professionals.* Heinemann Medical Books, London.

THE LAST HOURS AND DAYS

2 Managing distress

Claud Regnard
Margaret Kindlen
Janet Jackson
Sarah Alport
Margaret Younger

INTERMEDIATE LEVEL

Aim of this worksheet

To learn how to reduce patient distress in the last hours and days.

How to use this worksheet

- You can work through this worksheet by yourself, or with a tutor.

- Read the case study below, then work on the questions overleaf.

- The work page is on the right side, the information page is on the left.

- Work any way you want: you can try answering from your own knowledge (in which case, fold over the information page), you can use the information page (this is not cheating – you learn as you find the information) or you can use other sources of information.

- It should take you about 15 minutes. If anything is unclear, discuss it with a colleague.

- If you think any information is wrong or out of date, let us know.

- Use the activity on the back page and take this learning into your workplace.

Case study

Michael is a 57-year-old man with severe learning disability who lives in a community home with three other men with learning disability. Michael was diagnosed with gastric carcinoma some months ago, but presented too late for treatment. He has begun to deteriorate rapidly, is smoking fewer cigarettes and now has difficulty swallowing his tablets. He is extremely weak and unable to move in bed without assistance. Overnight he has become unsettled and distressed.

INFORMATION PAGE

Symptoms in the last 48 hours of life

Two hundred patients seen by a community palliative care service had the following problems in the last days of life:

Noisy/moist breathing 56%   Urinary incontinence/retention 53%   Pain 51%

Restlessness/agitation 42%   Dyspnoea 22%   Nausea and vomiting 14%

Sweating 14%   Jerking/twitching/plucking 12%   Confusion 9%

Lichter I and Hunt E (1990)

Managing symptoms

- *Noisy/moist breathing:* Positional change may be enough to reduce noise, otherwise consider hyoscine butylbromide 20 mg SC (less sedating) or hyoscine hydrobromide 400 microg SC (more sedating but longer acting). If cardiac failure is the cause consider frusemide 40 mg IV or IM. If necessary, use gentle suction.
- *Urinary incontinence:* This is likely to reduce in the last few hours and days as oral intake falls. If it persists, consider the use of pads or catheter (indwelling or intermittent), or use sheaths for male patients.
- *Urinary retention:* If possible, assist the patient to the toilet and maintain privacy. If all else fails, consider catheterisation (indwelling or intermittent).
- *Pain:* Finding the cause is the key (*see* CLIP worksheet *Diagnosing the cause of pain*). Disease-related pain does not usually worsen in the last stages of illness, but some new problems may cause pain and each needs a different treatment. Examples are urinary retention (catheterise), colic due to constipation (hyoscine butylbromide 20 mg SC), uncomfortable position (reposition, paracetamol PO or PR), infection (antibiotic PO or single dose of ceftriaxone 500 mg) and pressure sore pain (pressure-relieving mattress).

- *Restlessness/agitation/confusion:* Find and treat the cause if possible – it may be related to the above problems, fear or emotional distress (*see* CLIP worksheet *Confusion*). If other measures are inappropriate, consider sedation.
- *Breathlessness:* Find and treat the cause if appropriate (*see* CLIP worksheet *Breathlessness*). Consider changing the patient's position, increasing air movement (fan, open windows), oxygen, relaxation, and explanation. Consider drugs to (a) reduce any fear and (b) reduce the feeling of breathlessness.
- *Nausea/vomiting:* Continue antiemetics by the most appropriate route. Where the stomach is distended and the patient continually 'leaks' vomit, consider the brief insertion of a nasogastric tube to aspirate fluid and air.
- *Sweating:* Keep the patient cool, regularly change bed linen, and use cotton nightwear. Involve the family in sponging the patient if they wish.
- *Jerking/twitching/plucking:* Exclude causes of confusion (*see* CLIP worksheet *Confusion*). Alternatively, these may be myoclonic jerks due to their opioid, in which case reduce the dose or change opioid. Seizures may need low dose midazolam (2.5–5 mg buccally initially followed by 10–30 mg/24 hours SC infusion).

Managing an agitated confusion

Start with the simple things (not with drugs):
- Switch on a side light.
- Make sure the environment is quiet.
- Keep visiting strangers to a minimum.
- Explain what is happening to patient, partner and staff.

Treat the cause if you can: (*see* CLIP worksheet *Confusion*):
- Check for any drugs recently started (for adverse effects) or stopped (for withdrawal effects).
- Exclude chest or urinary infections, and exclude a full bladder or rectum.
- Start appropriate treatment if the patient *and* carer agree. The confused patient still has the right to refuse treatment (unless they are harming themselves or others). NB: There is no evidence that treating a chest infection lengthens a prognosis inappropriately.
- Hydration might help Michael's confusion if he is dehydrated.

MCQ answers:
1 F: Michael may be frightened and simply may need company. If the agitation is distressing for Michael he may need medication to allow a fuller assessment. Sedation is not the aim, although in severe agitation it may be necessary to use doses that result in some sedation.
2 T: Nicotine withdrawal is a cause of agitation. If smoking is not an option, then nicotine patches may help.
3 F: Darkness creates dark areas which can be frightening to a confused person.
4 F: A patient has the right to refuse treatment, even if the choice does not seem logical. The only exception is the patient who is at risk of harming themselves or others.
5 F: A chest infection can cause distressing airway secretions, pyrexia, pain and confusion.

WORK PAGE

Michael complains of pain on turning and rattly breathing.

Think Think of some causes for his pain and for his 'rattle'. How could you manage these?

	Possible causes	Treatment
Noisy breathing		
Pain		

Michael is on the following drugs: diamorphine SC infusion 40 mg daily; cyclizine SC infusion 150 mg daily; midazolam 5 mg as required. Initially settled, one evening Michael starts to become frightened, agitated and suspicious of people.

MCQ

1 Start by settling his agitation with sedatives	True	False
2 He might settle if he could have a cigarette	True	False
3 Switching on the light will make things worse	True	False
4 Refusing treatment can be ignored as he is confused	True	False
5 Treating a chest infection is always inappropriate	True	False

FURTHER ACTIVITY

Reflect on the last distressed patient you cared for at the end of life:

• What simple measures were used before drugs?

• If there were none, what was the reason?

FURTHER READING

Journal articles

Bolund C (1993) Loss, mourning and growth in the process of dying. *Palliative Medicine.* 7(2): 17–25.

Chapman CR and Gavrin J (1995) Suffering and the dying patient. *Journal of Pharmaceutical Care in Pain and Symptom Control.* 3: 67–90.

Edmonds P, Karlsen S, Khan S *et al.* (2001) A comparison of the palliative care needs of patients dying from chronic respiratory diseases and lung cancer. *Palliative Medicine.* 15(4): 287–95.

Frager G (2001) Improving end-of-life care: Listening to voices from the trenches. *Journal of Pain and Symptom Management.* 21(3): 249–50.

Higginson IJ, Astin P and Dolan S (1998) Where do cancer patients die? Ten-year trends in the place of death of cancer patients in England. *Palliative Medicine.* 12(5): 353–63.

Jaccaud M (1990) The dreams of dying cancer patients at the end of life. *Psychotherapies.* 10(2): 77–84.

Lichter I and Hunt E (1990) The last 48 hours of life. *Journal of Palliative Care.* 6(4): 7–15.

Luddington L, Cox S, Higginson I *et al.* (2001) The need for palliative care for patients with non-cancer diseases: a review of the evidence. *International Journal of Palliative Nursing.* 7(5): 221–6.

Owen C, Tennant C, Levi J *et al.* (1994) Cancer patients' attitudes to final events in life: Wish for death, attitudes to cessation of treatment, suicide and euthanasia. *Psycho-Oncology.* 3(1): 1–9.

Seamark DA, Williams S, Hall M *et al.* (1998) Dying from cancer in community hospitals or a hospice: Closest lay carers' perceptions. *British Journal of General Practice.* 48(431): 1317–21.

Steinhauser KE, Clipp EC and Tulsky JA (2002) Evolution in measuring the quality of dying. *Journal of Palliative Medicine.* 5(3): 407–14.

Wennman-Larsen A and Tishelman C (2002) Advanced home care for cancer patients at the end of life: a qualitative study of hopes and expectations of family caregivers. *Scandinavian Journal of Caring Sciences.* 16(3): 240–7.

Resource book

Stedeford A (1984) *Facing Death: patients, families and professionals.* Heinemann Medical Books, London.

THE LAST HOURS AND DAYS

3 The death

Claud Regnard
Sarah Alport

INTRODUCTORY LEVEL

Aim of this worksheet

To explore some issues for patients and carers at the time of death.

How to use this worksheet

- You can work through this worksheet by yourself, or with a tutor.

- Read the case study below, then work on the questions overleaf.

- The work page is on the right side, the information page is on the left.

- Work any way you want: you can try answering from your own knowledge (in which case, fold over the information page), you can use the information page (this is not cheating – you learn as you find the information) or you can use other sources of information.

- It should take you about 15 minutes. If anything is unclear, discuss it with a colleague.

- If you think any information is wrong or out of date, let us know.

- Use the activity on the back page and take this learning into your workplace.

Case study

Michael is a 57-year-old man with severe learning disability who lives in a community home with three other men with learning disability. Michael was diagnosed with gastric carcinoma some months ago, but presented too late for treatment. He has begun to deteriorate rapidly, is smoking fewer cigarettes and now has difficulty swallowing his tablets. In the last few days he has become extremely weak and unable to move in bed without assistance. He is now comatose and close to death.

INFORMATION PAGE

Death – how it is for the patient

For most patients with advanced illness there is a gentle 'winding down' of the body's systems. Even in cardiac and respiratory failure, sudden, unexpected, dramatic deaths are uncommon. At the end it is more a gentle absence of life, than a sudden presence of death. Peaceful silence is the most obvious feature.

Death – how it is for the carers

Some find it easy to cry, others feel as though they have dried up. Some feel the urge to speak, often to express relief. Others feel it's an anticlimax because, in a sense, the patient 'left' hours or days before.

Many are so numbed with grief that they feel helpless and useless, but they may not admit to this. Some cannot remember names, addresses and telephone numbers. This needs to be understood when it comes to giving information about registering a death – the information may have to be given to another member of the family.

Occasionally a relative or partner has been unable to adjust to the deterioration of the patient and reacts with shock or anger at what is obvious to everyone else. It is rare for such people to be truly ignorant of the facts, it is just that they have not been able to face the terrible reality. Experienced help and support from a palliative care specialist (doctor, nurse or social worker) may be needed.

(From Doyle, 1994)

Death – how it is for the professional carer

Awkward is how it feels.

There is an overwhelming feeling to:
- do something (check the pulse, breathing, move a pillow, make tea)
- say something (usually something like, 'Well, he's at peace now').

There are no rules, but there are some principles:
- Take your cue from the family or partner – enable them to do it their way.
- Silence is awkward, but is right in the right place (anyway, there's nothing you can say that will make it better).

- If those present want to talk, then talk; if they're silent, then let them be silent.
- Someone *will* need to check the patient has died. Don't pronounce death until at least several minutes have elapsed from the last breath, since some patients take an occasional breath for several minutes.
- After the death, ask those present if they want to stay, and if so, whether they want to be alone.
- Now go and make that cup of tea!

The arrangements

This gives you more things to do:
- Help the family contact friends and relatives.
- Ask them whether it's to be a burial or a cremation.
- Help them choose an undertaker.

- Explain what's on the certificate.
- If a post mortem is needed, obtain consent and explain the arrangements.
- Explain how to register a death.

The death certificate and post mortems

The death certificate should be filled out by the doctor who saw the patient within the last few days. The cause of death is what is put down (in Michael's case, 'Carcinoma of stomach'), *not* the mode of death (so not 'respiratory arrest' or 'coma').

There is no reason to seal the certificate in an envelope, it is better for the relative or partner to see the certificate and have the words on it explained. In some cases the patient or partner asks that the diagnosis is kept from other relatives (e.g. in AIDS). In this case the prime cause of death (e.g. 'Cerebral lymphoma') is put in and there is a box on the back of the certificate which ensures that the registrar contacts the certifying doctor later for the underlying cause.

Post mortems required by law: These are necessary where death is due to industrial disease (e.g. asbestosis), injury, neglect, suspicious circumstances, or within the normal recovery time of an operation. A relative's permission is helpful.

Post mortems as a valuable way of obtaining information: A relative's permission is essential and usually it is not difficult to ask if this is done sensitively ('It would help us to examine Michael to find out why he had problems with vomiting'). It needs to be made clear that the relative or partner can refuse.

It is unusual for a funeral to be delayed by a post mortem.

WORK PAGE

Think Think back to the last patient who died with you present. NB: If you find this hard because of a difficult personal experience then ask a colleague about their experience.

Q How did it seem for the patient?

. . . .

. . . .

. . . .

. . . .

Q How did it seem for the partner, relative or friend?

. . . .

. . . .

. . . .

. . . .

Q How did you feel?

. . . .

. . . .

. . . .

. . . .

Michael drifts into coma and dies peacefully four days later, with his family at his bedside.

What can you do and what can you say?

. . . .

. . . .

. . . .

. . . .

Michael's mother asks what is going to be put on the death certificate and whether a post mortem is necessary.

Q What do you say?

. . . .

. . . .

. . . .

. . . .

FURTHER ACTIVITY

Reflect on a patient who died recently:

- How did you feel?

FURTHER READING

Journal articles

Bolund C (1993) Loss, mourning and growth in the process of dying. *Palliative Medicine.* **7**(2): 17–25.

Chapman CR and Gavrin J (1995) Suffering and the dying patient. *Journal of Pharmaceutical Care in Pain and Symptom Control.* **3**: 67–90.

Edmonds P, Karlsen S, Khan S *et al.* (2001) A comparison of the palliative care needs of patients dying from chronic respiratory diseases and lung cancer. *Palliative Medicine.* **15**(4): 287–95.

Frager G (2001) Improving end-of-life care: Listening to voices from the trenches. *Journal of Pain and Symptom Management.* **21**(3): 249–50.

Higginson IJ, Astin P and Dolan S (1998) Where do cancer patients die? Ten-year trends in the place of death of cancer patients in England. *Palliative Medicine.* **12**(5): 353–63.

Jaccaud M (1990) The dreams of dying cancer patients at the end of life. *Psychotherapies.* **10**(2): 77–84.

Luddington L, Cox S, Higginson I *et al.* (2001) The need for palliative care for patients with non-cancer diseases: a review of the evidence. *International Journal of Palliative Nursing.* **7**(5): 221–6.

Owen C, Tennant C, Levi J *et al.* (1994) Cancer patients' attitudes to final events in life: Wish for death, attitudes to cessation of treatment, suicide and euthanasia. *Psycho-Oncology.* **3**(1): 1–9.

Seamark DA, Williams S, Hall M *et al.* (1998) Dying from cancer in community hospitals or a hospice: Closest lay carers' perceptions. *British Journal of General Practice.* **48**(431): 1317–21.

Steinhauser KE, Clipp EC and Tulsky JA (2002) Evolution in measuring the quality of dying. *Journal of Palliative Medicine.* **5**(3): 407–14.

Wennman-Larsen A and Tishelman C (2002) Advanced home care for cancer patients at the end of life: a qualitative study of hopes and expectations of family caregivers. *Scandinavian Journal of Caring Sciences.* **16**(3): 240–7.

Resource books

Doyle D (1994) *Caring for a Dying Relative: a guide for families.* Oxford University Press, Oxford.

Stedeford A (1984) *Facing Death: patients, families and professionals.* Heinemann Medical Books, London.

THE LAST HOURS AND DAYS

4 A friend dies . . .

Lynn Gibson
Dorothy Matthews
Claud Regnard
Margaret Kindlen

INTRODUCTORY LEVEL

Aim of this worksheet

To think about how to support fellow patients during and after the death.

How to use this worksheet

- You can work through this worksheet by yourself, or with a tutor.

- Read the case study below, then work on the questions overleaf.

- The work page is on the right side, the information page is on the left.

- Work any way you want: you can try answering from your own knowledge (in which case, fold over the information page), you can use the information page (this is not cheating – you learn as you find the information) or you can use other sources of information.

- It should take you about 15 minutes. If anything is unclear, discuss it with a colleague.

- If you think any information is wrong or out of date, let us know.

- Use the activity on the back page and take this learning into your workplace.

Case study

Michael is a 57-year-old man with severe learning disability who lives in a community home with three other men with learning disability. Michael was diagnosed with gastric carcinoma some months ago, but presented too late for treatment. He dies peacefully in his bedroom.

   Although all the men were aware of Michael's illness, Fred in particular has demonstrated some changes in behaviour and reluctance to participate in his usual activities. The staff are concerned that these changes are related to Michael's death and are unsure how to address these issues.

INFORMATION PAGE

- *Death of a relative or close friend:* This can happen during any illness and is an added burden on the patient.
- *Death of a fellow patient:* Many patients develop friendships with fellow patients through their shared experiences. This may be a recent friendship with someone in the same bay in hospital or hospice, or may be over months through attending the same day hospice, or over years through living in the same community home. Regardless of the length of the friendship, the death of one patient also can be a loss for fellow patients.
- *The effect of a death on staff:* Many staff get to know a patient well, seeing them through crises and listening to their fears and joys. The death of a patient can feel like the loss of a friend.

The consequences of not sharing loss

Every person will experience loss and bereavement at some point in their lives, but many people shy away from discussions involving death and dying. As a consequence these issues can become stigmatised by a team. This tendency to 'hide' death results in several typical practices at the time of death:

- 'hiding' the body by shutting the door, closing the curtains or putting the body in a box designed to look like a trolley
- talking in whispers
- not telling children
- a determination to continue as normal
- moving the body as soon as possible
- not telling fellow patients
- presenting a 'jolly' manner to cover the sadness.

This reluctance to share the loss results in fellow patients and staff suppressing their grief and having feelings of uncertainty, tension and fear. These problems have occurred because fellow patients and staff failed to view the death holistically from physical, psychological, social and spiritual points of view.

Starting to share the loss

1 *Unhelpful:* Honesty is the place to start. Every person is an individual in their own right and their specific needs will vary, but more harm will come from hiding fellow patients from the truth.
2 *Unhelpful:* Fellow patients are as likely to suffer from the loss of Michael as anyone else. Taking time to sit and talk with a fellow can be very beneficial and this includes people with alternative communication.
3 *Unhelpful:* It should be remembered that it is usual to feel sad and hurt during a time of loss, but it is not helpful for carers to try to 'jolly' the person along.
4 *Helpful:* For many people, reflecting back on a person's life (life story work) is a useful way to communicate significant life events, and can be seen as a vital element in helping the person bring back memories, both good and bad, that would otherwise be forgotten. The concept of life story books is also acknowledged in bereavement counselling.
5 *Helpful:* Look for changes in behaviour which might indicate difficulty in expressing an emotion. Assess Fred's overall condition – don't assume his behaviour changes are a result of his grief since they may be related to something else.

Remember that for some people, a grief reaction may take time to manifest.

6 *Unhelpful:* If memory is poor, reinforce the loss to assess Fred's understanding/feelings related to Michael's death. Repeat ideas to encourage learning.
7 *Unhelpful:* Adjusting to the change can be difficult. It can be tempting for staff to get on with normality. Both Fred and the care staff may need help and support whilst he is adjusting to living in an environment where Michael is missing.
8 *Helpful:* Families may not know how to break the news of the death to their relatives, especially if they are very young or have learning disabilities. They may try to protect the person from the effects of grief, which unintentionally makes matters worse, since the person may now wonder why they can no longer visit or see the person who has died. In cases where the mother has died, the child (or adult with a learning disability) has lost the person who understands them most. Informing the person that this important person is ill or dying allows the carer to prepare that person for their loss. They may need help to break this difficult news. (*See* CLIP worksheet *Breaking difficult news.*)

How do people with learning disabilities experience bereavement?

Historically, it was believed that people with learning disabilities were not capable of understanding or expressing grief.

Whether through ignorance or a misguided attempt to protect the person, the death of a relative or friend was often glossed over. Anecdotal evidence indicates that individuals were prevented from attending the chapel of rest or funeral following the loss of a loved one. Sometimes relatives and carers made a conscious effort to hide their true emotions from the person with learning disability.

Carers can test a person's understanding of the concept of death and what it means to that person by using issues raised on television as a starting point. There is evidence to suggest that although a person with learning disabilities uses the words 'death' or 'dead', this does not imply that they understand it as a concept. Keep ideas simple and concrete.

People with learning disability may not suffer all of the recognisable reactions to bereavement. However, they may have additional special difficulties due to poor intellect and complex needs, which deny them many of the social, verbal, auditory and visual opportunities of realising that death has occurred.

It is important to remember that people with learning disabilities have the same right to take part in family rituals as anyone else. This should include receiving/sending cards, sending flowers and helping to choose hymns or poems.

So, how should we treat people with learning disabilities following bereavement? The simple answer is easy – like any other person!

WORK PAGE

Think   Think about ways that staff avoid the issues around the death of a patient. Then think about the consequences of these actions and practices.

Things staff do to avoid issues about death	Consequences of those actions and practices
. . . .	. . . .
. . . .	. . . .
. . . .	. . . .
. . . .	. . . .
. . . .	. . . .
. . . .	. . . .
. . . .	. . . .

As you read the following list of possible phrases, decide whether they would be helpful or unhelpful when talking to Fred (Michael's friend).

Phrase	Helpful	Unhelpful
1 'Michael's gone away.'	☐	☐
2 'He won't realise that Michael's gone.'	☐	☐
3 'Don't worry, everything will be fine.'	☐	☐
4 'What do you remember about Michael?'	☐	☐
5 'Fred's been much quieter since Michael died.'	☐	☐
6 'It's time to move on – life's for the living.'	☐	☐
7 'Let's get the bed filled.'	☐	☐
8 'Fred, Michael has died.'	☐	☐

What can you do to support a person with learning disability who has just lost a fellow patient?

. . . .

. . . .

. . . .

. . . .

FURTHER ACTIVITY

Think about a recent death:

• What did you and the other members of the team do to support fellow patients?

FURTHER READING

Journal articles

Birchenall P (1993) Learning disabilities – bereavement and working with people with learning disabilities: when nursing goes beyond a duty of care. *Nursing Times.* **89**: 63.

Bolund C (1993) Loss, mourning and growth in the process of dying. *Palliative Medicine.* **7**(2): 17–25.

Chapman CR and Gavrin J (1995) Suffering and the dying patient. *Journal of Pharmaceutical Care in Pain and Symptom Control.* **3**: 67–90.

Frager G (2001) Improving end-of-life care: Listening to voices from the trenches. *Journal of Pain and Symptom Management.* **21**(3): 249–50.

Higginson IJ, Astin P and Dolan S (1998) Where do cancer patients die? Ten-year trends in the place of death of cancer patients in England. *Palliative Medicine.* **12**(5): 353–63.

Jaccaud M (1990) The dreams of dying cancer patients at the end of life. *Psychotherapies.* **10**(2): 77–84.

Moddia B (1995) Grief reactions in learning disabilities. *Nursing Standard.* **9**: 38–9.

Owen C, Tennant C, Levi J *et al.* (1994) Cancer patients' attitudes to final events in life: Wish for death, attitudes to cessation of treatment, suicide and euthanasia. *Psycho-Oncology.* **3**(1): 1–9.

Read S (1996) Helping people with learning disabilities to grieve. *British Journal of Learning Disabilities.* **5**: 91–5.

Seamark DA, Williams S, Hall M *et al.* (1998) Dying from cancer in community hospitals or a hospice: Closest lay carers' perceptions. *British Journal of General Practice.* **48**(431): 1317–21.

Resource books

Stedeford A (1984) *Facing Death: patients, families and professionals.* Heinemann Medical Books, London.

Blackman N (1999) *Helping People with Learning Disabilities Cope with Bereavement and Loss.* Pavilion Publishing, Brighton.

Cathcart F (1994) *Understanding Death and Dying: your feelings.* British Institute of Learning Disabilities, Kidderminster.

BEREAVEMENT

1 The loss begins . . .

Claud Regnard
Margaret Kindlen
Janet Jackson
Dorothy Matthews
Lynn Gibson

INTRODUCTORY LEVEL

Aim of this worksheet

To outline the responses to grief of patients, partners and professionals.

How to use this worksheet

- You can work through this worksheet by yourself, or with a tutor.

- Read the case study below, then work on the questions overleaf.

- The work page is on the right side, the information page is on the left.

- Work any way you want: you can try answering from your own knowledge (in which case, fold over the information page), you can use the information page (this is not cheating – you learn as you find the information) or you can use other sources of information.

- It should take you about 15 minutes. If anything is unclear, discuss it with a colleague.

- If you think any information is wrong or out of date, let us know.

- Use the activity on the back page and take this learning into your workplace.

Case study

Mary is a 39-year-old woman, divorced, with a 9-year-old boy and a 16-year-old daughter. She has very advanced breast carcinoma and was admitted to hospital urgently because of rapid deterioration. She is now deteriorating day by day and is insisting on returning home. Her recently widowed mother has been staying at home to look after the children.

INFORMATION PAGE

Every person will experience loss and bereavement at some point in their lives, but many people shy away from discussions involving death and dying, and as a consequence these issues have become stigmatised by society.

- *Loss* is a common experience with varying degrees of importance, from losing your car keys to losing someone close.

- *Grief* describes the feelings when someone dies.
- *Bereavement* is a term that describes the period of grief around the loss of someone close.
- *Mourning* is the public face of grief in the time immediately following a person's death.

Responses to loss

People experience grief differently. Grief is a common reaction to loss and can be understood more effectively when it is viewed within the emotional, cultural, social and psychological aspects of a person's life. Bereavement is one of life's most challenging periods. When each family member realised that Mary was gravely ill they will have gone through many different feelings:

- *Shock* at the news is inevitable. Any one of the family may have reacted with **numbness** or **denial** at the reality. They may also have reacted with **anger** or **frustration** that someone close is going to be taken from them, especially at the **meaninglessness** of the situation or its **unfairness**.
- *Anxiety* about this new situation can result in **fear**, with feelings of vulnerability and **loss of** security. Any of the family may feel **guilt**, which may have a good reason or be quite unjustified (children can feel that it's somehow their fault, that if only they'd been good . . .).
- *Relief* seems odd at first, but **relief** can result from the ending of any suffering and at release from the burden of caring. Although this relief is understandable, people often feel guilty that they feel such relief.

- *Sadness* is a feeling you would expect, especially one of **loss** of the future with a **yearning** that things were different.
- *Pining* for normality can occur with a mixture of many of the feelings already described. **Despair** can intervene and may even lead to **depression**.
- *Hyperactivity* can occur by '**keeping busy**', but **irritability** and **exhaustion** can develop.

Mary may be reacting with any of the same feelings. In particular, she will also have feelings of loss. She will grieve for the loss of her future with her family and not being able to see her children grow up.

When Mary dies, the family may go through many of these feelings again and again.

After the death, the family may have a few feelings that are different. They may develop a sense of **searching** for what has been lost, sometimes hearing, smelling or even seeing the person who has died. Paradoxically, this urge is accompanied by a conflicting **urge not to search** for the lost person (i.e. a wish to return to normal). Such conflicts are common in bereavement and result in the turmoil so often felt by bereaved people. This turmoil is particularly strong in the early bereavement, but becomes less as the loss and grief begin to resolve.

When does bereavement start?

What is clear from people's reactions is that they are almost identical before Mary died as after her death. All of these reactions are no different from those that occur after hearing bad or difficult news. This is not surprising, as such news usually tells someone about a loss they will suffer. Therefore it could be said that bereavement starts at the time of diagnosis, not just after the death.

It is now becoming clear that loss and grieving are felt by everyone before the death, *including the patient*. This has important implications since it means we can help partners and family in their bereavement in the weeks and months *before* the death. The patient becomes an important part of this bereavement care.

The stages of bereavement . . .

Kubler-Ross described different stages that bereaved people go through. This was wrongly interpreted by others as a fixed progression. Kubler-Ross realised that, although the responses occurred, they often did not occur in any particular order. In addition, people oscillate between different 'stages', especially in early bereavement.

In reality, bereavement is a chaotic, disruptive process that makes the individual feel out of control. It has been described as a 'whirlpool of emotions'.

WORK PAGE

Think   As they all look after and care for Mary, what sort of feelings do you think the family might be having?

Ex-husband:

. . . .

. . . .

Mother:

. . . .

. . . .

9-year-old son:

. . . .

. . . .

16-year-old daughter:

. . . .

. . . .

Think   What sort of feelings do you think Mary is having?

. . . .

. . . .

Mary continues to deteriorate and dies peacefully at home.

What *new* feelings might the family be having? What feelings are unchanged?

New feelings	Same feelings
. . . .	. . . .
. . . .	. . . .
. . . .	. . . .

Compare the lists you made above. What do you notice about the different lists? What does this tell you about the point at which bereavement starts?

. . . .

. . . .

Think   Do you think these reactions develop in any particular order?

. . . .

. . . .

FURTHER ACTIVITY

Think of a time you lost a valued or important *material* possession (e.g. house keys, credit card):

• What were your feelings and thoughts, and how did your behaviour change?

FURTHER READING

Journal articles

Ringdal GI, Jordhoy MS, Ringdal K *et al.* (2001) The first year of grief and bereavement in close family members to individuals who have died of cancer. *Palliative Medicine.* 15: 91–105.

Casarett D, Kutner JS, Abrahm J *et al.* (2001) Life after death: A practical approach to grief and bereavement. *Annals of Internal Medicine.* 134: 208–15.

Katz J, Sidell M and Komaromy C (2000) Death in homes: bereavement needs of residents, relatives and staff. *International Journal of Palliative Nursing.* 6: 274–9.

Resource books and website

Dickenson D, Johnson M and Katz JS (2000) *Death, Dying, and Bereavement* (2e). Sage Publications and the Open University, London.

Faulkner A (1995) *Working with Bereaved People.* Churchill Livingstone, Edinburgh.

Hindmarch C (2000) *On the Death of a Child* (2e). Radcliffe Medical Press, Oxford.

Kubler-Ross E (1989) *On Death and Dying.* Routledge, London.

Parkes CM (1996) *Bereavement: studies of grief in adult life* (3e). Routledge, New York.

Parkes CM (1996) *Counselling in Terminal Care and Bereavement.* BPS Books, Leicester/Baltimore.

Stedeford A (1984) *Facing Death: patients, families and professionals.* Heinemann Medical Books, London.

Worden JW (1991) *Grief Counselling and Grief Therapy: a handbook for the mental health practitioner* (2e). Routledge, London.

www.edc.org/lastacts – *Innovations at the End of Life Care*: peer-reviewed on-line journal.

BEREAVEMENT

2 The effect of death on staff

Claud Regnard
Margaret Kindlen
Dorothy Matthews
Lynn Gibson

INTRODUCTORY LEVEL

Aim of this worksheet

To explore the effects of a death on professional staff.

How to use this worksheet

- You can work through this worksheet by yourself, or with a tutor.

- Read the case study below, then work on the questions overleaf.

- The work page is on the right side, the information page is on the left.

- Work any way you want: you can try answering from your own knowledge (in which case, fold over the information page), you can use the information page (this is not cheating – you learn as you find the information) or you can use other sources of information.

- It should take you about 15 minutes. If anything is unclear, discuss it with a colleague.

- If you think any information is wrong or out of date, let us know.

- Use the activity on the back page and take this learning into your workplace.

Case study

Mary was a 39-year-old woman, divorced with a 9-year-old boy and a 16-year-old daughter. She had advanced breast carcinoma and required several hospital admissions, but insisted on returning home. Because of Mary's request, and with minimal preparation, the ward staff and the hospital palliative care team arranged for her to be discharged home urgently. She died peacefully at home a few days later.

INFORMATION PAGE

Issues in bereavement for staff

- *Acknowledging staff need:* Staff may be so involved in responding to the grief reactions of the remaining clients or patients that their own feelings go unrecognised. Sheer **workload** in some teams prevents staff exploring what they feel about the death of a patient.
- *Permission to cry:* Staff need '**permission to cry**'. Some health teams understand this and allow staff to show their feelings, but other teams cannot cope with such emotion, viewing it as '**unprofessional**', '**letting the team down**' or even as a seeing it as a **weakness**. This may lead to feelings being hidden and possible problems not being addressed. Staff most commonly **take their unresolved feelings home**. Although they may share the reasons with their partners or family, it is more common for them to '**dump the feelings**' on the unsuspecting partner or family without being able to explain the reason why. It will be harder if the staff member has recently had their **own bereavement**.
- *Reassurance:* Care staff usually perceive themselves as being able to make things better, so they may feel that they have failed in this situation. **Guilt** may be the result. This in-built desire to '**fix things**' can prevent staff from realising that, in reality, they made a difference by being with the patient and family, and that this was therapeutic and helpful.
- *Organisational issues:* Organisations should respect the needs of the patient and staff such as remembering to leave an appropriate length of time before re-allocating the bed. In a busy health service, stretched at times beyond its ability to cope, this is not always possible, but a **period of bereavement**, however brief, should be the aim when possible.
- *Time to reflect on the situation:* Now the rollercoaster has stopped; the **staff need time to reflect** on:
  - the progression of the client's disease
  - the nature of the death (was it peaceful and expected, or was it unexpected or distressing?)
  - how the death has impacted on both clients and staff.
- *Closure:* This typically North American term describes the completion of a grieving process. **Closure** is difficult in many health settings and it is not possible to achieve it with every death. **Attending the funeral** or service of just one patient can act to 'close the chapter' on other deaths. **Talking to bereaved relatives** may also help.

Complications of staff bereavement

- *Staff denial:* This works if the feelings are being channelled elsewhere, but it may cause that member of staff to remain **distant from the next dying patient** for fear of exposing unresolved feelings.
- *Team denial:* This can result in a team who are uncomfortable with dying patients, preferring instead to keep treatments going that are clearly no longer of benefit. Their discomfort will make it very difficult, if not impossible, to share the patient's fears or distress. Consequently they may miss problems that could be treated such as depression, or may ask for the patient to be moved elsewhere, believing that this is the kindest thing to do.
- *Stress and burnout:* Some stress is necessary to do our jobs well (it is possible to be *too* relaxed!). However, if this **stress** builds up because of blocked feelings then the staff member may eventually suffer from an anxiety state, clinical depression, along with physical symptoms of **exhaustion**, **difficulty making decisions**, and **feeling unable to come to work**. They feel **guilty** that they haven't been 'stronger'. This is known as 'burnout' and usually catches people unawares, since the sufferer is often the last to acknowledge that they are suffering from stress.

How you can help yourself

If there are team difficulties with emotions or death, don't try to sort this out yourself – this needs organisational change and education, neither of which can occur overnight or without the help of others. In the meantime:

- Find someone you can talk to about coping with staff deaths – an understanding colleague at work is often better than taking the issue home and dumping it on your partner.
- Even if you can't cry with your team, find somewhere quiet and have a good cry, with a colleague if you can.
- Look back on the things you did that made a difference, keeping the patient comfortable, looking after the relatives. It's often the small things that make a difference.
- Try to go to one funeral of a patient – it often helps to 'close the chapters' of many other deaths. Don't be ashamed of using a funeral in this way – funerals are about the dead, but they are meant for the living.

Support mechanisms

- *Colleague:* Ask a colleague to talk over the death. The local palliative care team can help.
- *Specialist help:* Persistent or complicated grief will need more specialist help from a bereavement service, counsellor or psychiatrist. Trusts and health organisations often have support teams but the availability of these services depends on local resources.

WORK PAGE

What factors *at work* do you think help staff to resolve a death and what factors *at work* do you think hinder its resolution?

Factors at work that help	Factors at work that hinder (i.e. risk factors)
. . . .	. . . .
. . . .	. . . .
. . . .	. . . .
. . . .	. . . .
. . . .	. . . .
. . . .	. . . .
. . . .	. . . .
. . . .	. . . .
. . . .	. . . .

Think (Ring) issues that would make you concerned about a team or individual following Mary's death.

Feeling guilty	Unable to make decisions
Easily exhausted	Talking to bereaved relatives
Crying after the death	Recent family bereavement
Unable to come to work	Wanting time to reflect
Attending funeral	Distant with dying patients

Think What can you and your team do to reduce the risks?

. . . .

. . . .

. . . .

. . . .

. . . .

FURTHER ACTIVITY

Think of a relative who has suffered bereavement:

* How could they have been supported differently?

FURTHER READING

Journal articles

Casarett D, Kutner JS, Abrahm J *et al.* (2001) Life after death: A practical approach to grief and bereavement. *Annals of Internal Medicine.* **134:** 208–15.

Katz J, Sidell M and Komaromy C (2000) Death in homes: bereavement needs of residents, relatives and staff. *International Journal of Palliative Nursing.* **6:** 274–9.

Ringdal GI, Jordhoy MS, Ringdal K *et al.* (2001) The first year of grief and bereavement in close family members to individuals who have died of cancer. *Palliative Medicine.* **15:** 91–105.

Resource books and website

Dickenson D, Johnson M and Katz JS (2000) *Death, Dying, and Bereavement* (2e). Sage Publications and the Open University, London.

Faulkner A (1995) *Working with Bereaved People.* Churchill Livingstone, Edinburgh.

Hindmarch C (2000) *On the Death of a Child* (2e). Radcliffe Medical Press, Oxford.

Parkes CM (1996) *Bereavement: studies of grief in adult life* (3e). Routledge, New York.

Parkes CM (1996) *Counselling in Terminal Care and Bereavement.* BPS Books, Leicester/Baltimore.

Stedeford A (1984) *Facing Death: patients, families and professionals.* Heinemann Medical Books, London.

Worden JW (1991) *Grief Counselling and Grief Therapy: a handbook for the mental health practitioner* (2e). Routledge, London.

www.edc.org/lastacts – *Innovations at the End of Life Care*: peer-reviewed on-line journal.

BEREAVEMENT

3 Assessing risk

Claud Regnard
Margaret Kindlen
Janet Jackson
Tessa Nichol
Dorothy Matthews
Lynn Gibson

INTERMEDIATE LEVEL

Aim of this worksheet

To describe the important factors which can help in deciding bereavement risk.

How to use this worksheet

- You can work through this worksheet by yourself, or with a tutor.
- Read the case study below, then work on the questions overleaf.
- The work page is on the right side, the information page is on the left.
- Work any way you want: you can try answering from your own knowledge (in which case, fold over the information page), you can use the information page (this is not cheating – you learn as you find the information) or you can use other sources of information.
- It should take you about 15 minutes. If anything is unclear, discuss it with a colleague.
- If you think any information is wrong or out of date, let us know.
- Use the activity on the back page and take this learning into your workplace.

Case study

Mary was a 39-year-old woman, divorced, with a 9-year-old boy and a 16-year-old daughter. She had advanced breast carcinoma and required several hospital admissions, but insisted on returning home where she died peacefully a few days later.

   Her recently widowed mother had been staying with them and has stayed on to look after the children. Her ex-husband had been visiting regularly but has had to return back to work as a lorry driver.

INFORMATION PAGE

The bereavement journey

We react to grief and loss in very different ways. People oscillate between experiencing loss and working towards restoration. In the early stages these oscillations are rapid and intense, gradually reducing over time and moving more towards restoration. The extent of these oscillations will depend on many different past experiences, on personality and on current issues. Not surprisingly, it is not possible to talk about 'normal' or 'abnormal' grief. The one clear feature, however, is that most people find they begin to cope and function more effectively as time passes.

For many, this journey started at the time of diagnosis when they were first faced with the possibility of such profound losses. Some will have used that time (and been supported) to work through some of the issues they are having to face. The distressing 'oscillations' of loss–restoration will have lessened and they will be better prepared for the death. Others will not have been able to use this time for the reasons below.

What helps or hinders the resolution of bereavement?

- *Factors which help resolution* include close relationships, the perception of a good network of support, strong spiritual beliefs of any sort, a good relationship with the person who died, a feeling of 'closure' about the life and death of the person (i.e. no 'unfinished business), a peaceful and expected death, being present at the death, and a healthy status of the bereaved.
- *Factors which can hinder resolution* include poor relationships, little or no social support, a difficult or poor relationship with the person who died, unfinished business, difficulty in shedding tears, a sudden or unexpected death, a distressing death, being unable to fulfil a wish to be present at the death or funeral, illness in the bereaved, bad experiences of previous deaths, the presence of other sources of stress (e.g. recent divorce or death), lack of planning in financial or business affairs, and absent or inadequate care arrangements for children.
- *High risk factors:* In reality, any factor could indicate a high risk in certain circumstances. **All of the factors** previously indicate a risk that bereavement may resolve slowly. Other risk factors include **persisting anger or guilt**, extreme or **obsessive crying** after the first few months, **previous psychiatric history** or **suicidal tendencies, drug or alcohol dependence**. Being absent at the time of the death is less of a risk if the bereaved person felt they had already said all that needed to be said. On the other hand, **missing the opportunity to say goodbye** or express their love could seriously hinder resolution of their bereavement.

Mary's family

- *Mary's mother* will be **at risk from two bereavements** – her husband and now her daughter. She is likely to feel how 'unnatural' it has been that her daughter died before she did and may **feel she would rather have died**. For the time being, however, she will be **occupied** looking after the children and this may help her to resolve her grief, although it could also **occupy her so much** that she does not have the time to address her own losses and may **not be able to enjoy her old age**. Many of Mary's admissions were because of the lack of help at home and this will have made her mother feel **guilty** that her own problems prevented her from being there more often.
- *9-year-old boy:* The loss of his mother will be a major impact on his life. Like the adults he will **not be able to make sense of what has happened**, but unlike them his imagination may feed beliefs that he was to **blame**, or that if he had been better behaved she would not have died. He may not have been allowed to see his mother in the last days, or attend the funeral because of well intentioned but **misguided protection** by his father and grandmother. He may feel **anger at staff** for diagnosing Mary's illness and then not being able to treat the cancer. He may also be **angry at his mother** for spending time away and 'leaving' by dying, compounded by **anger towards his father**. This may have been worsened if there is **uncertainty about Mary's wishes for the care of the children** and might need guardianship or residency orders to be arranged.
- *16-year-old daughter:* Her mother's death will have taken away an important support and guide at a time when she was only just starting to understand adulthood. She may **'take over' the role of her mother** in caring for her brother, and **spend her energies** supporting her father and grandmother, **giving herself little or no time** for her own grief. She also may have been prevented from seeing her mother in the last days. She may become **hyperactive** trying to do everything, eventually becoming **exhausted**. Bereavement is a drastic, disruptive process and she may feel **out of control**. She may be **ambivalent or angry towards her father. Uncertainty about home tenancy or ownership** will add to the complications.
- *Mary's ex-husband:* His job will isolate him and if he is living alone he will be at further risk. He may **feel guilty** about the failure of the marriage and about moving away from home and the children.

Getting help

It is obvious from discussion with relatives and acknowledging their feelings that they may require further support/help to work through the bereavement process, using the following networks:

- opportunities to discuss feeling/concerns with staff who have cared for Michael
- the clergy: support for the family could be gained both in the short and long term
- medical staff: support for the family and to discuss unresolved issues. The general practitioner is often the first line of help and should be meeting the bereaved within a few weeks, and again after a few months
- specialist help: persistent or complicated grief will need more specialist help from a bereavement service, counsellor or psychiatrist.

The aims of counselling the bereaved correspond to the four tasks of grieving:

- to increase the reality of loss
- to help the survivor come to terms with both his/her expressed and latent feelings
- to help with making the readjustments necessitated by the loss
- to encourage the survivor to make a healthy emotional withdrawal from the deceased and to feel comfortable reinvesting that emotion in another relationship.

The availability of these services depends on local resources.

WORK PAGE

Write a list

In general, what factors do you think help resolve bereavement and what factors do you think hinder its resolution?

Factors that help   Factors that hinder (i.e. risk factors)

. . . .

. . . .

. . . .

. . . .

. . . .

. . . .

. . . .

. . . .

. . . .

Circle Circle

Now look at your right hand list (factors that hinder). (Ring) those risk factors you think are a *high risk*.

What factors could be a risk for individual members of Mary's family?

Mary's mother:

. . . .

. . . .

9-year-old boy:

. . . .

. . . .

16-year-old daughter:

. . . .

. . . .

Mary's ex-husband:

. . . .

. . . .

FURTHER ACTIVITY

Cast your mind back to the recent death of one of your patients:

- What factors might have *hindered* the relative's bereavement?

- What factors might have *helped* the relative's bereavement?

FURTHER READING

Journal articles

Casarett D, Kutner JS, Abrahm J *et al.* (2001) Life after death: A practical approach to grief and bereavement. *Annals of Internal Medicine.* **134**: 208–15.

Katz J, Sidell M and Komaromy C (2000) Death in homes: bereavement needs of residents, relatives and staff. *International Journal of Palliative Nursing.* 6: 274–9.

Ringdal GI, Jordhoy MS, Ringdal K *et al.* (2001) The first year of grief and bereavement in close family members to individuals who have died of cancer. *Palliative Medicine.* **15**: 91–105.

Resource books and website

Couldrick A (1988) *Grief and Bereavement. Understanding Children.* Sobell House Publications, Oxford.

Couldrick A (1991) *When Your Mum or Dad Has Cancer.* Sobell House Publications, Oxford.

Dickenson D, Johnson M and Katz JS (2000) *Death, Dying, and Bereavement* (2e). Sage Publications and the Open University, London.

Faulkner A (1995) *Working with Bereaved People.* Churchill Livingstone, Edinburgh.

Hindmarch C (2000) *On the Death of a Child* (2e). Radcliffe Medical Press, Oxford.

Holland J (2001) *Understanding Children's Experiences of Parental Bereavement.* Kingsley, London.

Lewis CS (1961) *A Grief Observed.* NW Clerk, London.

Markham U (2002) *Bereavement: your questions answered.* Vega, London.

Parkes CM (1996) *Bereavement: studies of grief in adult life* (3e). Routledge, New York.

Parkes CM, Relf M and Couldrick A (1996) *Counselling in Terminal Care and Bereavement.* British Psychological Society, Leicester.

Parkes CM (1996) *Counselling in Terminal Care and Bereavement.* BPS Books, Leicester/Baltimore.

Relf M, Couldrick A and Barrie H (1986) *Grief and Bereavement.* Sobell House Publications, Oxford.

Stedeford A (1984) *Facing Death: patients, families and professionals.* Heinemann Medical Books, London.

Stokes J and Crossley D (2001) *A Child's Grief: supporting a child when someone in their family has died.* Winston's Wish, Gloucester.

Walsh F and McGoldrick M (eds) (1991) *Living Beyond Loss. Death in the Family.* Norton, New York/London.

Webb NB (ed.) (2002) *Helping Bereaved Children. A Handbook for Practitioners.* Guilford, London.

Worden JW (1991) *Grief Counselling and Grief Therapy: a handbook for the mental health practitioner* (2e). Routledge, London.

www.edc.org/lastacts – *Innovations at the End of Life Care*: peer-reviewed on-line journal.

Index